Elise S. Ahn and Juldyz Smagulova (Eds.)
Language Change in Central Asia

I0130254

Contributions to the Sociology of Language

Edited by
Ofelia García
Francis M. Hult

Founding editor
Joshua A. Fishman

Volume 106

Language Change
in Central Asia

Edited by
Elise S. Ahn
Juldyz Smagulova

DE GRUYTER
MOUTON

ISBN 978-1-5015-1626-9
e-ISBN (PDF) 978-1-61451-453-4
e-ISBN (EPUB) 978-1-5015-0043-5
ISSN 1861-0676

Library of Congress Cataloging-in-Publication Data
A CIP catalog record for this book has been applied for at the Library of Congress.

Bibliographic information published by the Deutsche Nationalbibliothek

The Deutsche Nationalbibliothek lists this publication in the Deutsche Nationalbibliografie;
detailed bibliographic data are available on the Internet at http://dnb.dnb.de.

© 2016 Walter de Gruyter Inc., Boston/Berlin
This volume is text- and page- identical with the hardback published in 2016
Cover image: sculpies/shutterstock
Typesetting: RoyalStandard, Hong Kong
Printing and binding: CPI books GmbH, Leck
♾ Printed on acid-free paper
Printed in Germany

www.degruyter.com

We would like to thank our families, friends, contributors, and colleagues for their support and encouragement throughout the different stages of this project.

Preface

The idea for this edited volume emerged out of the conference stream that we organized for the 19th Sociolinguistics Symposium in Berlin (2012). This book is intended to raise Central Asia's sociolinguistic profile by bringing it to the attention of the international community of language researchers. This volume goes beyond simply documenting and providing descriptive cases from particular societies; we, as authors and editors, were motivated to draw attention to recent empirically-based research that has been conducted in the region in order to demonstrate Central Asia's potential in contributing to (as well as problematizing) language and education-related theoretical and methodological frameworks.

We would like to thank the many people that have contributed to the development of this book. We are grateful to Joshua Fishman and Ofelia Garcia, for their vision and commitment to scholarship on issues related to the broader field of the sociology of language and for allowing us to the contribute the series with this volume. Additionally, we are thankful to the anonymous external reviewers who provided comprehensive feedback on an earlier version of this volume and to Lara Wysong for her efficient handling of the publication process, quick turnaround regarding our questions, and overall patience with our project.

Although it was a small group of presenters and participants in the Berlin panel, a number of people expressed interest in contributing to the volume and kindly agreed to share their expertise across a variety of languages and contexts. It was a long process of putting all of the chapters together; the volume has undergone multiple cycles of internal review and revision. Thus, we owe the biggest debt of gratitude to all of the chapter contributors for the time and effort they have put into conducting research throughout Central Asia and its borders, writing, and patiently collaborating with us on this project. Any errors or oversights in the volume that remain are fully our responsibility.

Elise S. Ahn and Juldyz Smagulova
Almaty, Kazakhstan

Table of contents

List of illustrations

List of tables

List of abbreviations

ASSR	Autonomous Soviet Socialist Republic
EMI	English Medium Instruction
FSU	Former Soviet Union
LOI	Language of Instruction
LWC	Language of Wider Communication
MOI	Medium of Instruction
OECD	Organisation for Economic Co-operation and Development
SSR	Soviet Socialist Republic
UN	United Nations
USSR	Union of Soviet Socialist Republics

Juldyz Smagulova and Elise S. Ahn
1 Introduction

1 Overview

In the foreword to the second edition of the classic, *The Great Game*, Peter Hopkirk (2006: xiii) wrote that "[s]uddenly, after many years of almost total obscurity, Central Asia is once again in the headlines, a position it frequently occupied during the nineteenth century, at the height of the old Great Game between Tsarist Russia and Victorian Britain". The unexpected dissolution of the Soviet Union in 1991, the subsequent socio-political reforms developed in each of the then newly independent Central Asian countries, and the continued broader geo-political instability has turned the area back into a "hot spot" drawing the attention of policy makers, social scientists, academics, and journalists.

Narrowly, Central Asia (sometimes referred to as Central Eurasia) geo-politically consists of the former Soviet Union (FSU) Turkic republics, which includes Kazakhstan, Kyrgyzstan, Turkmenistan, Uzbekistan, along with Tajikistan. However, when taking into consideration transnational minorities and historical population migration patterns, a broader conceptualization of Central Asia could include parts of Western China (e.g., Xinjiang), southern Siberia, the East European Plains, Afghan Turkestan, and the Pamiri and Kashmiri regions which straddle Tajikistan and Afghanistan (Figure 1.1). This book looks at Central Asia through both lenses, narrow and broad, in an attempt to delineate the different pathways the republics have followed as well as elucidating cross-national language and education-related issues.

The linguistic map of the modern Central Asian region displays enormous diversity and complex interaction patterns between the indigenous Turkic and Iranian languages and the Russian language (Figure 1.2). Many communities are historically multilingual, e.g., the Tajik-Uzbek-Russian speakers of Samarkand, Uzbekistan or the Kazakh-Uyghur-Chinese speakers of Kulja, China.

However, despite the region's importance geo-politically and historically, empirically-based research on Central Asia is still in a nascent stage. Particularly regarding language-related research, language change efforts vis-à-vis numerous language change reforms "went largely unnoticed by the linguistic community" and many processes that could enrich sociolinguistic research were left undocumented and unanalyzed (Pavlenko 2013: 263).

Twenty four years after the dissolution of the Soviet Union, the region is still undergoing numerous socio-economic and political changes. A top priority for the national governments is their establishment as independent and legitimate

The Caucasus and Central Asia

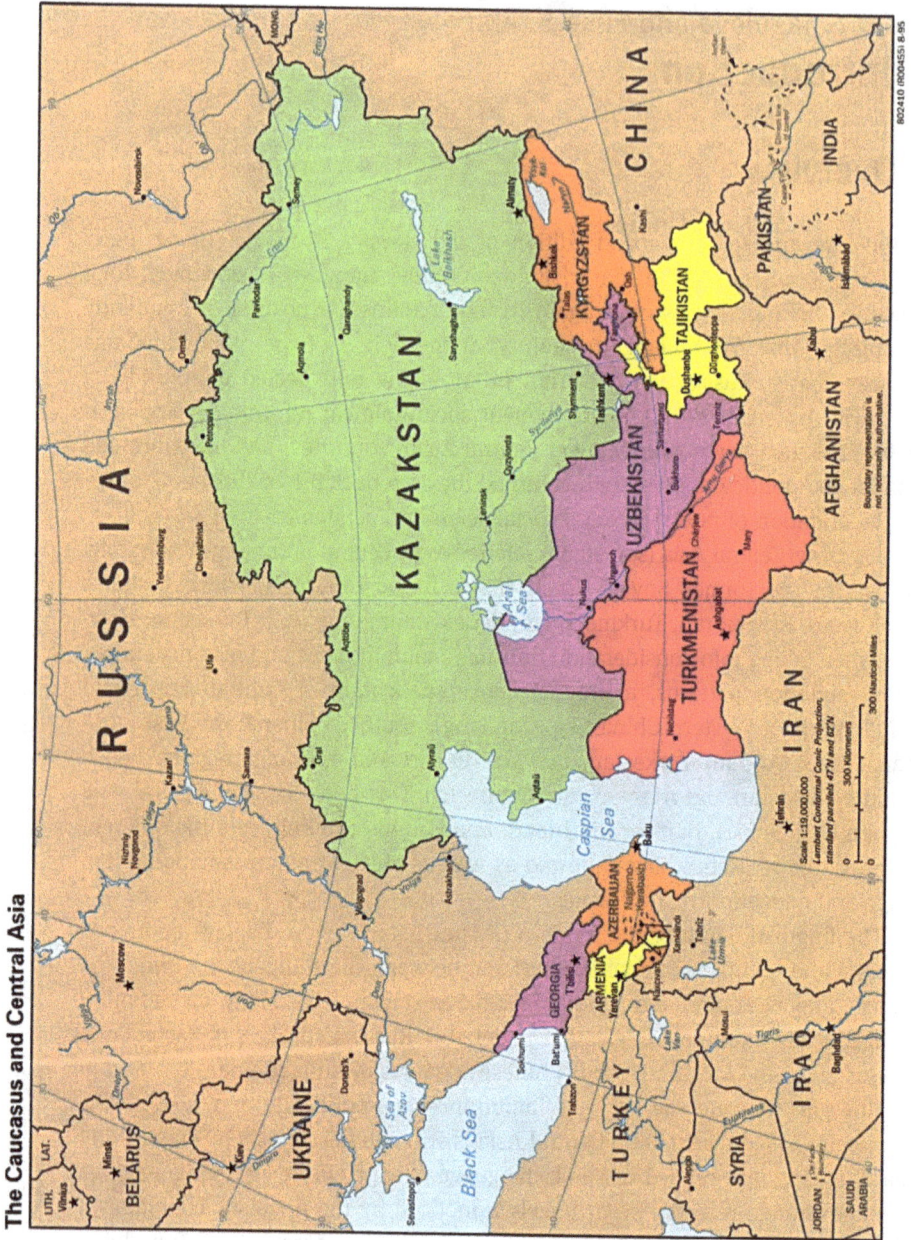

Figure 1.1: A map of Central Asia and its neighbors
Source: http://commons.wikimedia.org/wiki/File:The_Caucasus_and_Central_Asia_-_Political_Map.jpg

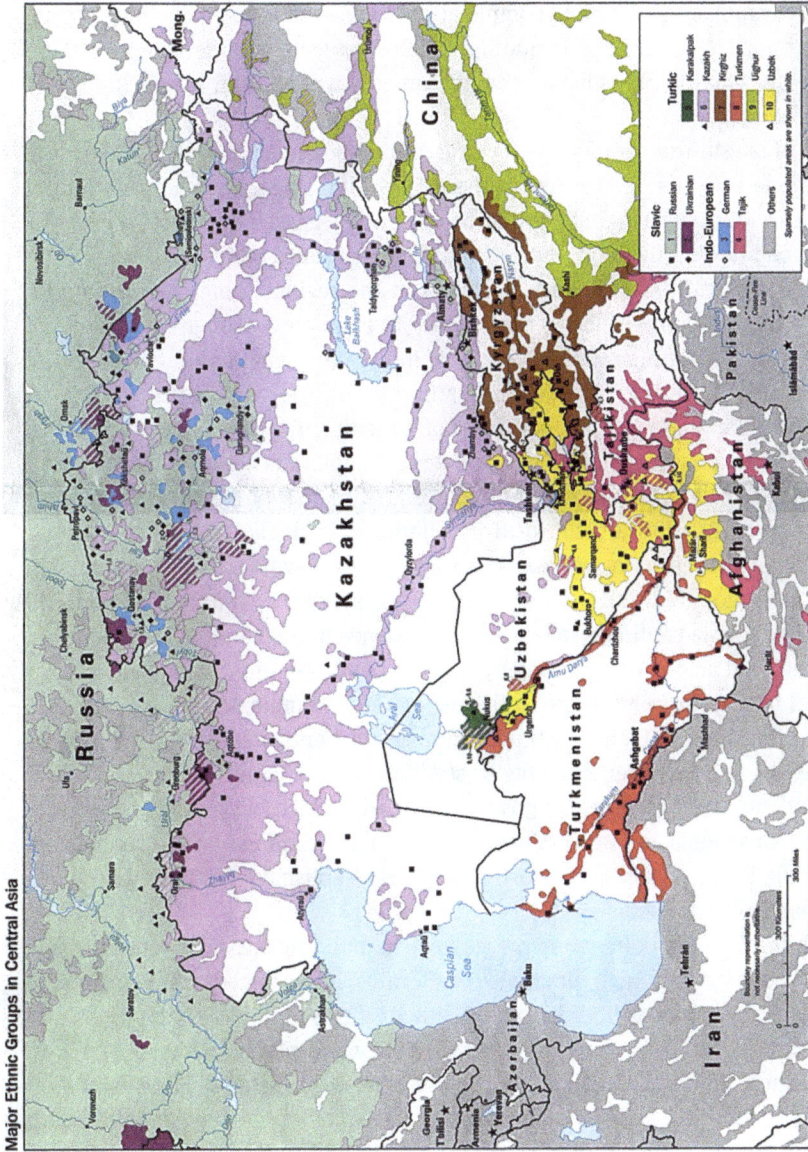

Figure 1.2: The ethnolinguistic patchwork of Central Asia in the later years of the Soviet Union
Source: http://en.wikipedia.org/wiki/Soviet_Central_Asia#/media/File:Central_Asia_Ethnic.jpg

political and global entities. Equally important is the construction of national identities. An added layer of complexity is the continuation of the political maneuvering from the international community that took place during the last few centuries, i.e., the "Great Game" which continues today in soft power domains, e.g., economics, language, and culture. These external and internal power dynamics are further complicated by the enormous challenges that these countries are facing including: ethno-linguistic and religious conflict, security, population movement, poverty, unemployment, and increasing social stratification.

To illustrate the complex geo-political and sociolinguistic dynamics in the region, one can look at the case of the Russian language. The sharp decline of Slavic and Russian-speaking population in Central Asia, in conjunction with the widespread de-Russification policies in the newly formed states has significantly decreased the cultural influence of Russia in the region. There has appeared a whole new generation of locals particularly in rural areas who are monolingual speakers of their titular languages. Despite these demographic changes and policy shifts, the Russian language is still wide-spread; it remains the lingua-franca, the language of pop-culture, mass-media, new media, education, as well as the language of academic and business communication. In fact, Russia's economic growth and its rising political influence has propelled a resurgence of interest in Russian among local populations (Pavlenko 2013). Russian was also acknowledged as a working language of the newly established Eurasian Economic Union (May 2014), further reifying its symbolic capital in the region.

While Russia continues to reassert its influence throughout the FSU countries, other regional actors are pursuing their own agendas in order to gain economic, political and cultural influence in the region. For example, the Chinese government is funding Confucius Institutes throughout Central Asia, while providing funding for Central Asian students to study in China (30,000 scholarships over the next 10 years). The Turkish government and Turkish businessmen are funding Turkish schools and universities, and funding is coming into the region from the Middle East to finance the construction and establishment of Islamic religious schools, i.e., *medresses*.

While different political actors engage in building ties to and within the region, poverty and high unemployment rates have forced many people to migrate to other places both in and outside of the region, in search of jobs and opportunities. In addition to the language policy and planning efforts that have been established and implemented by the states, this type of labor migration has thus provided additional impetus to learn other languages/dialects for mobility and employment purposes.

These and many other factors (both macro and micro) have informed the political defragmentation process that have been taking place in these linguistically, culturally and socially diverse societies. But in the context of growing social fragmentation, promoting and maintaining a dominant Westaphalian nation-state model (i.e., "one state, one language") has been difficult for new nation-states in light of issues related inequality, labor mobility, diversity, and change (Heller 2011).

However, while the Central Asian republics share socio-cultural, historical, and linguistic similarities, along with a Soviet legacy that has remained entrenched in various institutions, they have pursued different development pathways. By focusing on language-related issues, this edited volume is thus an attempt to describe the how social change has been conceptualized, implemented, and experienced within and across the transnational complex of the Central Asian republics. Thus, this book broadly revolves around the following questions:

- How has the institutionalization of language and literacy policies through education with a focus on affirming titular languages contributing to the reproduction of particular types of national identities or nationalist discourses?
- How do (new) language practices and changing notions of what constitutes socio-cultural-linguistic capital reflect wider global and local, social and cultural changes?
- What has been (and continues to be) the impact of urbanization and demographic change on language change, particularly as it relates to language shift and revival, as well as education reform in Central Asia? and
- How has language been used as a geo-political tool in the politicization of transnational identities and histories (e.g., pan-Turkism, pro-Russian, pro-EU movements)?

All of the chapters in this book provide insight into one or more of the aforementioned questions in relation to current discussions about national identity, language policy and planning processes, education, and changing notions of socio-cultural capital in the Central Asian context. The overall aim of this book is to encourage discussion about these different lines of research that will contribute to the broader field of the sociology of language by examining this under-published but dynamic region.

2 Context

To situate this volume in terms of language research, this section provides a brief overview of sociolinguistic research on language change in post Soviet countries. Pavlenko (2013) lists several reasons for the scarcity of sociolinguistic research of post-Soviet contexts in the West, particularly in the United States. This includes: a lack of an appropriate methodological foundation for the study of sociolinguistic changes and linguistic reforms in the post-Soviet space; a lack of systematic sociolinguistic fieldwork and an overreliance on surveys and analysis of policy documents; and a lack of collaboration between Western and local scholars (Pavlenko 2013: 263). Similar problems have more generally hindered the development of sociolinguistic research in post-Soviet academia.

Briefly looking at its intellectual history, one of the key assumptions under-girding Soviet linguistic research was the understanding that language was a type of a social activity and that it was dialectically linked to both social consciousness and interaction (Desheriev 1968; Jakubinsky 1986; Krysin 1977; Polivanov 1931; Shveitser 1976; Shveitser and Nikolsky 1978). But despite this conceptualization of language as a social phenomenon contemporary to the work being conducted by Labov (1972a, 1972b) and others, Soviet sociolinguistics was fundamentally constrained by ideology. Because the socialist society was theoretically egalitarian and therefore classless, to posit that language variation could be due to social inequality and/or power differentials or that it was ideo-logically driven was not permitted. This is exemplified in how the analysis of Soviet researchers regarding language planning in African post-colonial con-texts was framed as a critique of urban Western bourgeois policies (and thus aligned with narratives produced by Soviet ideology). Additionally, language planning studies in the Soviet Union advanced the notion that the Soviet lan-guage policy was enriching for both the Russian language as well as the milieu of minority languages (Desheriev 1966, 1987; Isayev 1979; Khasanov 1976).

Moreover, foundational to the creation a homogenous Soviet nation was the establishment of Russian as the language of the Union. This process of *sblizhenie* (getting closer) and *sliianie* (merging) of ethno-linguistic groups further confined research related to bilingualism and language contact to "safe" areas including comparative linguistics and examining language transfer as it related to the improved acquisition of Russian by non-Russian speaking populations.

Research was also constrained by methodological limitations. Within the Soviet research tradition, few methods were considered legitimate sources of knowledge production. Public opinion surveys, textual and comparative analysis methods were central in sociolinguistic work, which limited the research that could be conducted to policy documents and quantitative, taxonomic-type of work. This vein of research was then appropriated for state-usage to inform the Soviet policy-making apparatus which was interested in how numbers and research reflected an alignment with its ideological agenda. This was different from language-related research (язык), where language as the main of object of study led to extensive analysis of literary works, usually authored by famous and state-approved writers like the Russian poet, Alexander Pushkin or the Kazakh novelist, Mukhtar Auezov. Language-in-use oriented research was, thus, essentially non-existent during that period.

The fall of the Soviet Union brought along a collapse of this research tradition which was based on its own version of Marxism-Leninism. However, at a macro-level, the epistemological void left behind was then filled by nationalist discourses within the nascent, post-Soviet nation states. While language-related research previously existed to scaffold the Soviet social meta-narrative, the same research and research ideologies then became re-appropriated by the different titular nationalities in attempts to reproduce similar meta-narratives within their geo-political borders.

However, the appropriation of the language-ethnicity-land link was not new to the post-1991 FSU countries. During the late 1980s, a number of local publications on language as a way of preserving and reviving ethnic identity and language were circulated throughout the Soviet Union and within regions with large ethnic populations with historic ties to the land. Thus, the idea of a titular language then as being the sole state language was easy to recycle (Kertzer and Ariel 2002; Tishkov 1997). As a result, the post-1991 political conditions then created contexts in which "new" political elites could use the "discourse of language and nation-state, linking land and political control" to establish these nation-states (Heller 2011: 16). But while the euphoric, nationalist discourses across the FSU countries in the 1990s was characterized by the move towards privileging the languages of their titular ethno-linguistic groups, the reality of reconciling symbolic language policy discourse and the implementation of language planning activities has held numerous challenges, which is examined throughout the rest of this book.

3 Overview of this book

The first section of this volume looks at different frameworks and data collection methods that can provide insights into how language change can be understood in Central Asia's multilingual contexts. In Chapter Two, Stephen Bahry looks at how using a linguistic ecology framework better captures both the historical and contemporary multilingualism and social complexity of language networks and language change in Central Asia. Tracing back the interactions between different ethnolinguistic groups, Bahry provides an overview of the long history of language networks in the region highlighting both the longevity and breadth of the existing linguistic diversity. In Chapter Three, Nathan Light uses ethnographic interviewing to examine the function of aspect in Kyrgyz narratives about cultural practices and personal experiences. Drawing from two years of recorded interviews, Light uses linguistic analysis to investigate different modes of narrative expression. In Chapter Four, Elise Ahn and Antonia Jensen provide a glimpse into the Turkmenistani education system, different education-related language reforms and the various policies that provide a conflicted picture regarding broader socio-political aims through the lens of an English language lecturer that spent several years teaching in Turkmenistan. By using an auto-ethnographic approach, Ahn and Jensen utilize this method as a way of engaging in research under constrained conditions.

The second section of this book focuses specifically at language policy and planning activities as part of the nation-state building process in Central Asia. Chapters Five and Six provide analysis of language change in Kazakhstan. In Chapter Five, Juldyz Smagulova describes the re-acquisition of Kazakh in Russian-dominated urban areas in Kazakhstan. She focuses specifically on the role of Kazakh language Medium of Instruction (MOI) and its impact on Kazakh language revitalization efforts. In Chapter Six, Maganat Shegebayev examines the corpus building process by looking at the Kazakhstani oil and gas sector, drawing interviews that were conducted at several different Kazakhstani gas companies.

Chapters Seven and Eight examine language and education policy Tajikistan from the vantage point of different minority populations. Stephen Bahry explores multilingualism among Pamiri communities in Tajikistan using a linguistic ecology lens and Daniyar Karabaev and Elise Ahn describe the lived language and schooling experiences of Kyrgyz populations in Badakhshan, Tajikistan. Chapters Eight and Nine focus on language change in the broader Central Asian areas. In Chapter Nine, using text analysis, Ruth Bartholomew examines the way Tatar nation-state construction was articulated in debates regarding Tatar language script change in the 1990s. Chapter Ten describes language use by Uyghur students in the Autonomous Region of Xinjiang, China. Here, Ablimit Baki Elterish uses a mixed method approach (i.e., surveys, interviews, and documents) in order to situate language use and attitudes of these students in their complex socio-political context.

The last section takes a brief look at how globalization is affecting and introducing new issues into the broader Central Asian context. In Chapter Eleven, Leroy Terrelonge, Jr. examines the complex relationship between Tajik migrant workers migrating to Russia and the role of language in helping/hindering this opportunity, which are situated in a broader context of increasing tension in Russia and increased nationalism in Tajikistan. And in the final chapter, Dilia Hasanova studies the role of English in Uzbekistan, where the government has aggressively pursued a nationalist language policy agenda, yet desires to be able to participate in the international community.

The chapters and contributors were selected to represent a range of language practitioners and researchers, e.g., researchers, linguists, anthropologists, educationalists, educators, and sociolinguist, in order to look at the region from an interdisciplinary perspective using a range of methodologies and tools.

We believe that the methodological diversity reflected in this book helps to provide a fuller picture of the language change in Central Asia. By no means do the papers in this volume exhaustively answer the questions identified earlier. However, as Martha Brill Olcott (2014) argued, "[m]any of the current discussions about Central Asia do a real injustice to what has happened over the more than two decades of statehood in this part of the world and totally remove it from the context of global trends and problems more generally." Thus, our aim in bringing together this collection was was two-fold. The first was to raise emergent language and education-related issues. The second was to demonstrate that this region deserves a closer attention from researchers as it can provide invaluable data and insights to question many normative assumptions widely accepted among language researchers.

References

Alpatov, Vladimir. 2000. *150 языков и политика. 1917–2000 гг. Социолингвистические проблемы СССР и постсоветского пространства* [150 languages. 1917–2000. Sociolinguistic problems of the USSR and post-Soviet space]. Moscow: Kraft.

Blommaert, Jan & Ben Rampton. 2011. Language and superdiversity: A position paper. *Working papers in urban language & literacies.* http://www.kcl.ac.uk/sspp/departments/education/research/ldc/publications/workingpapers/70.pdf (accessed on 7 September 2014).

Desheriev, Yunus. 1977. *Социальная лингвистика. К основам общей теории.* [Social linguistics. An introduction to general theory]. Moscow: Nauka.

Desheriev, Yunus. 1968. *Язык и общество* [Language and society]. Moscow: Nauka.

Desheriev, Yunus. (ed.). 1966. *Закономерности развития и взаимодействия языков в советском обществе* [The regularity of development and interaction of language in Soviet society]. Moscow: Nauka.

Desheriev, Yunus. (ed.). 1987. *Взаимовлияние и взаимообогащение языков народов СССР* [The mutual interaction and mutual enrichment of language of the people of the USSR]. Moscow: Nauka.

Gans-Morse, Jordan. 2004. Searching for transitologists: Contemporary theories of post-communist transitions and the myth of a dominant paradigm. *Post-Soviet Affairs* 20(4). 320–349.

Heller, Monica. 2011. *Paths to post-nationalism: A critical ethnography of language and identity*. Oxford: Oxford University Press.

Hopkirk, Peter. 2006. *The Great Game: On secret service in High Asia*. London: John Murray.

Isayev, Magomed. 1979. *Языковое строительство в СССР* [Language planning in USSR]. Moscow: Nauka.

Jakubinsky, Leo. 1986. *Избранные работы. Язык и его функционирование* [Selected works: Language and its functioning]. Moscow: Nauka.

Kertzer, David & Dominique Arel (eds.). 2002. *Census and identity: The politics of race, ethnicity, and language in national censuses*. Cambridge: Cambridge University Press.

Khasanov, Bakytzhan. 1987. *Казахско-русское двуязычие* [Kazakh-Russian bilingualism]. Almaty: Nauka.

Khasanov, Bakytzhan. 1976. *Языки народов Казахстана и их взаимодействие* [Languages of people of Kazakhstan and their interaction]. Almaty: Nauka.

Kopylenko, Moisey & Saaya Saina. 1982. *Функционирование русского языка в различных слоях казахского населения* [The use of Russian among Kazakhs in different social strata]. Almaty: Nauka.

Krysin, Leonid. 1977. *Язык в современном обществе* [Language in modern society]. Moscow: Nauka.

Labov, William. 1972a. *Sociolinguistic patterns*. Philadelphia: University of Pennsylvania Press.

Labov, William. 1972b. *Language in the Inner City: Studies in the Black English Vernacular*. Philadelphia: University of Pennsylvania Press.

Larin, Boris. 2003. *Филологическое наследие: Сборник статей* [Philological heritage. Collection of articles]. Saint Petersburg: Saint Petersburg University Press.

Olcott, Martha Brill. 2014, June 4. Central Asia today: An afterthought. *The global think tank*. http://carnegieendowment.org/2013/06/04/central-asia-today-afterthought/g8dz?reload-Flag=1 (accessed 10 June 2014).

Pavlenko, Aneta. 2013. Multilingualism in post-soviet successor states. *Language and Linguistics Compass* 714. 262–271.

Pavlenko, Aneta. (ed.). 2008. *Multilingualism in post-Soviet countries*. Clevedon: Multilingual Matters.

Pavlenko, Aneta. 2006. Russian as a lingua franca. *Annual Review of Applied Linguistics* 26. 78–99.

Polivanov, Evgeny. 1931. *За марксистское языкознание. Сб. популярных лингвистических статей* [For Marxist linguistics. A collection of popular linguistic articles]. Moscow: Federatsia.

Rivers, Williams. 2002. Attitudes towards incipient *mankurtism* among Kazakhstani college students. *Language Policy* 1. 159–174.

Thelen, Tajana. 2011. Shortage, fuzzy property and other ends in the anthropological analysis of (post)socialism. *Critique of Anthropology* 31(91). 43–61.

Tishkov, Valery. 1997. *Ethnicity, nationalism and conflict in and after the Soviet Union. A mind aflame*. London: Sage.

Shveitser, Alexander. 2012 [1976]. *Современная социолингвистика. Теория, проблемы, методы* [Modern sociolinguistics. Theory, problems, methods]. Moscow: Librocom.

Shveitser, Alexander & L. Nikolsky. 1978. *Введение в социолингвистику* [Introduction to sociolinguistics]. Moscow: Vyshaya shkola.

Stephen A. Bahry
2 Language Ecology: Understanding Central Asian Multilingualism

Abstract: Central Asia is extremely multilingual. Each of the five republics is named for a titular nationality, with, in turn, its own titular language. Kazakh, Kyrgyz, Turkmen and Uzbek are classified as Turkic languages; however, Tajik is an Indo-Iranian language. However, speakers of these languages are found not only in their titular republics, but also in the neighboring republics. Each language has a number of regional dialects with transitional varieties that share their features, creating complex Turkic and Iranian dialect continua. Adopting a language ecology framework, this chapter explores several diachronic stages of Central Asia's language history and ends examining contemporary Central Asia through an ecological lens. The chapter argues that an ecological approach to language change in Central Asia provides a richer lens for analysis. Furthermore, I argue that incorporating both comparative diachronic and synchronic perspectives provides deeper insight into the processes of change that may also shed some light on the current language dilemmas faced within the region.

Keywords: Central Asia; language ecology; bilingualism, multilingualism, plurilingualism; language hierarchies; Chaghatai; Kazakh; Kyrgyz; New Persian; Soghdian; Tajik; Tatar; Turkmen; Uzbek; Turkic languages; Iranian languages

1 Introduction

This chapter provides an overview of multilingualism over space and time in Central Asia from two perspectives. The first is that of societal multilingualism, i.e., the co-existence of multiple languages within a territory or society, and second, that of personal plurilingualism, i.e., individual proficiency in one or more languages. This chapter argues that adopting a language ecology approach in examining language diversity in this region can provide a more nuanced understanding of complex language issues.

1.1 Background information

Central Asia is ethno-linguistically diverse. Each republic is named for its politically dominant titular nationality, which has a corresponding titular language.

Thus, there is Kazakh in Kazakhstan, Kyrgyz in Kyrgyzstan, Tajik in Tajikistan, Turkmen in Turkmenistan, and Uzbek in Uzbekistan, with speakers of these languages are found also in the neighboring countries (Figure 1.1). Kazakh, Kyrgyz, Turkmen and Uzbek are classified as members of the Turkic language family, while Tajik, an Indo-Iranian language, is a Central Asian variety of Persian (Landau and Kellner-Heinkele 2012).

However, there remains the issue of boundaries: where does one language end and another begin? Each language has a number of regional transitional dialects that share some features, creating a complex Turkic and Iranian dialect continua with boundaries less sharp than geo-political and language maps suggest (Fierman 1991; Schlyter 2013). Besides this geographic variability, there is social variation related to differing status assigned to particular language varieties (Chambers 2008; Wardhaugh 2010).

2 Conceptual framework: Ecological approaches to language in society

Work in linguistics has historically been situated within a monolingual perspective with some attention given to bilingualism. Yet when we consider the daunting number of languages and bi- and multilingual individuals in contemporary societies, the inadequacy of monolingual approaches is apparent. However, the concept of language ecologies as proposed by Charles and Frances Voegelin (1964) captures both the richness and fluidity of social linguistic diversity. They argued that "[I]n linguistic ecology, one begins not with a particular language but with a particular area, not with selective attention to a few languages but with comprehensive attention to all the languages in the area" (Voegelin and Voegelin 1964: 2). Haugen (1972) further developed the approach in examining the Norwegian vernacular dialect continuum and contention between a Danish-based standard language and a Norwegian-based standard, which arguably parallels the creation of modern Central Asian standard Turkic languages distinctive from classical Turkic. Haugen encouraged researchers to ask what languages are used, in what domains; what standards and language variation exist, how they are used in writing and supported institutionally; and what attitudes exist towards these language varieties and their uses (1972: 336–337).

More recent attempts to apply ecological frameworks to better understand complex multilingual contexts see language(s) more as the practices of people or communities in unique settings for particular purposes, than as abstract system(s) (Calvet 1999, 2007; Hornberger 2002; Hornberger and Hult 2008;

Mühlhäusler 1997, 2002). Proponents of this frame draw out different aspects. Some adopt a conflict-based perspective, in which languages devour each other in an either-or competitive dynamic (Nelde 2002). Others see potential for non-conflictual, symbiotic relations between languages, in the linguistic equivalent of ecological niches (Mühlhäusler 1997, 2002). Still others call for protection of endangered languages, parallel to calls for protection of endangered species (Hornberger and Hult 2008; Nettle and Romaine 2000).

To the extent that language is an individual, social, economic and political phenomenon, and that societies and the language(s) within them, are rarely monolithic, an ecological frame seems to capture the richness of various connections, interactions, and influences. Furthermore, since social relations and language are neither deterministic nor atomistic, but fundamentally involve both human agency and manmade institutional structures, an adequate social science must go beyond idealized linguistic systems to account more fully for how languages are actually used in all their complexity.

3 Methodological approach

The remainder of this chapter examines the literature on languages in Central Asia, both diachronically and synchronically, through a language ecology frame by reviewing moments of change in Central Asia's language ecology. These moments are points in time when new languages were introduced into this "language ecology system". This review is then followed by a discussion of research relevant to the contemporary contexts in order to better understand the current linguistic situation. To provide one more layer of complexity, this chapter explores these languages within a High (H) and Low (L) social function perspective. Ferguson (1959) examined cases of extreme difference between varieties of a language used for informal, or low, social functions, and those associated with high status domains and functions. Cases where the gap between H and L forms of a language are so great that speakers of L forms cannot understand H forms without instruction and/or formal study were termed by Ferguson as "diglossic contexts". Examples cited included Arabic, Bengali, and Greek, where classical languages or classically-influenced contemporary languages were used for H functions while their vernacular descendants were used for L functions. Diglossia has serious implications for education, presenting children unexposed to H varieties before starting school with serious challenges to learning when lessons are taught via H varieties.

Fishman (1967) added bilingualism to the consideration of diglossia distinguishing two types of diglossic situations: those with and without bilingualism (according to whether the high prestige variety is a different language or a dialect of the same language), and two types of bilingualism (those where diglossia is and is not present). Examining the historical and contemporary H and L functions of languages in Central Asia through an ecological lens reveals a suggestive, if somewhat incomplete, portrait of Central Asia's language ecology at different moments in time.

4 Central Asia's language ecology

Since attempts to deal with language policy on a territorial principle rather than the principle of personality (Calvet 1996: 60–61) have proven extremely complex, an ecological approach to linguistic analysis seems particularly suited in the Central Asian context. Yet awareness of the utility of such a theoretical frame still lags. For example, recent works on language politics in Central Asia largely focus on macro-political aspects of language choice in the region, and do not fully exploit the burgeoning micro-level research on language and use in the region that can be seen as implicitly taking an ecological approach to language in the region (Bahry, Karimova and Shamatov 2013).

4.1 Historical multilingualism in the Central Asian language ecology

4.1.1 Soghdian as a regional contact language[1]

For almost 500 years (est. 300–800 A.D.), Soghdian, an eastern Iranian language was spoken by a core population settled near Samarkand (in today's Uzbekistan). The Soghdian alphabet, derived from Aramaic script, was used for written Uighur, and later, Mongolian. Soghdian traders and settlers along the Silk Road were often proficient in languages such as Turkic Uighur, Indic Sanskrit, as well as

---

1 There are multiple spellings found in the English language literature of the name of the language, Soghdian and Sogdian, and the land, Soghdia and Sogdia, depending on how closely it adheres to the phonetics of the language, with *gh* used as a closer approximation than *g* to the Soghdian sound [ɣ]. This chapter uses the spellings with *gh* as based more on Soghdian, Persian and Tajik pronunciation than on the Russian approximation of this sound. Similarly, this chapter uses Yaghnobi rather than Yagnobi.

Chinese. The Soghdians functioned as administrators within the Old Uighur Turkic Empire which was ostensibly facilitated by their literacy and bi-/multilingualism (Harmatta 1996; Yoshida 2009).

Bi- and multilingualism among Soghdian speakers are evidenced by numerous borrowed vocabulary from neighboring languages as well as numerous borrowings from Soghdian into Old Uighur and New Persian (Henning 1939; Yoshida 2009). Archaeological evidence from the Turfan Basin region located in today's eastern Xinjiang suggests that during the Sui (581–618 A.D.) and Tang (618–907 A.D.) dynasties speakers in that area were multilingual in a variety of Chinese, Indo-Iranian and Turkic languages (Skaff 2012). While the Soghdians were known for their bilingualism (which allowed them to serve as Chinese-Turkic interpreters in the Tang Empire), how much others learned Soghdian is unclear (Lung 2011).

With the Arabic conquest and the coming of Islam to parts of Central Asia from 670 to 750 AD, Soghdian was replaced in both its H functions and written form first by Arabic and later by New Persian. Soghdian, however, did continue to exist for some time; according to Al-Kashgari[2], there were bilingual Soghdian-Turkic districts in today's northern Kyrgyzstan/south-eastern Kazakhstan. Today, Soghdian survives only in the form of one of its descendants, i.e., Yaghnobi, a language spoken in a few isolated valleys in Tajikistan (Golden 2006; Paul et al. 2010; Starr 2013; Tetley 2008; Yoshida 2009).

4.1.2 The case of New Persian

Speakers of some form of Middle Persian entered Central Asia with the Arabic armies, but the particular variety of Persian and its relation with other Central Asian languages remains uncertain. However, based on different texts and the time period, one can conjecture that Turkic, Arabic, Soghdian and other eastern Iranian languages were spoken along with Middle Persian. Two hundred years later, New Persian appeared in the written record in L uses. Among its earliest documented uses was for business correspondence in Hebrew script (Utas 2009), and for popular literature in Arabic script (Lazard 1975). Written New Persian was criticized by proponents of Arabic for its lack of specialized vocabulary rendering it unsuitable for scholarship and administration (Richter-Bernburg 1974; Tetley 2008). Some mocked its pretensions to fill the H functions of Arabic, saying, "If one looks at a scientific book which has been translated into Persian, its beauty has gone, its importance is eclipsed, its face blackened, and it loses all usefulness, because this language is no use except for tales of kings and

---

2 Kashgari is also spelled in the literature as Kāšyarī, Kāshgharī and Kashghari.

night-time story-telling" (Biruni 1973: 12, as cited in Tetley 2008: 27). Despite this, there were others who resisted this, e.g., Ibn Sina (Avicenna), a Persian speaker who composed most of his scientific works in Arabic. When he wrote his *Book of Sciences [Daneshname]* in Persian for a non-scholarly audience, he avoided direct usage of Arabic vocabulary; instead, he innovated Persian equivalents for Arabic technical terms and demonstrated that Persian could be adapted for H uses (Afnan 1958).

Written New Persian did eventually replace Arabic for most H language uses in Central Asia. The H variety of Persian ultimately developed; however, it did not reflect Avicenna's practice. Rather, it directly borrowed enormous amounts of classical Arabic vocabulary (Richter-Bernburg 1974). Some have speculated that New Persian developed as a contact language. Besides its many Arabic borrowings, much of its lexicon derived from Parthian and Soghdian (Lazard 1975; Yoshida 2009). Lazard (1975: 597–598) noted several anomalies regarding New Persian's origins, asking:

> What necessity gave rise to it [New Persian]? How does it happen that, in spite of its [Middle Persian's] original connection with the regions of the south-west, it seems to have appeared first in the east ...? Why did literature develop initially in Transoxiana [Central Asia], an outlying region where... the common and literary language was Soghdian, a fundamentally different Iranian language?

Utas (2006, 2009) speculated that the Arab conquest had created a need for an interethnic language, filled by New Persian, which had perhaps as a result undergone either creolization or koineization. McWhorter argued that Persian's extreme structural simplicity relative to other Iranian languages could best be explained by massive pidgin or creole-like contact processes (2007, 2011). As a contact language, New Persian's resulting simpler structure and high learnability may have been a factor contributing to its spread as an LWC in L uses, and to its later replacement of Arabic as the language of administration and literature by the Central Asian Samanid Empire, eventually becoming the H language of Iran and much of Central Asia (Starr 2013).

4.1.3 Classical Chaghatai Turkic and Persian-Turkic diglossia and bilingualism

Mahmud Kashgari, an 11th century Central Asian Turkic intellectual familiar with Arabic and Persian, documented multilingualism in the late 11th century in the Central Asian region with a special focus on the Turkic languages. Although multilingual, Kashgari expressed a preference for forms of Turkic languages that were relatively uninfluenced by borrowed Persian terms, further characterizing the Turkic speech of Turkic-Persian bilinguals as "slurring" (Golden 2006: 23–24). During that period, there were several H languages in the region, i.e., classical Arabic, Middle Persian, Turkic, and multiple L varieties, e.g., New Persian. Additionally, there were remnants of eastern Iranian languages like Khworezmian and Soghdian.

Despite the purist sentiments expressed by Kashgari, Chaghatai, a written Central Asian Turkic language emerged largely based on southeastern Turkic languages (e.g., Old Uighur, Karluk), but with considerable lexical and even syntactic influence from Arabic and Persian. In the Central Asian context, Chaghatai has even been termed by some as *koine* language (Prior 2012).[3] Chaghatai was also used as H written language in areas where the southwest (e.g., Oghuz and Turkmen) and northwest (e.g., Kazakh, Kyrgyz, and Tatar) languages varieties were spoken. In these areas, its lexicon was supplemented by vocabulary and syntax derived from these varieties (Bodrogligeti 2009; Boeschoten and Vandamme 1998; Doerfer 1991, 1992). It even reached the Volga Tatars whose written language before the 19th century was "a more or less [T] atarized version of the Chagatay language" (Strauss 1993: 565). Chaghatai was used across Central Asia and beyond, perhaps because its lexical richness and phonological flexibility allowed it to transcend dialect differences, supporting its use by non-southeast Turkic speakers (Doerfer 1992).

4.1.4 The emergence of Volga Tatar as a language of wider communication and written H language

From the 16th until the 20th century, Volga Tatars traveled broadly across the Siberian steppes and Central Asia and as far as the western fringes of Qing China. This was first a response to the conquest by Moscow of the Khanate of Kazan and Moscow's subsequent anti-Muslim policy, and later a consequence of Catherine the Great's emancipation of her Muslim subjects, events which drew many Tatars eastward. In the 18th and 19th centuries, Tatar traders, speakers of a northwest Turkic language, interacted largely with speakers of other northwest Turkic languages (Kazakh and Kyrgyz). Because they could speak Turkic languages and some knew Russian, these Tatar traders helped maintain connections between the Tatar diaspora, Russia, the Volga region, and Central Eurasia.

---

3 There are multiple spellings of Chaghatai in the literature, Chaghatai, Chagatai, Chaghatay, Chagatay, Čayataj, and Jaghatai. It is also termed Turki, and in Soviet scholarship, Old/Middle Uzbek.

As with the Soghdians, this dispersed trading network with a multilingual capacity mediated the transmission of ideas as well as goods. For example, while involved with trading, Tatars were also involved in conversion of non-Muslims and strengthening people's attachment to Islam through the construction and staffing of mosques and local Islamic schools throughout Siberia and Central Asia (Dowler 2001; Sultangalieva 2012; Yemelianova 1999; Zenkovsky 1953).

Language vernacularization then was a branch of a broader movement for modernization of culture and society that developed in response to contact with other languages and societies that had begun modernization earlier. The Tatar written language had been Chaghatai with Tatar and Ottoman elements. In the 19th century, Volga Tatars began developing a written standard which reflected vernacular Tatar more. During this period, there were debates about the merits of an Ottoman or Central Asian standard, and whether to base new forms of Tatar on the standards developing among Crimean Tatars or following Volga Tatar usage (Strauss 1993: 565–566). A guiding principle of Tatar language reformers as put by Isxaki (1909) was that of simplification "in order to make it understandable even for the common people" (as cited in Strauss 1993: 569). Indeed, some reformers promoted the value of Tatar-Russian bilingualism and translation of works in Russian into Tatar (Zenkovsky 1953: 313).

As the Russian empire expanded into Central Asia between the 18th and 20th centuries, it initially relied on Tatar-Russian bilinguals and the Tatar language for administration in Turkic-speaking regions. However, Russian authorities also apparently feared that Tatarization and Islamicization of the Kazakh and Kyrgyz languages was taking place. Consequently, Cyrillic-based Kazakh alphabets were taught to students in Russian-Kazakh boarding schools, evidence of language being able to simultaneously occupy a space in which it is both a resource and a political weapon (Dowler 2001; Sultangalieva 2012; Zenkovsky 1953).

4.2 Contemporary Central Asia's language ecology

The coming of the Soviet regime disrupted the historical ecological relations between the different Central Asian languages. Firstly, all three of the aforementioned classical languages were rejected as potential bases for developing modern standard languages in Central Asia. Instead, 19th century European notions linking state, language, nationality and identity were introduced with a Marxist veneer. The dialect continuum of spoken vernaculars was divided broadly into today's five Central Asian titular languages. Writing systems were designed for many of the region's languages, for use in at least elementary education and basic literacy. The titular languages were granted special privileges as languages of education in neighboring republics as well. There were debates over which dialects would form the basis of the modern Soviet Central Asian standard languages. However, except among language specialists, the study of transitional dialects intermediate between the titular languages, the range of actual sociolinguistic variation in language use within the republics, and the degree and forms of local-local bilingualism and/or diglossia during the early Soviet liberal language policy period has, to date, received little attention (Fierman 1991; Lewis 1972; Schlyter 2013).

In the later years of Soviet Union, studies on bilingualism based largely on census data with some attention to Central Asia began to appear, e.g., Kazakhstan (Desheriev 1976; Dzhunusov 1980; Guboglo 1986; Khasanov 1987). Census questions asked respondents to name their native language, and the studies focused on local-Russian bilingualism and factors promoting its spread. Unfortunately, census responses on native language arguably reflected loyalty to a particular ethno-linguistic identity more than actual language use (Anderson and Silver 1983). Regardless, local-local bilingualism and Russian-local bilingualism are barely touched on in this literature, leaving the extent and nature of local-local and Russian-local bi- and multilingualism still relatively unexplored.

Similar asymmetrical bilingualism can be observed in neighboring minority language areas of western China, where research has established that there is also local-local bi- and multilingualism, e.g., Tajiks in Xinjiang who speak either Sarykoli or Wakhi Pamiri languages as first languages, are bilingual in oral Kyrgyz, literate in Uighur, with some proficiency in Chinese (Luo and Zhao 2004). Furthermore, while like Russophones in Central Asia, Han Chinese in minority areas of China are said to rarely learn local languages (Dwyer 1998), both of these groups, when settled in rural areas where minorities form a local majority, develop some oral proficiency in the minority language (Hansen 2005; Ma 2007). Unspoken taboos on acknowledging asymmetrical bilingualism seem to have restricted explicit study of this phenomenon.[4]

4.3 Late-Soviet language ecology

Some late Soviet work explored bi-, multi-, and plurilingualism in the region and its asymmetrical nature. Various chapters on Central Asia in the *Atlas of*

---

[4] The exception might be some work that was done in the Ukrainian Soviet Socialist Republic using the frame of 1920s Leninist language policy to critique the strong promotion of Russian at the expense of republican languages like Ukrainian conducted under Brezhnev (Dzyuba 1974).

Languages of Intercultural Communication in the Pacific, Asia, and the Americas lay out the types of bilingualism in each republic, going beyond local-Russian bilingualism to enumerate multiple cases of local-local bilingualism and the limited Russian-local bilingualism in the region. Despite appearing in 1996, much of the Central Asia material was produced during perestroika in the late 1980s (Baskakov 1996a, 1996b, 1996c, 1996d; Baskakov and Džuraev 1996; Baskakov and Xasanov 1996; Nasyrova 1996).

4.3.1 An ecological perspective on multi- and plurilingualism research: Uzbekistan

It is thought that in urban Uzbekistan many H language functions were conducted in Russian, but that elsewhere penetration of Russian is low. An estimated 17–22% of Uzbeks, Karakalpaks and Tajiks and 12–14% of Kyrgyz and Turkmen in Uzbekistan were proficient in Russian as a second language, while bilingualism in Uzbek or languages of other nationalities of Uzbekistan is said to be an uncommon phenomenon among Russians and other groups for whom Russian is the dominant language (Baskakov and Džuraev 1996).

Baskakov and Džuraev (1996) estimated the degree of bilingualism in Uzbek among non-Uzbek ethnicities as (in descending order): 37% (Tajiks), 30% (Kyrgyz), 20% (Turkmen and Uighurs), 3–6% (Russians, Ukrainians, Germans and Koreans). Russian functioned as first language for ethnic Russians and European nationalities, and as a second language for many educated non-Russian urban dwellers. It also functioned as an H language in domains such as science and technology and as the language of interethnic communication in urban areas.

Nasyrova (1996) closely examined the interrelationships among the languages in the Karakalpak Autonomous Region. Karakalpak is a northwest Turkic language which is spoken in Uzbekistan, but that is more similar to the Kazakh language, with some Uzbek and Turkmen-like features (Kirchner 1998; Wurm 1951). In the Karakalpakstan Autonomous Republic[5] within Uzbekistan, the Karakalpak language has some official status in addition to Uzbek and is used in local schools and to some extent in administration and media. Besides speakers of Karakalpak and Uzbek, Karakalpakstan also has speakers of Kazakh, Turkmen, Tatar and Korean. Russian is spoken there by Russians and others who have adopted Russian as their primary language (Schlyter 2005, 2013) (Figure 2.1).

---

5 In Karakalpak, the territory is Karakalpakstan; in Uzbek, Karakalpakistan. This chapter uses the Karakalpak term.

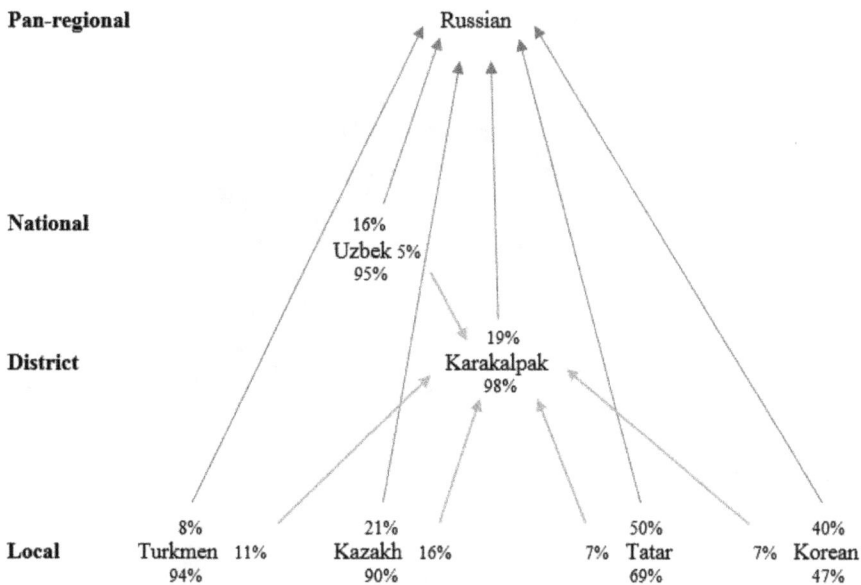

Figure 2.1: Karakalpakstan's hierarchical language ecology
Source: Adopted by author from Nasyrova (1996: 927)

Adopted from Nasyrova (1996: 927), Figure 2.1 broadly illustrates Karakal-pakstan's language ecology based on the percentage of each nationality claim-ing its language as their native language and their self-reported proficiency in Russian and Karakalpak. Figure 2.2 also manipulates the reported data in Nasyrova (1996: 927) by showing the directionality of bi- and trilingualism. This revealed a two-way bi- and trilingualism linking similar Turkic languages (Turkmen-Uzbek-Karakalpak) and (Uzbek-Karakalpak-Kazakh), and one-way Tatar-Karakalpak, Tatar-Uzbek, and Korean-Karakalpak bilingualism.

In Figure 2.2, two-way bilingualism and trilingualism are represented by the double-headed, orange arrows while one way bilingualism by the uni-directional, green arrows. "Two-way passive" bilingualism is an interesting type of bilingual communication, found most frequently among speakers of two Turkic languages. This is when each interlocutor speaks their own language, while understanding what their counterpart is saying in the other language (Baskakov and Džuraev 1996: 921). Baskakov and Džuraev (1996) posited that there might, in fact, be regional variation in the type and degree of bilingualism, e.g., they noted that there is extensive Tajik-Uzbek and Uzbek-Tajik bilingualism in Samarkand and Bukhara, with Tajik often functioning as language of interethnic communication in these districts.

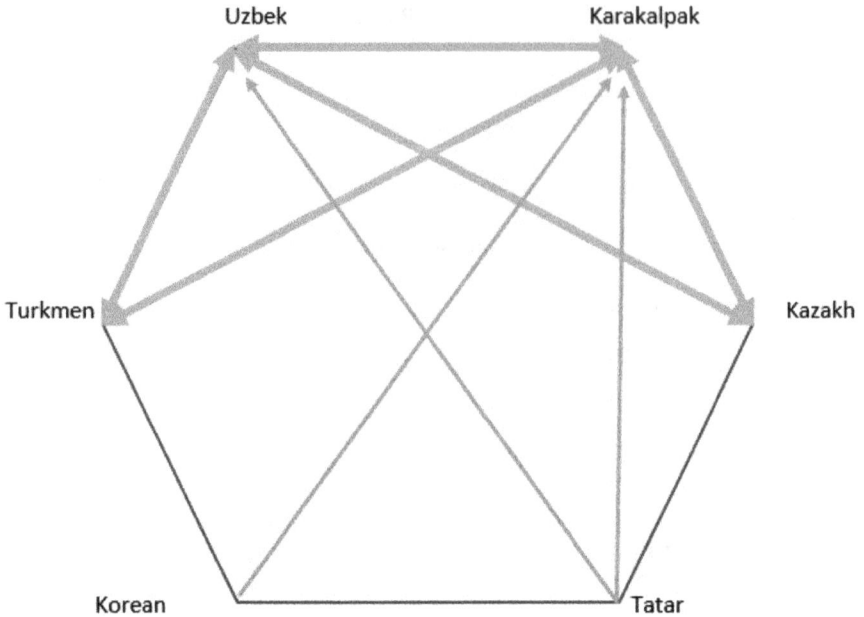

Figure 2.2: Plurilingualism in Karakalpakstan's language ecology. Notations: two-way bilingualism and trilingualism (double-headed thick arrows); one way bilingualism (one-headed thin arrows).
Source: Adopted from Nasyrova (1996: 927)

Regardless of type, Nasyrova's data suggests a certain resilience of Uzbek and local minority languages in the face of competition from dominant Russian and Uzbek languages, and a greater degree of bilingualism than some reports might suggest. However, although published in 1996, the major data sources seem to be Nasyrov (1976) and the last Soviet census in 1989. Given that the commitment to Karakalpak status in the 1995 post-Soviet revision of the Uzbekistan language law is somewhat weaker in comparison to its local state language status granted before independence in 1989 (Schlyter 2005, 2013), there is a need to ascertain how policy changes have affected Karakalpakstan's language ecology and the status of the Karakalpak language.

The authors' classification of the languages of Uzbekistan by the domains and functions in which they are found revealed a language hierarchy with Russian the language of wider communication and prestige, particularly seen in H functions in technical scientific domains such as medicine, while Uzbek's H functions were in administration, media, publishing and education. Besides Uzbek, Kazakh, Kyrgyz, Tajik, Turkmen, and Karakalpak were used locally for H functions in education and media. Baskakov and Džuraev (1996) reported considerable passive bilingualism in L language uses, particularly among Turkic-languages. Interestingly, some Russian-local bilingualism was found outside the capital, with some Russians using a local language rather than Russian as a language of interethnic communication, Uzbek in Andijan, and Tajik in Samarkand (Baskakov and Džuraev 1996: 921–922).[6]

4.3.2 An ecological perspective on multi- and plurilingualism research in the other republics

Research that is informed or can be seen through an ecological perspective is increasingly being conducted in Central Asia. Baldauf (2006) argued for the importance of micro-level language studies through an ecology lens as part of language planning processes and policy research pointing out an ethnographic study conducted by Delorme (1999) of a Kazakhstani dual-medium school as an exemplar. Korth (2005) investigated attitudes towards Kyrgyz, Russian and Uzbek languages in Kyrgyzstan. She found that tolerance of bilingualism and code-switching co-existed alongside linguistic purism which persisted from the Soviet period. In the Kyrgyz case she found that there was a compartmentalization of Kyrgyz in L functions and Russian for H, which were associated with attitudes of superiority, modernity and urbanity. Similarly, Smagulova (2014) found that among educated urban Kazakhs, the titular language is used for early linguistic socialization of but infants, as time passed, the same parents would shift to using Russian as the general home language, thereby relegating Kazakh being limited to the "baby talk" L function domain.

Fierman (2012) has contributed a discussion of the status of the Uzbek language outside Uzbekistan in the other republics of Central Asia, which could serve for example as a model for the ecological study of other titular languages outside their home republic. Bahry et al. (2008) surveyed the linguistic ecology of school education across the region. Clement (2005) has examined the history of language planning and implementation in Turkmenistan with a particular focus on the changing relation between the Turkmen, Chaghatai and Russian languages from 1904 to 2004. Elsewhere in this volume, Bahry looks at the interaction between Russian, Tajik, and several local languages in the western Pamiri region, while Karabaev and Ahn examine the perspectives of Kyrgyz language speakers in Tajikistan's eastern Pamiri region. Such research into

---

6 It is possible that the structural resemblance of Tajik and Russian and many transparent cognates (*zan, žená*, [woman]; *hast, jest'* [is]; *sad, sto/sot*, [hundred]) contribute to Russian-Tajik bilingualism.

micro-, meso- and macro-language policy contexts provide insight into the ecologies of Central Asia by elucidating and highlighting the complexity of language use dynamics and networks of practice.

Looking through a wider lens, in the highly multilingual Bortala prefecture of neighboring Xinjiang, China, speakers go beyond passive bilingualism to an even stronger accommodation to speakers of other languages as a sign of respect through mutual active bilingualism. For example, in the market, Uighur sellers try to speak in the language of prospective buyers, who in turn address the sellers in Uighur, while guests are said to speak in the language of their hosts. Such active accommodation seems to occur mainly between speakers of Uighur, Kazakh, and Mongolian with Chinese speakers receiving this accommodation, but not reciprocating, and generally only using Chinese (Lee-Smith 1996: 901).

Were such forms of respect shown through mutual linguistic accommodation to become widespread in Central Asia, it might be anticipated that there would be major effects on language practices and attitudes with unpredictable effects on choice, development and form(s) of languages of wider communication used for face to face interaction for L uses. Indeed, it is hypothesized that prolonged folk bilingualism in areas where Tajik and Uzbek have long been in intimate contact has led to neighboring Tajik and Uzbek dialects becoming structurally parallel (Soper 1987), a phenomenon which is occurring with contemporary Kazakh influenced by Russian (Muhamedowa 2009).

In this vein, a recent ethnography from neighboring Tajik-speaking, Uzbek-speaking and mixed Tajik-Uzbek speaking villages outside Bukhara, Uzbekistan demonstrates such a positive attitude towards bilingualism and identity as typical (Finke and Sancak 2012). In families where the parents are from different language communities, children are often expected to adopt the language of their father as their dominant language. In reality, children were observed often adopting the language of their mother or grandmother, who typically spoke their own primary language in the home, which thus becomes the de facto of the home. At the same time, there is extensive bilingualism outside the household with virtually all having receptive understanding of the other language and many productive proficiency as well. The major finding of Finke and Sancak's ethnography (2012) seems to be that this traditional identity is alive and well in today's rural Bukhara with no seeming interruption by the Soviets.

However, while the local custom makes no distinction between Tajik and Uzbek languages in L functions, the state is now actively promoting the use of Uzbek for H functions through education. In the Soviet period, the choice of attending an Uzbek- or Tajik-medium village school had little bearing on a child's chance to learn enough of the then dominant language Russian to improve future educational and career opportunities, since education in both languages was equally disfavored. Now that Uzbek is the state language and its prestige is increasing, there are very few Tajik-medium schools even in Tajik-dominant villages. For the moment, the consequence seems to be that Tajik-speakers educated only in Uzbek will not have the "somewhat richer and more diverse vocabulary" in Tajik that they might otherwise have developed (Finke and Sancak 2012: 63). For Finke and Sancak (2012), Bukhara seems to be a dynamic language ecology with both social and individual passive and active bilingualism in L uses for personal interaction in which passive bilingualism in a variety of languages is becoming more predominant, a process that currently favors the greater transmission of active ability in Uzbek.

5 Areas for future research

There are a numerous areas open for studying language use and language change in the Central Asian context. This includes examining aspects of horizontal variation among and between language dialects, vertical variation within different language registers, observing different contact phenomena, e.g., such as koineization as a process (Kerswill 2013), interlanguages, the politics of language policy and the study of language attitudes. Again, in the Uzbek case, recent calls have been made about the use of Uzbek language in university entrance exams for ethnic Uzbeks living in Kazakhstan (Oka 2011). However, to situate this protest, little information about the language repertoires of Kazakhstan's Uzbeks and their relation to standard Uzbek and standard Kazakh is available. Moreover, it is unclear from the secondary literature, for example, how contemporary standard Uzbek, Karakalpak, Kypchak dialects of Uzbek, and Uzbek dialects within Kazakhstan differ from each other.

This highlights the fact that the study of the non-titular languages, their speakers and their language practices, to date, has received little attention. Take, for example, the case of the Uighur language in Central Asia. In what settings, domains and functions do Uighurs in the region use the Uighur language and/or other languages in the ecology? When Uighurs learn other H language(s), do they gravitate towards languages in the same linguistic family, e.g., another Turkic language like Turkish, or to Russian or English (or some combinations thereof), or do they demonstrate some preference toward Uzbek, the Turkic language most similar to Uighur? When using other languages, how do they navigate these languages and what factors influence these different language choice strategies? What are the language practices of Uighur youth in schools?

To what extent do Uighurs in the region have or wish to have use of their language in schools and in the media? Similar questions may be asked for a range of non-titular languages, such as Balochi and other eastern Iranian languages as well as those ethnolinguistic groups that have links to a heritage country, e.g., Central Asian Koreans (*Koryo saram*) and Dungan Chinese (*Hui*).[7]

6 Concluding thoughts

The cases reviewed in this chapter are each, in and of themselves, brief and incomplete, and perhaps unpersuasive. Certainly in order to more systematically and elaborately describe each linguistic ecology (and overlapping ecologies), each case is deserving of an entire monograph, demanding an interdisciplinary approach bringing to bear the expertise of a broad range of scholars. However, by conducting a survey of the literature available through a particular lens, the hope is that these cases informed each other, thereby strengthening findings.

In the Soviet Union and today's independent Central Asian republics, we have seen a belief by language planners and policy makers that one H language should predominate in the territory and that the education process should favor a single state language. This approach, what Ruiz (1988) calls orientations towards language as right (the state language) versus language as problem (other languages), historically led to numerous people who attended Russian-only boarding schools successfully being able to learn Russian. However, the educational methods that produced this elite did not produce additive bilinguals, but subtractive bilinguals with ability to use their heritage language in progressively fewer functional domains from generation to generation, and less and less productive ability. Ultimately this creates the status quo, where many urban Central Asians know their heritage language poorly or not at all, while acquiring an attitude of condescending superiority over rural residents due to their lower proficiency in Russian (Korth 2005).

This attitude is relatively new in history, and has little historical precedent in Central Asia. This chapter briefly highlighted the continuous multilingual character of Central Asian society and plurilingualism of many individuals and communities and the co-existence of multiple H languages within Central Asia. Thus, 20th and 21st century language policy approaches which favor one language over another are the historical rarity in Central Asia.

---

7 Balochi is also spelled as Baluchi.

The different approaches to L and H languages in Central Asia in the 20th century share similarities with the historical contexts discussed earlier. Three major alternatives continue to inform establishment of languages for H functions in the region, then and now. The first alternative is Externalism, where an external language such as Arabic or Russian becomes adopted as an exclusive H language in a territory where it had no base as an L language. The second is localism where a local language is developed for H purposes on the analogy of an external H language by using local language neologisms rather than by overt borrowings from an external language. The third alternative is a mixed externalism-localism approach, where a local language is developed for H language uses by extensive borrowing of specialized external language H function terminology in place of developing of equivalent neologisms.

At the same time, trade and traders taking their languages with them and learning others' languages contributed to language contact and the establishment of languages of wider communication in the region for centuries, as with Soghdian and Tatar. Today, the growing trade routes and relations between China and the Central Asian republics is largely conducted with Xinjiang, by Uighurs, Kazakhs, Kyrgyz, Uzbek and Dungan, along with Pamiri-speaking Tajiks in the Mountainous Badakhshan Autonomous Province of Tajikistan and Tashkuergan Tajik County in Xinjiang, China (Sadovskaya 2012).[8,9] While sources say little about the linguistic aspects of this trade, this type of transnational interaction inherently requires plurilingual participants, and each of these languages is spoken in Xinjiang and Central Asia. The potential impact on the language ecology of cross border multilingualism and plurilingualism on the entire region is enormous, but remains largely unstudied.

References

Afnan, Soheil M. 1958. *Avicenna, his life and works*. London: G. Allen & Unwin.

Anderson, Barbara A. & Brian D. Silver. 1983. Estimating Russification of ethnic identity among non-Russians in the USSR. *Demography* 20. 461–489.

Bahry, Stephen A., Yuliya Karimova & Duishon Shamatov. 2015. Review of Jacob M. Landau & Barbara Kellner-Heinkele (2012), *Language politics in contemporary Central Asia*, London: I.B. Tauris. *Language Policy* 14(1). 95–97. DOI: 10.1007/s10993-013-9295-6.

---

8 Chinese-speaking Muslims are also referred to as the Hui people in China and in Central Asia.
9 While working in 1998 at Khorog State University, Mountainous Badakhshan, Tajikistan, the author conducted informal classes in oral Chinese in anticipation of the opening of the new road to Xinjiang, China.

Bahry, Stephen A., Sarfaroz Niyozov & Duishon Shamatov. 2008. Bilingual education in Central Asia. In Jim Cummins & Nancy H. Hornberger (eds.), *Bilingual education* [Encyclopedia of Language and Education 5], 205–221. New York: Springer Science + Business Media LLC.

Baldauf, Richard B., Jr. 2006. Rearticulating the case for micro language planning in a language ecology context. *Current Issues in Language Planning* 7(2–3). 147–170.

Baskakov, Aleksandr N. 1996a. Languages of interethnic communication in the area of Central Asia and Kazakhstan. In Stephen A. Wurm, Peter Mühlhäusler & Darrell T. Tryon (eds.), *Atlas of languages of intercultural communication in the Pacific, Asia, and the Americas*, Vol. 2, 913–918. Berlin: de Gruyter.

Baskakov, Aleksandr N. 1996b. Languages of interethnic communication in Turkmenistan. In Stephen A. Wurm, Peter Mühlhäusler & Darrell T. Tryon (eds.), *Atlas of languages of intercultural communication in the Pacific, Asia, and the Americas*, Vol. 2, 929–932. Berlin: de Gruyter.

Baskakov, Aleksandr N. 1996c. Languages of interethnic communication in Kirgizistan. In Stephen A. Wurm, Peter Mühlhäusler & Darrell T. Tryon (eds.), *Atlas of languages of intercultural communication in the Pacific, Asia, and the Americas*, Vol. 2, 937–940. Berlin: de Gruyter.

Baskakov, Aleksandr N. 1996d. Languages of interethnic communication in Tajikistan. In Stephen A. Wurm, Peter Mühlhäusler & Darrell T. Tryon (eds.), *Atlas of languages of intercultural communication in the Pacific, Asia, and the Americas*, Vol. 2, 941–944. Berlin: de Gruyter.

Baskakov, Aleksandr N. & Aziz B. Džuraev. 1996. Languages of interethnic communication in Uzbekistan. In Stephen A. Wurm, Peter Mühlhäusler & Darrell T. Tryon (eds.), *Atlas of languages of intercultural communication in the Pacific, Asia, and the Americas*, Vol. 2, 919–924. Berlin: de Gruyter.

Baskakov, Aleksandr N. & Bakhytzhan X. Xasanov. 1996. Languages of interethnic communication in Kazakhstan. In Stephen A. Wurm, Peter Mühlhäusler & Darrell T. Tryon (eds.), *Atlas of languages of intercultural communication in the Pacific, Asia, and the Americas*, Vol. 2, 933–936. Berlin: Mouton de Gruyter.

Bodrogligeti, Andras J. E. 2009. Turkic-Iranian contacts. Chaghatay language and literature. *Encyclopaedia Iranica.* http://www.iranicaonline.org/articles/turkic-iranian-contacts-ii-chaghatay (accessed 25 January 2014).

Boeschoten, Hendrik & Marc Vandamme. 1998. Chaghatay. In Lars Johanson & Éva Á. Csató (eds.), *The Turkic languages*, 166–178. New York: Routledge.

Calvet, Louis-Jean. 1996. *Les politiques linguistiques.* Paris: Presses Universitaires de France.

Calvet, Louis-Jean. 1999. *Pour une écologie des langues du monde.* Paris: Plon.

Calvet, Louis-Jean. 2007. Pour une linguistique du désordre et de la complexité [For a linguistics of disorder and complexity]. *Carnets d'Atelier de Sociolinguistique* 1. 1–71.

Chambers, J. K. 2008. *Sociolinguistic theory*, 2nd edn. Chichester: Wiley-Blackwell.

Clement, Victoria. 2005. *Rewriting the "nation": Turkmen literacy, language, and power, 1904–2004.* Columbus, OH: Ohio State University dissertation.

Delorme, R. Stuart. 1999. *Mother tongue, mother's touch: Kazakhstan government and school construction of identity and language planning metaphors.* Philadelphia, PA: University of Pennsylvania dissertation.

Desheriev, Iunus D. 1976. *Razvitie natsional'no-russkogo dvuiazychiia* [The development of national Russian bilingualism]. Moscow: Nauka.

Doerfer, Gerhard. 1991. Chaghatay language and literature. *Encyclopaedia Iranica*, Vol. V, Fasc. 4, 319–343. London: Routledge and Kegan Paul. http://www.iranicaonline.org/articles/chaghatay-language-and-literature (accessed 3 November 2013).

Doerfer, Gerhard. 1992. Central Asia xiv. Turkish-Iranian language contacts. *Encyclopaedia Iranica*, Vol. V, Fasc. 2, 226–235. http://www.iranicaonline.org/articles/central-asia-xiv (accessed 3 November 2013).

Dowler, Wayne. 2001. *Classroom and empire: The politics of schooling Russia's eastern nationalities, 1860–1917*. Montreal: McGill-Queen's University Press.

Dwyer, Arienne M. 1998. The texture of tongues: Languages and power in China. *Nationalism and Ethnic Politics* 41(2). 68–85.

Dzhunusov, Makhsud S. 1980. Vzaimoobogashchenie natsionalnykh kultur i razvitiia natsional'no-russkogo dvuiazychiia [The mutual enrichment of national cultures and the development of National-Russian bilingualism]. In Iunus. D. Desheriev & Eteri G. Tumanian (eds.), *Vzaimo-otnoshenie razvitiia natsional'nykh iazykov i natsionalnykh kultur* [The interrelation of development of national languages and national cultures], 42–64. Moscow: Nauka.

Dzyuba, Ivan 1974. *Internatsionalizm chy rusifikatsiya* [Internationalism or russification? A study in the Soviet nationalities problem]. New York: Monad Press.

Ferguson, Charles A. 1959. Diglossia. *Word* 15. 325–40.

Fierman, William. 1991. *Language planning and national development: The Uzbek experience*. New York: de Gruyter.

Fierman, William. 2012. The fate of Uzbek language in the 'other' Central Asian republics. In Harold Schiffman (ed.), *Language policy and language conflict in Afghanistan and its neighbors: The changing politics of language choice*, 208–262. Leiden: Brill.

Finke, Peter & Meltem Sancak. 2012. To be an Uzbek or not to be a Tajik? Ethnicity and locality in the Bukhara oasis. *Zeitschrift für Ethnologie* 137. 47–70.

Fishman, Joshua A. 1967. Bilingualism with and without diglossia; Diglossia with and without bilingualism. *Journal of Social Issues* 23(2). 29–38.

Golden, Peter B. 2006. Turks and Iranians: An historical sketch. In Lars Johanson & Christine Bulut (eds.), *Turkic-Iranian contact areas: Historical and linguistic aspects*, 17–38. Wiesbaden: Harassowitz.

Guboglo, Mikhail N. 1986. Factors affecting bilingualism in national languages and Russian in a developed socialist society. In Bernard Spolsky (ed.), *Language and education in multilingual settings*, 23–31. Clevedon: Multilingual Matters.

Hansen, Mette E. 2005. *Frontier people: Han settlers in minority areas of China*. Vancouver: University of British Columbia Press.

Harmatta, Janoś. 1996. The languages of the 'silk route' up to the 16th century. In Stephen A. Wurm, Peter Mühlhäusler & Darrell T. Tryon (eds.), *Atlas of languages of intercultural communication in the Pacific, Asia, and the Americas*, Vol. 2, 949–954. Berlin: de Gruyter.

Haugen, Einar. 1972. The ecology of language. In Anwar S. Dil (ed.), *The ecology of language. Essays by Einar Haugen*, 324–329. Stanford: Stanford University Press.

Henning, Walter B. 1940. Sogdian loan-words in New Persian. *Bulletin of the School of Oriental and African Studies* 10(1). 93–106.

Hornberger, Nancy H. 2002. Multilingual language policies and the continua of biliteracy: An ecological approach. *Language Policy* 1. 27–51.

Hornberger, Nancy H. & Francis M. Hult. 2008. Ecological language education policy. In Bernard Spolsky & Francis M. Hult (eds.), *The handbook of educational linguistics*, 280–296. Oxford: Blackwell.

Kerswill, Paul. 2013. Koineization. In J. K. Chambers & Natalie Schilling-Estes (eds.), *The hand-book of language variation and change*, 2nd edn., 519–536. Chichester, England: Wiley-Blackwell.

Khasanov, Bakhytzhan Kh. 1987. *Kazakhsko-russkoe dvuiazychie* [Kazakh-Russian bilingualism]. Alma Ata, Kazakh SSR: Nauka.

Kirchner, Mark. 1998. Kazakh and Karakalpak. In Lars Johanson & Éva Á. Csató (eds.), *The Turkic languages*, 318–332. London: Routledge.

Korth, Britta. 2005. *Language attitudes towards Kyrgyz and Russian: Discourse, education and policy in post-Soviet Kyrgyzstan*. Bern: Peter Lang.

Landau, Jacob M. & Barbara Kellner-Heinkele. 2012. *Language politics in contemporary Central Asia*. New York: I. B. Tauris.

Lazard, Gilbert. 1975. The rise of the New Persian language. In Richard N. Frye (ed.), *The Cambridge history of Iran: From the Arab invasion to the Saljuqs*, Vol. 4, 595–632. Cambridge: Cambridge University Press.

Lee-Smith, Mei W. 1996. An example of multilingualism in the great northwest of China. In Stephen A. Wurm, Peter Mühlhäusler & Darrell T. Tryon (eds.), *Atlas of languages of inter-cultural communication in the Pacific, Asia, and the Americas*, Vol. 2, 901–903. Berlin: Mouton de Gruyter.

Lewis, Glyn E. 1972. *Multilingualism in the Soviet Union*. The Hague: Mouton.

Lung, Rachel. 2011. *Interpreters in early imperial China*. Philadelphia: John Benjamins.

Luo, Jiayun & Jianguo Zhao. 2004. *Tajike zu: Xinjiang Tashiku'ergan xian Tizinafu cun diaocha* [Tajik nationality: Xinjiang Tashkurgan county, Tizinafu village investigation]. Kunming, China: Yunnan University Press.

Ma, Rong. 2007. Bilingual education for China's ethnic minorities. *Chinese Education and Society* 40(2). 9–25.

McWhorter, John H. 2007. *Language interrupted: Signs of non-native acquisition in standard language*. Oxford: Oxford University Press.

McWhorter, John H. 2011. *Linguistic simplicity and complexity: Why do languages undress?* Berlin: de Gruyter.

Mühlhäusler, Peter. 1997. Language ecology–contact without conflict. In Martin Pütz (ed.), *Language choices: Conditions, constraints, and consequences*, 3–16. Amsterdam: John Benjamins.

Mühlhäusler, Peter. 2002. Ecology of languages. In Robert B. Kaplan (ed.), *The Oxford handbook of applied linguistics*, 374–387. New York: Oxford University Press.

Muhamedowa, Raihan. 2009. The use of Russian conjunctions in the speech of bilingual Kazakhs. *The International Journal of Bilingualism* 13(3). 331–356.

Nasyrov, Dogžan. S. 1976. *Stanovlenie karakalpaksogo obščenarodnogo razgovornogo jazyka I ego dialektnaja sistema*. [The establishment of the Karakalpak common spoken language and its dialectal system]. Nukus, Uzbek SSR: Academy of Sciences of Uzbekistan.

Nasyrova, Ol'ga D. 1996. Languages of interethnic contact in Karakalpakistan, the former Karakalpak ASSR. In Stephen A. Wurm, Peter Mühlhäusler & Darrell T. Tryon (eds.), *Atlas of languages of intercultural communication in the Pacific, Asia, and the Americas*, Vol. 2, 925–928. Berlin: Mouton de Gruyter.

Nelde, Peter H. 2002. Language contact. In Robert B. Kaplan (ed.), *The Oxford handbook of applied linguistics*, 326–334. New York: Oxford University Press.

Nettle, Daniel & Suzanne Romaine. 2000. *Vanishing voices: The extinction of the world's languages*. New York: Oxford University Press.

Oka, Natsuko. 2011. Neither exit nor voice: Loyalty as a survival strategy for the Uzbeks in Kazakhstan. IDE Discussion Paper 286. Chiba, Japan: Institute of Developing Economies, Japan External Trade Organization.

Paul, Daniel, Elisabeth Abbess, Katja Müller, Calvin Tiessen & Gabriela Tiessen. 2010. The ethnolinguistic vitality of Yaghnobi. Dallas, Texas: SIL International. http://www.sil.org/ resources/archives/9107 (accessed May 25, 2014).

Richter-Bernburg, Lutz. 1974. Linguistic shuʻūbīya and early Neo Persian prose. *Journal of the American Oriental Society* 94(1). 55–64.

Ruiz, Richard 1988. Orientations in language planning. In Sandra Lee McKay, & Sau-ling Cynthia Wong (eds.), *Language diversity: Problem or resource?* 3–25. New York: Newbury House.

Sadovskaya, Yelena Y. 2012. The dynamics of contemporary Chinese expansion into Central Eurasia. In Felix B. Chang & Sunnie T. Rucker-Chang (eds.), *Chinese migrants in Russia, Central Asia and Eastern Europe*, 85–105. New York: Routledge.

Schlyter, Birgit N. 2005. The Karakalpaks and other language minorities under Central Asian state rule. In Birgit N. Schlyter (ed.), *Prospects for democracy in Central Asia*, 157–187. Swedish Research Institute in Istanbul. London: I. B. Tauris.

Schlyter, Birgit N. 2013. Multilingualism and language renewal in ex-Soviet Central Asia. In Tej. K. Bhatia & W. C. Ritchie (eds.), *The handbook of bilingualism and multilingualism*, 2nd edn., 871–898. Oxford: Wiley-Blackwell.

Skaff, Jonathan K. 2012. *Sui-Tang China and its Turko-Mongol neighbors: Culture, power, and connections, 580–800*. Oxford: Oxford University Press.

Smagulova, Juldyz. 2014. Early language socialization and language shift: Kazakh as baby talk. *Journal of Sociolinguistics* 18(3). 370–387. DOI: 10.1111/josl.12078

Soper, John D. 1987. *Loan syntax in Turkic and Iranian: The verb systems of Tajik, Uzbek and Qashqay*. Los Angeles, CA: University of California dissertation.

Starr, S. Frederick. 2013. *Lost enlightenment: Central Asia's Golden Age from the Arab Conquest to Tamerlane*. Princeton, NJ: Princeton University Press.

Strauss, Johann. 1993 Language modernization-The case of Tatar and modern Turkish. *Central Asian Survey* 12(4). 565–576. DOI: 10.1080/02634939308400839

Sultangalieva, Gulmira S. 2012. The Russian Empire and the intermediary role of Tatars in Kazakhstan: The politics of cooperation and rejection. In Tomohiko Uyama (ed.), *Asiatic Russia: Imperial power in regional and international contexts*, 52–79. New York: Routledge.

Tetley, Gillies E. 2008. *The Ghaznavid and Seljuk Turks: Poetry as a source for Iranian history*. New York: Routledge.

Utas, Bo. 2006. A multiethnic origin of New Persian. In Lars Johanson & Christine Bulut (eds.), *Turkic-Iranian contact areas: Historical and linguistic aspects*, 241–251. Wiesbaden: Harassowitz.

Utas, Bo. 2009. Iranian languages as gardens. *Iranian Journal of Applied Language Studies* 1(1). 142–160.

Voegelin, Charles F. and Florence M. Voegelin. 1964. Languages of the world: African fascicle one. *Anthropological Linguistics* 6(6). 1–149.

Wardhaugh, Ronald. 2010. *An introduction to sociolinguistics*, 6th edn. Oxford: Wiley-Blackwell.

Wurm, Stefan A. 1951. The Karakalpak language. *Anthropos* 46(3/4). 487–610.

Yemelianova, Galina M. 1999. Volga Tatars, Russians and the Russian state at the turn of the nineteenth century: Relationships and perceptions. *The Slavonic and East European Review* 77(3). 448–484.

Yoshida, Yutaka. 2009. Soghdian. In Gernot Windfuhr (ed.), *The Iranian languages*, 279–335. New York: Routledge.

Zenkovsky, Serge A. 1953. A century of Tatar revival. *American Slavic and East European Review* 12(3). 303–318.

Nathan Light

3 Being Specific About Generalization: Kyrgyz Habitual Narratives in Ethnographic Interviews[1]

Abstract: This chapter develops a linguistic anthropological analysis of the ways habitual aspect is used in Kyrgyz narratives within interviews. Based in research on habitual aspect in linguistics, linguistic anthropology and narratology, the analysis shows how respondents alternate among expressions describing singular and repeated events. Despite the broad relevance of this topic to ethnographic interviewing, the pragmatics of habitual aspect have not been systematically examined. This introductory overview of the wide spectrum of Kyrgyz uses of habitual aspect in describing cultural practices, personal experiences and historical accounts, demonstrates the value of this approach to understanding the relationship of social activities and habitual narrative.

Keywords: ethnographic interviewing; Kyrgyzstan; habitual aspect; narrative; generalization

1 Introduction

Habitual aspect is an important element of many narrative genres and generally expresses the narrator's understanding that a practice or event was consistently repeated. While the study of verbal aspect in narrative has long been considered important in linguistics, it has received only limited attention from linguistic anthropologists (Richland 2005, 2010; Silverstein 1974, 1996). There are many ways of expressing repeated action but in this chapter, I focus on aspect forms known as "generic" (emphasizing a general character or pattern, e.g.,

---

1 I have many people to thank for help with this project: many colleagues at the Max Planck Institute for Social Anthropology and particularly co-director Chris Hann who supported my research; Professor Éva Csató and Birsel Karakoç in the Department of Linguistics and Philology of Uppsala University; Dr. Gulnara Aitpaeva and the many helpful people at Aigine Cultural Research Center in Bishkek; my fieldwork assistants Damira Imanalieva, Asel Turganbaeva, Nazira Satïsheva, Zemfira Inogamova and Gulmira Aldakeeva; and the many people from my fieldwork sites who have been supportive of my work. Gulmira Aldakeeva was particularly helpful with her timely transcriptions of difficult passages.

"dogs bark" or "people make mistakes"), "habitual" or "iterative" (for repeated or typical events or actions), and "gnomic" (a form of generic aspect that is a less expected characterization and is sometimes called "proverbial"). Habitual aspect can also be used to refer to all types when the distinctions seem less important. Gnomic forms are not usually in past tense but are used to characterize and comment upon events. Additionally, within my analysis, I use the terms "intraterminal" and "postterminal" to indicate the point of view on the action being described in distinction to its iterative or generic character (Johanson 1996, 2000).

This chapter examines grammatical aspect in Kyrgyz narratives about the past, specifically the alternation of generic, habitual and iterative descriptions of events with singular narratives of events that only happen once. The central goal of this examination is to connect ethnographic interviewing with narrative and linguistic analysis in order to better understand the role of generalization in narrative. The questions I ask here include:

- Why and how do interview respondents alternate among aspectual forms?
- How do they use these forms to convey information?
- How do uses of habitual aspect change with changing oral genres?
- What do these forms accomplish in contexts of anthropological interviewing and cultural description?

Habitual aspect is used to connect specific narratives about past events and processes to generalized patterns of events. Narrators use these imperfective aspect forms for a number of reasons. They provide generalized and typical accounts that are more relevant and concise than multiple discrete sequences of events. Such accounts may provide background information for more specifically narrated events or a narrator may wish to point out a characteristic pattern of events. The narrator may have limited knowledge about or wish to avoid revealing details of a particular case. Moreover, the narrator or audience may indicate that a shorter account is more efficient or that there is a limited need for details. In contrast, narratives about specific singular events emphasize the value of details and their narrative realization, either as information or entertainment. Generic narratives reduce details and downplay their value as specific elements in a sequence of events.

Despite extensive discussions of the constitutive role of details in sociolinguistic and anthropological analysis of narrative performance (Hill and Irvine 1993; Ochs and Capps 2009; Shuman and Bohmer 2004), the use of habitual and generic aspect forms has received little attention. Similarly, the burgeoning linguistic literature on aspect has only begun to examine aspect within narrative discourse genres with most studies of aspect focusing on historical change and formal typologies.[2] Most narratologists do not recognize narratives which use habitual or iterative forms as "proper narratives" and this *a priori* classification prevents careful investigation of the differing uses of narrative forms. The present chapter identifies and analyzes the uses of habitual and generic aspect to suggest ways that ethnographic and discourse analysis can fill gaps in understanding of aspect.

2 Kyrgyz sociolinguistics

This project contributes to the underdeveloped fields of linguistic anthropology and sociolinguistics in Kyrgyzstan. Other than studies of language preferences, collections of oral narratives, and analysis of their cultural and historical contents, little work has been done on the relationships of language and society in Kyrgyzstan. Studies of Soviet and post-Soviet bilingualism and language attitudes have led to a number of publications, and the more productive scholars among these have also published in English on language attitudes and code switching among bilinguals in the Kyrgyz Republic, with particular reference to educational contexts (Huskey 1995; Korth 2005; Orusbaev et al. 2008).

The comprehensive grammatical presentation by Guy Imart (1981) discusses parallels among Kyrgyz and other Central Asian Turkic languages. He carried out his research through extensive consultation with native speakers so he offers many comments about variations in use and meaning. Imart's detailed analysis allowed him to draw nuanced conclusions about new forms emerging from Soviet-era contact with Russian (Imart 1981: para. 843, 1275, 2694, 2754, 2800, 2880, 2915). He also critiques academic misunderstandings of Kyrgyz grammar caused by the adoption of Russian concepts, especially in relation to analyzing aspect (Imart 1981: para. 1417–1431, 2006). Some linguistic changes appeared to result from the influence of literary forms on the spoken language (Imart 1981: para 1704). Nonetheless, Imart provides only occasional comments about regional variants and dialectology and little about sociolinguistics.

---

2 In both linguistic anthropology and linguistics, there is a need for more study of the discourse function of aspect forms. As Binnick (2006: 259) argues, an "explanatory account of aspect depends on understanding the function of aspect in discourse." Thelin's edited volume (1990a) and chapter (1990b) contribute to this effort but linguistic analysis dominates: the chapters by Jensen (1990) and Holk (1990) are valuable contributions and help fill Paul Friedrich's call for more investigation of pragmatic functions of aspect (1974: S8).

3 Aspect theory in linguistics

Aspect is a complex topic in contemporary linguistic theory with significant ongoing debates, although some consensus can be identified around several fundamental insights (Binnick 2012; Comrie 1976; Sasse 2002; Vendler 1957). Differences among theoretical models and widely varying terminology for temporal relations in tense and aspectuality reflect the complexity and dynamic development of this field. The major models for tense-aspect are not mutually exclusive but involve different theoretical emphases and in this section, I briefly summarize and link the important concepts rather than exploring contrasts among theories (Binnick 2006). In the "relational model" of tense and aspect, tense expresses the relationship of time of speaking to the time of events spoken about while aspect expresses the relationship of two events in time (known as "taxis") without regard to the time of speaking. The "boundedness model" emphasizes the ways that aspect forms define the boundaries of events in time, i.e., events may be separated, connected, partially or fully overlapping, or one may include the other. Finally, the "phasic model" emphasizes the ways that morphemes and other operators situate expression in relation to the structure of an action, such as prospective (about to start), inchoative (beginning), progressive (ongoing), or retrospective (describing completed action, hence close to perfective in sense).

Grammatical aspect can be expressed by verbal forms or periphrastic expressions, while lexical aspect relates to the intrinsic meanings of words, often called "Aktionsart". In lexical aspect, boundaries are shaped by verbal semantics and are characterized by duration (or its lack) and telicity (uniform action vs. reaching a defined end). In one effort to refine the terminology for these forms, Johanson (1996, 2000) distinguishes viewpoint operators that modify terminality features from the internal phase structure: the latter he terms the "actional content of a phrase". He analyzes grammatical aspect forms as morphosyntactic "viewpoint operators": at the point in time from which the action is "viewed", the actional content may be ongoing (intraterminal), attaining an end (adterminal) or having ended (postterminal). Johanson (1996, 2000) suggests these are more precise than the more idiosyncratic and variable categories imperfective and perfective. In analyses below I rely on these terms to distinguish perspectives on narrated action, but modify it with terms necessary to distinguish, *inter alia*, the continuing or intermittent nature of ongoing actions.

3.1 Habitual, iterative, generic and gnomic aspect

The categories of perfective and imperfective aspect continue to dominate most discussions, and until the past few decades there was limited attention to habitual, iterative, generic and gnomic aspects. The imperfective has continued to be the catch-all category for forms that describe repeated actions: such expression implies that each element in a sequence is completed, but the overall sequence nonetheless continues (Croft 2012; Silverstein 1974). Habitual aspect forms thus involve elements of both perfective and imperfective (progressive, durative) aspects rather than simply being imperfective in the sense of a single ongoing process viewed from within (Binnick 2006: 258–259; Croft 2012: 92–126; Johanson 2000: 29). In this chapter I focus on narrative discourse rather than developing precise linguistic analyses. The narrative examples here involve primarily habitual and iterative aspect forms, but a few generic and gnomic forms appear as well.

3.2 Aspect in Turkic languages

Turkic languages have a wide range of means to express past and present imperfective, habitual and iterative meanings using both periphrastic and grammatical forms, including auxiliary verbs. Johanson has developed his extensive discussion of aspect, viewpoint operators and actional markers since his dissertation (1971, 1995, 1996, 1999). He has shown the important interaction of tense-aspect with evidentiality (2000, 2003) and the effects of language contact on the meanings of tense-aspect forms (2002).

3.3 Habitual aspect in oral and written Kyrgyz narratives

Imart (1981: para. 1938–1943) describes several forms used for expressing habitual aspect rooted in the *-chU* suffix for verbal nouns: *-chU bolgon, -chU boldu* and *-GAn bolchu.* He also discusses the habitual meaning of *-Ar ele* (para. 2027–2030). Further, he identifies the uncommon evidential form *-chU eken* which designates reported or presumed information, as also conveying a nuance of habituality (para. 2055).

Morphological expressions of habitual aspect appear rarely in Kyrgyz oral genres. In the Manas epic (Hatto 1990) and other traditional oral and written narratives (Prior 2012), verbal forms using *-chU* in a habitual sense are very uncommon. Perhaps this can be attributed to the strong tendency of Kyrgyz oral narratives to focus on a punctual, concrete past, although this focus is often doubled by characters' thought and speech about events in their past, immediate present and future. The lack of habitual aspect forms that can be translated into English with "would" or "used to" reflect the infrequency of descriptions of ongoing and repeated actions in traditional Kyrgyz oral narratives. The habitual forms presented by Imart are drawn from literary sources and grammatical studies, suggesting that they are used more in contemporary Kyrgyz.

4 Narratology and habitual narratives

Few narrative theorists have carefully described and analyzed of the role of grammatical aspect in expressing different kinds of event sequences. Narrative theory has commonly defined narratives as singular sequences of events while habitual or iterative expression within narrative has been neglected. Some of the few studies of habitual aspect in narratives include the work of Charlotte Linde (1986) and others on what they term "habitual narratives." Linde (1986) discusses the contrasts in reportability – whether a narrative is relevant and informative – between habitual narratives and those made up of sequences of distinct events (Norrick 2005). She writes

> Note that habitual narratives, which are of great interest to sociologists, anthropologists, etc., are exempt from the constraint of current reportability. That is, a habitual narrative tells how we used to do something; even if the actions reported were completely common at the time of the story, they have become rare or obsolete at the time of narration, and hence are reportable. (Linde 1986: 197)

Linde (1986) places her account within the event structure approach to narrative of William Labov (1972, 2013) and Livia Polanyi (1985), who discuss habitual narratives as one of a number of varieties of generic or pseudo-narratives. In Labov's definition, a narrative consists minimally of two past-tense main clauses, whose order is to be taken as the order of events. These linguistically marked event clauses present the "facts" of the narrative in the sense of reporting what happened. Labov and Polanyi distinguish narrative proper from several other types: the generic narrative, the hypothetical narrative, and the pseudonarrative (Polanyi 1985; as cited in Linde 1986: 186).

Polanyi (1982: 510) rigidly defines proper narratives with a careful exclusion of habitual aspect forms, noting that

In narrative discourse, a precise time line is established through the telling, made up of discrete moments at which some instantaneous occurrence took place in the "world" created through the narration. In the text of the telling, this time line is communicated through the ordering of "event clauses" in the surface structure of the narrative... [E]vent ... denote[s] an occurrence in some world which is encoded in a proposition which receives an instantaneous rather than durative interpretation... Events are linguistically realized in syntactically main clauses which are semantically punctual, non-iterative, and completive.

Polanyi's complex specification of differences among narrative categories suggests that it is easier to distinguish such narratives in practice than in analytic definitions. Studies of personal narratives show that speakers generally lack names for such distinctions but alternate among the forms according to their goals in discourse.

Narrative researchers with less prescriptive concepts of narrative have studied forms that do not fit Labov and Polanyi's strict definitions. In studies of life history narratives, Riessman (1990, 1991) points out that background information tends to be presented using habitual aspect while foregrounded events are put into perfective, punctual forms (Hopper 1979). More recently prescriptive (etic) definitions of narratives have been challenged through closer attention to the variety of ways people embed narratives in social life (Fina and Georgakopoulou 2011). Examining such embedding reveals how speakers organize and use linguistic forms within utterances. The present chapter similarly examines the pragmatics of aspect forms, people's individual stylistic repertoires, and the shifting roles of habitual aspect in narrative genres. Kyrgyz narrative representations of events within interviews are understood through balanced investigation of contextual embedding, personal style and linguistic forms.

5 Ethnographic interviewing

Through analysis of interview data from northwest Kyrgyzstan villages I show how oral narrators employ grammatical aspect and periphrasis to express singular, repeated, typical and generic events: this analysis thus contributes to the rather underdeveloped field of the "anthropology of interviewing".[3] The role of habitual and generic aspect in ethnographic interviews has received little attention, apparently because it was not seen as a relevant dimension of pragmatic

---

3 See Briggs (1986, 2007). The problematics of interviews and their discursively formulated descriptions of culture practices and events are generally eschewed in the more purist paradigms of ethnomethodology, conversation analysis and interactional sociolinguistics (Gumperz 1999).

practice. Increased attention to issues of generalization, vagueness, relevance and narrative ideology may lead to more theoretical interest in this topic. Most linguistic anthropologists tend to focus on "naturally occurring" discourse and avoid close work on interviews, but the linguistic behaviors explored here do appear in a variety of narrative contexts as well as in interviews.

Among linguistic anthropologists, Michael Silverstein (1974: S64) was one of the earliest to explore the role of "usitatives" or habituals in cultural description noting that

> These forms are used in describing cyclically repeated activities, though, it is clear, the segmented actions are completed each time they occur... [P]assages entirely in usitatives are frequently employed to describe traditional customs in the texts. It should be observed that this category does not negate in any way the perfectivity of the action, but "quantifies" it as cyclically segmentable.

Here Silverstein alludes to the concept of quantification developed by Roman Jakobson. Binnick (2005: 346) expands upon how the concept of quantification can help distinguish between habitual and generic aspects:

> Generic sentences concern recurrent eventualities but differ from habitual sentences in that we can neither individuate... nor quantify... the occurrences in the series of situations referred to, in the way that we can in the case of habitual sentences... because the generic, unlike the habitual, does not concern a series of actual eventualities.

Binnick distinguishes here between habitual sentences with definite actors and events of the type "each time a squirrel finds a nut he will eat it" and generic sentences such as "squirrels eat nuts." But there are many shades of meaning between the restrictive specificity of particular squirrels carrying out particular actions repeatedly under particular conditions, and generic squirrels that make generalized actions without quantification. Quantification appears to be a distinctive feature, but not the only criterion for distinguishing habitual from generic aspects, and perhaps the continuing ambiguities are one reason that the habitual/generic distinction has not been more commonly investigated by linguistic anthropologists.

Charles Briggs (1985: 300) describes the habitual forms used in Mexicano pedagogical discourse, both in interviews and in other conversations about cultural characteristics, observing that

> References to "nowadays" are inflected in the present tense and the indicative mood, while verbs that refer to "bygone days" are marked for past tense and habitual aspect. By marking the verbal elements of such expressions as *sembraban* for past + habitual, we are left with the impression that such actions occurred so frequently in "bygone days" that they are characteristic of life during that era.

Despite these examples, the lack of detailed discussion of typification in narratives suggests that it has not been seen as important to analyze and differentiate among the various forms, pragmatics and contexts. The topic may be overlooked because it is obvious – generic and habitual forms are widely used to describe regularities – but more careful consideration of semantic and pragmatic dimensions should uncover more subtle distinctions and develop a framework for comparative analysis.

The work of a legal anthropologist, Justin Richland (2005, 2010) suggests the potential value of such research. He has shown that the pragmatics of habitual aspect in Hopi legal narrative shape the presentation of legal precedent and can be the subjects of judgments about cultural practices. The judge in a Hopi court case attempted to use the generalizing force of the habitual aspect to impose an interpretation of the case upon elders charged with establishing the facts. However, the elders resisted accepting this generalizing view of tradition and would not "subsume their normative understandings of tradition to the norms of an Anglo-American style legal system that requires general norms to be applied by triers of fact (here the Judge) to the facts of the case. To the elders… this was nothing more than a power grab" (Richland 2010: 443).

5.1 Power and personal ideals in narrative forms

My attention to this problem emerges from my personal response to generic and habitual narratives. I am concerned about the ways that assertions of tradition impose the power of ideals on real behavior. This is similar to the situation in legal discourse about normative practices. Interviews also rely upon institutionalized frames and involve negotiations over power relations (Briggs 1986). In interviews I generally seek to explore dialogically what interlocutors wish to discuss, and thus am reluctant to steer narrators according to my own preferences. Nonetheless, because most ethnographic description relies upon concrete cases, I prefer narratives about particular, singular events, rather than generalized cultural descriptions or even hypothetical descriptions and examples. Hence I appear to share Labov (1972, 2013) and Polanyi's (1985) evaluative commitment to "proper narratives".

When Kyrgyz tell stories in everyday social interaction, they generally narrate stories of specific singular sequences of events with few habitual and generic elements. They participate in an aesthetic preference for compact and specific narrative accounts, often with humorous elements. Narratives are often interesting because of unusual or unexpected and funny events. This suggests that generalizing elements remain implicit: the narrator does not include generic elements because she can rely upon her knowledge of the shared understand-ings of her listeners to lead them to distinguish the usual from the distinctive, and hence reportable.

In contrast, when I ask open-ended questions about practices, it appears that people often tell me generalized accounts because I am not seen as having the shared background that makes a specific account relevant. Almost anything told to me is seen as new information, and it becomes similar to the situation pointed out by Linde (1986: 197) above where actions that were "common at the time of the story... have become rare or obsolete at the time of narration, and hence are reportable". Rather than discussing concrete narratives and actual events in interviews, people present didactic generalizations or express thoughts, observations and concerns about what they consider to be generally the case. Interestingly, in Kyrgyz, as in English, the introductory phrase "for example" (*misal üchün* or simply *misal* in Kyrgyz), is often used to present a hypothetical case. It is possible that this has been introduced through contact with narrative patterns from Russian or another language, and this suggests that there might be a widespread connection of such rhetorical forms with a modern Western approach to formulating cultural descriptions, as suggested also by Richland's (2010) Hopi case above.

One problem in interviews is asking questions that lead people to provide specific and detailed accounts rather than generalizations. There is no con-venient metalanguage for distinguishing among aspect forms, and this is an indication of the degree to which aspect forms are subconscious reflections of the communicative goals of the narrator. It is not easy to elicit narratives that use particular aspect forms since use is determined by semantics. In my inter-views, open-ended questions allowed interlocutors to present what they thought were relevant narratives, but they also often took the opportunity to give gener-alizing descriptions. In one *ad hoc* strategy aimed at eliciting singular accounts, I would identify them by the genre term *okuyilar* (stories). One of my fieldwork assistants would sometimes use the word *pakït*, the Kyrgyz form of the Russian word *fakt*, when seeking examples. Below I give another example showing how another assistant suggested other genres.

6 Narrative examples

The narrative examples I present here have been selected because they include repetition and habitual accounts, and thus are candidates for carrying gram-matical aspect morphological markers. I also sought examples of skilled narrators presenting accounts of intrinsic interest, including diverse aspects of religious and economic life in the Soviet period and after. Due to space limitations I provide limited contextualizing commentary, but further discussion of Kyrgyz religious experience and Soviet religious persecution can be found in the literature cited in this chapter.

6.1 Baktïgül Abdïvalieva

In spoken and written Kyrgyz, habitual aspect verb forms are used, but in contrast to English, they tend to be optional, with periphrastic forms expressing frequency and repeated action being more common. Here I give an extended example from a published life history that was collected as part of a project on Kyrgyz spiritual practices, particularly pilgrimages to sacred sites, healing, dreaming and spirit initiation (Aitpaeva and Egemberdieva 2009a, 2009b). The life histories collected in this project were transcribed from recorded interviews and then given to the interviewee to correct. Hence they combine oral and written production. In the life history of Baktïgül Abdïvalieva, a healer, her uses of the habitual past expressed with *–chU + personal ending* and the intraterminal (imperfective) past with *-Ar ele + personal ending* are noteworthy in the initial section where she describes her childhood spiritual experiences.

(1) *Бул дарыгерлик шыпаагерчилигим 6–7 жаш эс тартып калган[4]*
   учурумда пайда болду. Ошол убакта өлгөн адамдарды көп көрүп, алар
   мени менен жүргөндөрүн байкап, көп ирет коркуп, качып, жашынып
   калган күндөрүм эсимде. Күндөрдүн биринде уктап жаткан жеримден
   мени жетелеп тышка, же башка бөлмөгө алып кетип, көптөгөн
   сөздөрдү айтаар эле. Алардын баарысын балалыгым менен байкабап-
   тырмын. Көпчүлүк учурда аян түшүмдөгү окуялар көп болоор эле, көбү
   кызыктуу. Алар менен чогуу асманга учуп кетчүмүн, кээде жакшы,
   кооз жерлерде, гүлдестелердин арасында, же алма бактын ичинде, же
   болбосо көлдүн ичинде, кээде аскер баатырлар менен согушта
   жүргөндөй болуп, же Мекке таштын жанында тегеренип жүрүп,
   же Пирамидага чыгып, чокусунда болуп калар элем. (Aitpaeva and
   Egemberdieva 2009a: 189)

[My healing abilities appeared when I became able to reason at about 6–7 years old. I remember days when I often saw dead people, and they would walk attentively with me, and many times I suddenly became afraid, ran

---

4 Iudakhin (1965: 964) gives *эс токтогон калган бала*—and the implied synonym *эс тартып калган бала*—meaning "a child who has already begun to reason" (*соображать, рассуждать*).

away and hid. Waking me one day from my sleeping place, leading me outside, or taking me to another room, they would say many things. Because I was young I did not pay attention to everything [they said]. Many times the stories in my dream visions would be many with lots of meaningful elements. Together with them [the spirits] I would fly to the heavens, sometimes to nice and beautiful places amidst flower-filled fields or within apple orchards, or otherwise amidst lakes. Sometimes I would be (suddenly) accompanying warrior-heroes in battle, or walking around the stone in Mecca, or climbing up a pyramid and standing on the summit.] (Aitpaeva and Egemberdieva 2009b, 174, translation modified)

Following this passage she tells a specific (punctual) account of a dream encounter, and then returns to habitual and imperfective forms when she mentions meetings with the epic hero Manas, Friedrich Engels, Vladimir Lenin, Iosif Stalin and Leonid Brezhnev and visits to sacred sites. After these, in the rest of her brief life history – only two pages – she does not use intraterminal past forms (Aitpaeva and Egemberdieva 2009a: 189–91).

The distinction between durative or habitual intraterminal past forms is usually not clear here: whether the action was continuing or repeating has to be inferred from context. The second sentence uses periphrasis and *-Ip* gerunds to connote the intraterminal sense. What is particularly interesting in these past tense sentences is that the narrator provides multiple verbs and predicates to make explicit the sense of a repeated activity. In other words, the narrator uses not only the intraterminal and habitual forms but puts explicit alternative events within the sentence using either the gerund in *-Ip* or alternative nouns with locative endings. She also extends the *kalar elem* auxiliary form of the last line to impart an intraterminal meaning to all the *-Ip* gerunds in the sentence. As we shall see below, neither this use of morphological habitual and intraterminal verb forms nor the giving of multiple alternatives within one sentence are common in oral Kyrgyz narratives.

6.2 Burul Apa

The next example I consider comes from a videotaped interview with Burul Apa, one of the best narrators from the rural village of Beshbulak where I did fieldwork in northwestern Kyrgyzstan.[5] She was born in 1932 and married through an arranged marriage to her husband in 1949, and has lived in the same house

---

5 Beshbulak is considered an *ayïl* [village] in Kyrgyzstan even though it has a population of roughly 4,000 residents living in 700 homes. I have changed the name of the town and people mentioned here to protect identities. In the story of Sïdïgalï Moldo, I name him and the villages mentioned because these will not identify living interlocutors.

since then. Her husband passed away more than 20 years ago. She has 11 children, including four daughters, one of whom was adopted from her eldest son (a common practice among Kyrgyz). I interviewed her several times between 2007 and 2010. She was always a generous and tireless teller of stories drawn from her own life and from those of her extended family. I worked with an assistant who Burul Apa chooses to address in these interviews because she is female and more competent culturally and linguistically. Because she is addressing this local native speaker, Burul Apa only provides explanatory asides relevant to someone from the region.

In this interview, Burul Apa shares some shorter narratives about her life history and then we ask her open-ended questions about her relatives. She speaks for more than 15 minutes about the persecution of her grandmother-in-law's father in the 1930s and 40s. I begin with a question about the *uruu* (lineage) she was born into and that into which she married. Then I ask her if she knew any stories (*okuyilar*) about these uruu. My assistant follows my question by suggesting legends (*ulamïsh*) or histories (*tarïkhi*). Identifying these narrative genres prompts Burul Apa to think a moment before deciding to tell us a story she implies is not a legend but resembles one. She states that she did not know any legends but then launches into a description of the *moldos* (mullahs, religious specialists) of the family she married into. She begins with her husband's parents, their grandparents and how many children each had. After three minutes, she reaches the story she wanted to tell about the father of her grandmother-in-law. Sïdïgalï Moldo had been an important *moldo* from the town of Krupskoe who had been condemned in the 1930s to death by execution in the Siberian tundra along with two other moldos from the nearby towns of Bakayïr and Suulu-Maimak.[6]

(2) *Apparat, apparïp turup munday jer tamga ki:p kamayt iken...*[7] [They were taken [to Siberia] and imprisoned in an earthen house like this [gesturing to show size]...]

Ushu kamaganda, bayu üch moldo olturawalïk, munday bulan karawaler, shu kitep okuwaler shu, ötön okugan moldolor olturiveret iken da, bulanni karawayli. [Imprisoned like this these three moldos sat facing this way, reading from a book, the moldos were apparently sitting, looking this way [gestures to show they were facing the wall].]

---

6 Being sent to Siberia implies that he was actually sentenced to imprisonment in a labor camp rather than to execution.

7 All transcriptions from oral Kyrgyz are rendered as closely as possible to local spoken forms but without resorting to IPA symbols. Hence many, standard written Kyrgyz forms are reduced to oral contractions.

Anan bayan militsioner kelet. [Then this guard came.]

Mïnï:nday mïnday birtke nan berip, birtke suu berip koewu, ushunday. [Like so like so he gave a bit of bread, he gave a bit of water, something like this [gestures the length of her forefinger].]

Anan kiyin anna eshikta kulptap, kulptap turup, ketet militsiyalar. [After that the guards locked the door, locked it up and left.]

Militsiyalar kulptap ketse-dalï bayagï kulp jerge tüshüp kalat ushunche, kulptanbayt achïlïp, munday jerge tüshöt, boldu. [After the guards locked it and left that lock suddenly fell to the ground, it did not stay locked and fell to the ground, that was it.]

The guards come back and ask if anyone had gone out and how the lock had fallen off but the prisoners answer that they know nothing. The guards tell the commander of the prison. Burul Apa pauses to explain that the commander is a Tatar and a Muslim, as is his wife.

(3) *Anan kiyin bayagï militsiyalar aytïp barat da ushundai ushundai. Eshik achïlïp kalat, bilbeybiz. Kulptaybïz, tartabïz, kelermiz, kayra barsak eshik, kulp jerde jatat. Emne ekenin bilbeybiz ushiga dep. Anda orto jerde bir kishi bar, ushu ech jakta karabayt, ushu okuy beret okuy beret, deyt.*

[After that the guards came saying such and such: "The door suddenly opens, we do not know [how]. We lock it, we pull it, we come [here], and when we go back, the door, the lock is lying on the ground. We do not know why. And in the middle there is a man who does not look to either side but is praying and praying."]

The commander asks them to bring him the one in the middle, Sïdïgalï Moldo, and they do so. When they take him from the prison cell, Burul Apa describes the other two moldos as "holy men with spiritual abilities" (*kasiettüü bar oliya kishiler*) who can foresee the future, and she narrates their parting comments in parallel lines:

(4) *Ey Sïdïgalï Moldo deptir,* [Hey, Sïdïgalï Moldo they apparently said,]

Sen eldu körösen deptir, [You will see your people they apparently said,]

Biz körbeybiz deptir, [We will not see (them) they apparently said,]

Bizden salam aytïp koy barïp kalsang deptir. [Could you go and give (them) greetings from us, they apparently said.]

After thus quoting the moldos' words, Burul Apa returns to a more discursive account of what happens to Sïdïgalï Moldo. He is taken to the prison office building, which is a two story building, to meet the commander. The height of the building is significant because Burul Apa says that Sïdïgalï feared he would be shot on its roof and thrown off. However, the commander tells him that although he is condemned to death, he will be given his freedom if he can pray and cure his 18-year old son whose face has been twisted around backwards by an illness. Sïdïgalï Moldo tells the commander that his power comes only through praying to God (*birinchi Kuday sevep deyt*) but he will pray and use his breath (*dem salam deyt*) to try to cure the boy. The commander and his wife give Sïdïgalï Moldo good food and allow him to take a hot bath (*moncho*).

(5) *Kechinde anan keyin okuyum deyt, Kudayga siyinip. . .* [He says he will come to pray each evening to God. . .]

    Üch kün okugan, bet mïnday kelgen deyt. [After praying for three days the boy's face came like this [gestures to show the head turning half-way to the front].]

    Bet, ushunday keldi deyt. [The face came like this.]

    Jeti kün shert bolgondo mïnday, togra bet mïnday tüz keldi deyt. [After seven days of this treatment the face turned straight like this.]

In the interest of space I do not detail here the successful outcome of his prayers, the adoption of Sïdïgalï Moldo as the father of the commander and his wife, and his eventual freedom. After further adventures he returns to his home in Krupskoe (Talas Oblast) where he dies in 1953. The passages I have given with Kyrgyz language transcription above are the ones where repeated action suggests that habitual aspect forms could be used. But Burul Apa uses reduplication to indicate something is ongoing, as in *okuy beret okuy beret* ("went on reading and reading") in (3) which actually redoubles the already continuous form constructed with the auxiliary *ber-/-ver-*, also appearing in the combined form *olturiveret* ("continued to sit") in (2). The events that the guards report to the commander are also clearly a repeated experience, with the present indicative verbs in sequence providing one indication. In (3), "*Eshik achïlïp kalat, bilbeybiz, kulptaybiz, tartabïz*" and ending "*kayra barsak*" ["when we go back"] suggesting an assertion based on repeated experience. And finally, the most obvious case of repetition, in which he goes every night for three days to pray, is expressed with the indefinite past *-GAn*: *üch kün okugan, bet munday kelgen deyt* (5) and then the definite past in *-Di* to describe the resulting effect on the boy's face.

Although Burul Apa is not narrating in the same genre as epic narratives, she skillfully presents an extended narrative alternating narration, explanation and comments with key points in the plot presented in parallel lines of quoted speech marked by *deyt* ("he/she says") or *deptir* "he/she apparently said" (4). These quoted speech markers report the speech within the story, as well as what Sïdïgalï Moldo said when telling the story. In epic narrative quoted speech marked with *deyt* often emphasizes lines and links them into rhyming passages. In the epic context, this is reported speech only in the sense that it repeats the words of a putative prior performer of the epic. An exceptional example found on one page of Manas consists of 70 lines of poetry with 27 lines ending in *deyt* (Hatto 1990: 360).

In other interviews, people make more detailed arguments and explanations, either to me or my assistants, or both. When addressing me they often provide more details and background to the topics they present, rather than presenting concrete singular narratives. On the one hand, they do not seem to feel I have the necessary background knowledge to make a specific narrative relevant, and on the other, they seem to want to impart more general ideas and facts. I have argued elsewhere that adult male Kyrgyz, usually not elders, tend to be more willing to make broad claims about history (Light under review). Adult men seem somewhat more willing to assert general facts about the past while women seem more confident speaking about their own or others' lives in concrete narratives. However, gender and cultural difference are only some of the interpersonal dimensions that shape narrative and other elements in interviews. Since I have not considered this question in much detail I leave it as an area for further investigation.

6.3 Amanbek

An interview I did in 2009 involved habitual and generic narratives about past problems with *jamaat*, which are self-help credit associations. Jamaats in Kyrgyzstan began to be established early in the 2000s as part of a development scheme that enabled villagers to obtain loans to use for investing in projects. The legal framework for these cooperative microcredit organizations was established in 2004 (Ibraimova 2009: 65–7). Because jamaats were prone to loan default at least in Beshbulak, they were not very successful, although there are reports of greater success in other parts of Kyrgyzstan (Babajanian 2009).

Amanbek, an agronomist and one-time village government official, explained to me that jamaats involved people coming together and pooling equal contributions to create a fund from which members could borrow at low interest rates to fund business activities. Unfortunately there was no way to ensure that people would repay their loans except social pressure and the trustworthiness of each member. When people made poor investments they often could not or would not return the funds.

(6) *Misal, jamaatta, on kishi bolsa özgür orto akcha salganda. Misal, ellu somdon salat, on kishi besh jüz som. Besh jüz somdo bir ayda siz alasiz, besh protsent menen. Jigirma üch som koshup beresiz, anan ekinchi tegi alat bul akïrïn akïrïnïp koyup koyoturup alti jüz ellu, alti jüz jetmish, mïng somgo jetip kalat barïnï chogulup kalïngïz. Jakhshï bashlangan. Anan bir eki üch jil buzulup buzulup ketti-da jigirma ottuz mïngdan algan, on mïngdan kaytip kaytar bolat... Sotko barsak bolboyt iken.*

[For example, in a jamaat, if there are 10 people they each put in money. For example, they put in 50 som each, 10 people (would have) 500 som. You take 500 som for one month at five percent, and return it with an additional 23 som [sic]. And then the second takes, and gradually gradually adding adding it would reach 650/670/1000 som. It began well. And then one two three years it began breaking breaking, and 20 or 30,000 borrowed and only 10,000 would be returned... And going to court is not possible.]

Amanbek goes on to point out that although the government established the legal framework to create jamaats there was no provision for enforcing the jamaat loan contracts. In fact, he reports that if one brought a suit in court, the court would argue that the money-lending was an unregistered business activity and the participants should have been paying taxes.

It is unclear whether Amanbek avoids details about the operation of particular jamaats and legal cases because he feels they are unnecessary, would not interest me, or because he himself does not know the specifics. He gives enough information to make his points clear but the narrative depends upon his generalizing assertions rather than concrete examples of particular events or cases. He expresses most of the repeated actions within these processes through reduplication, but in the final description of people returning less than they borrowed he does use the intraterminal form -*Ar bol-*. In fact, further into the interview Amanbek does admit that from the 30 jamaats originally established in Beshbulak there is one with 18 members that still operates successfully after seven years. This kind of specific detail might have led to deeper ethnographic analysis but in this case he was not a member of the jamaat so could not explain why it had been able to prevent defection and default on loans.

6.4 Jamila

Jamila was born in 1951 and married at age 17 right after finishing middle school. She had wanted to study accounting but her father would not let her go to Bishkek. Instead, she was married by arrangement between her father and the father of the groom. Her husband drank too much and she took her baby daughter and left her husband when the girl was eight months old. In 1970, she remarried a widower who was 25 years older than she with three children of his own already. Her second husband worked breeding sheep on the state farm (*sovkhoz*). He died at age 77 in 2001. She was still maintaining a flock of more than 50 sheep when I interviewed her in 2009. She has given birth to two daughters and three sons of her own and also proudly told of organizing the marriage of her second husband's younger son who was born in 1961. He now has 12 children of his own.

Our interview begins as a discussion of the *chernaya kassa* or rotating credit associations that are popular, mostly among women, as a way to pool funds in order to make larger household purchases. *Chernaya kassa* became more common after the end of the Soviet period, and involve up to 10 people of similar age and background who come together on the same day each month to eat a large meal hosted by members in turn. They each give the host the monthly fixed donation, usually 300–1000 som, or roughly 5–15 Euros. The host slaughters a sheep and provides a feast and guests also take home shares of meat and other food from the feast. Jamila participates in two *chernaya kassa* because she enjoys the social activity. The money left over after providing the feast is usually only enough for a moderate household purchase.

In this interview Jamila frequently describes past conditions and events using the *−chU + personal ending* form seen in the written example above but in both the durative and habitual sense.[8] When she talks about her remarriage, she says that to preserve her father's honor (*namïs*), she married a man 25 years older than herself.

(7) *Emneyalam. Jashoo shundai. Al ubakta uyat bolchu.* [What could I do? Life is like that. At that time it was shameful [to be divorced].]

She then comments,

(8) *Jigirma besh jash uluu bolchu.* [He was 25 years older.]

---

8 For further discussion, see Kirchner (1998: 351) where he uses *-chI* for the form that Imart (1981) writes as *-chU*.

When I ask her if they had had yaks (*topoz*) she replies

(9) *Topoz bolchu bolgon, ilgeri bolgon, azïr jok.* [There used to be yaks, before they were here, but now there are not.]

In detailing her work with sheep, she says,

(10) *Sovkozdïn koyi, alt jüz koy digen tughchu.* [The sovkhoz sheep, 600 sheep would give birth.]

Kashar bar bolchu, azïr kashar barï jok. [There were kashars and now they are all gone.]

Koy tughanda jardäm berchim, maga aylïkka jazïlchï. [When the sheep were giving birth they would register me for a salary.]

Jayloogo ketchik, jayloodon kelchik. [We would go to jayloo and would come back from jayloo.]

She describes the different aspects of tending the sheep when they give birth, and the process of artificial insemination that was used to breed the thousands of pure-bred Merino sheep that the state farm maintained. Her husband would use a syringe to take sperm from a ram and inseminate twenty or thirty ewes each day. She worked alongside him to manage and prepare the equipment. Around 1985 they moved from the *kashar* in the mountains where they took care of 600 sheep, to the village where she took up a village job. Her husband's children took over the *kashar* and worked as shepherds (*chaban*).

It is not clear why Jamila uses the -chU form so often to describe past practices while others seem to avoid it. She seems to find it more convenient than the periphrastic forms that we noted above, and uses it extensively to describe intraterminal states such as the shame of divorce or the presence of yaks, as well as iterated actions.

Generic aspect forms, sometimes termed gnomic, are common in Kyrgyz proverbs as part of moving from specific cases to relevant generalizations. A good proverb summarizes and defines an easily remembered rule. Kyrgyz often consider proverbs intrinsically interesting and worthy of commentary for their unusual metaphorical imagery or clever logical ideas.

Two examples appeared in our interview with Jamila. When discussing the harvest in 2009 which was unusually poor for some crops such as dry beans because of the wet spring, but very good for apples and other fruit, she used the following proverb:

(11)   *Beti jakshï bolgon jïlï, tubu jakshï bolboyt. Tubu jakshï bolgon jïlï, beti*
       jakshï bolboyt. [In a year when its face is good, its root will not be good.
       When its root is good its face will not be good.]

During the harvest season in the village, people often mentioned this idea that
a good harvest in one category would be balanced by a poor harvest in other
categories, sometimes changing from the two-way classification of underground
and above-ground crops to three categories: root crops (potatoes, carrots), surface
crops (beans, wheat, cabbage), and tree crops (apples, plums).

   Jamila uses this phrase to explain that she had had to buy fruit preserves
because the previous year she had a poor fruit crop. The present year was
much better. Then she explains the proverb at some length because this is the
first time I and my assistant had heard this idea. The exchange begins when my
assistant says that the jam she serves us tastes good and asks if it was from her
own garden. Jamila replies, somewhat contradicting the proverb's implication
that there should be a balance in any given year:

(12)   *Satiwaldik-da. Munu tigiyalbaym, satiwaldim. Jüz somdon boldughu anda.*
       [We bought it. I was not able to grow them, I bought [them]. They were
       100 som each.]

       Bu jïl Kudaga shukuri barï bar boldu. [This year, thank God, there was
       everything.]

       Bïltïr echteke jok... Kartoshka bïltïr azrak bolchu. [Last year there was
       nothing... Potatoes were few.]

Then she states the above proverb (11) and explains it.

   Later in the interview Jamila discusses local people who grow and sell
marijuana. She admits to knowing little about it but claims that everyone who
has been able to build a two story house must have gotten rich from growing
marijuana. Ordinary people like herself only make enough money to build one
half of their house while letting the other half deteriorate. She does not like
marijuana for moral reasons and because it is dangerous. She states that people
should make an honest living, and then uses the following proverb.

(13)   *Beshenenge emne jazïlgandï körüp olturush kerek.* [[You] must live
       according to what is written in your fate.]

Beshene literally means "forehead" and Kyrgyz often tell legends about unfor-
tunate events befalling a person and only after their death are these events
discovered to have been foretold by words carved into the bone of the skull.

These two examples suggest that analyses of proverbial and generic aspect forms have to take discourse function into account to understand the meanings of tense-aspect morphology. Proverbs can state general rules but still take change into account: the rule about crops suggests that years are different, but in any given year there will be a balance of successful and unsuccessful harvests according to categories of crops.

The second proverb offers a rule for moral action: not doing things contrary to one's fate functions here as a warning against pursuing wealth to the extent of doing something illegal and dangerous. Although the proverb appears to specify a strict rule it is actually ambiguous because one cannot know in advance what is written in one's fate (although foreknowledge may come through spiritual abilities as with the moldos above in (4)). Hence, living according to what is written in one's fate is an exhortation not to violate good sense and attempt to exceed the limits of one's circumstances, i.e., not striving to get more than one's due. The sentence combines a generic statement and the modal *kerek*, and thus is not a direct command but an enduring principle that should guide behavior.

Finally, although both proverbs are not narrative in form, they are closely related to narratives and appear as integral parts of them. Linguistically, both proverbs here do have temporal juncture, although not exactly as envisioned by Labov (1972, 2013) and Polanyi (1982, 1985) in their discussion of "proper" narratives. The one proverb describes changes from year to year that produce alternations among crops. The other implies (however paradoxically) that judgments can be made about behavior based on whether someone reads her fate and obeys its dicta. Hence the first establishes the causal principle that results in the narrative about the annual harvests, while the second offers a moral principle for judging whether villagers live modestly and do not engage in immoral activities as a result of aspiring to more than their destiny affords.

7 Conclusions

In this chapter I have given a few examples that show the complex relationships among specific, singular narratives, habitual narratives and those using generic or gnomic aspect forms. Kyrgyz speakers use these forms in a wide variety of narratives for different purposes, and the strict linguistic analysis of morphology can only provide a rough outline of how these semantic domains are expressed in practice. My analysis is a preliminary exploration of complex issues, undertaken to demonstrate how diverse aspect forms are used to accomplish pragmatic goals within narratives, and to suggest that the movement from the specific to habitual and generic forms reflects logics of generalization. Work within both linguistic anthropology and narratology has only begun to explore the many ways that generalization, cultural description and specific narratives interact.

The first narrative I analyzed above comes from a written source, but was initially transcribed from an interview. In keeping with a pattern frequently noted for life histories (Riessman 1991), Baktïgul presents her early years as background information using intraterminal and habitual past forms. But these forms are less common in oral examples presented from my own fieldwork interviews in the rest of this chapter.

Burul Apa's extended and well-developed narrative with iterated events is longer and more vivid than most and describes the persecution and liquidation of religious leaders in the early Soviet period. The narrative combines an important event in early Soviet history with Kyrgyz beliefs about the spiritual powers of moldos, because Burul Apa is strongly committed to these beliefs and an enthusiastic proponent of the spiritual powers of the family she married into. The narrative links traditional supernatural content with a historically-situated narrative that Burul Apa heard first-hand from those involved. She stylizes the account and develops it according to a narrative logic, recalling descriptive elements in relation to their function in the story. The quoted speech in parallel lines marked with forms such as *deyt* or *deptir* (4) resemble the poetry of epic narrative. Such quoted passages also explain and anchor major plot turning points, while the two-story building is mentioned because Sïdïgalï Moldo described his fear of being shot and thrown from its roof.

To describe the repeatedly failing lock and the nightly prayers over the injured boy, Burul Apa uses both the progressive forms made with the *ber-/-ver-* auxiliary as well as reduplicating verb phrases to indicate repetition. In the narrative told by Amanbek, he also uses reduplication rather than verb endings to generalize about the repeated activities that led to the failure of the jamaat self-help credit groups. Burul Apa is specific about who the actors are in her narrative, and exactly what they do, but she narrates repetitions without specifying how many times actions happened. For his part, Amanbek uses generalized descriptions that do not refer to particular actors or actions, but outline a process that happened in roughly the same way in all jamaats. He puts this general process into a larger narrative about the government failing to provide an adequate legal framework and thus bearing responsibility for the failure of the jamaats and people's resulting financial losses. The general claim that Burul Apa makes through her narratives is less explicit: she demonstrates the powers of Sïdïgalï Moldo and other moldos condemned to prison camp with him, and hence by extension moldos in general, especially among her husband's kin group. But she does this through details of specific events within a poetically elaborated narrative performance: the legend-like narrative does not explicitly generalize about a class of events but links them to a category that is only mentioned by the interviewer.

Amanbek made an explicit argument to me within a less specific account while Burul Apa told my assistant a longer, more specific account. However, when we interviewed Jamila she mostly addressed my assistant and yet told more general accounts, using mostly past durative forms in *-chU+personal ending*. These durative descriptions of how they would do things provide accounts of typical patterns from her life with her second husband and from her work in the sovkhoz. Jamila's choice of more generic narrative forms in this broad account of her life shows that her primary concerns are the general conditions rather than specific events. More detailed analysis of our interview might reveal how and why she chose this focus, but I suspect that this reflects a personal style of narration: she also told specific accounts, but did not dwell on them and develop them in the same way. Her use of generalization can also be seen in the reliance upon proverbs to explain the balance among crops and to justify her view that marijuana producers aspire to immoral wealth beyond their assigned lot.

Through ethnographic examples of narratives produced within interviews, this chapter has shown how complex and poorly understood are the many pragmatic dimensions of aspect. In addition to classifying linguistic forms, we have to understand the variety of uses these forms can have, and more generally attend to the wide range of expressive forms available to express continuing action, repetition, generality and degrees of specificity in narrative. Only more comprehensive study of the ways different Kyrgyz speakers develop these meanings and making comparisons with similar repertoires in other languages will allow us to be more specific about what people generalize about, when, and why.

The examples presented here suggest that the infrequent occurrence of habitual aspect morphologies in Kyrgyz epic narrative has changed over time to occasional or even common use in contemporary personal narratives, both to describe the general conditions of one's earlier life as Baktïgül and Jamila do, or to make broader arguments about social patterns as Amanbek does. People's preferences and narrative practices appear to be changing: older people such as Burul Apa prefer more traditional genres such as belief legends, marked by vivid quoted speech and reduplication to convey iterative or habitual aspect, while younger people and those with more literate education have adopted styles from written prose, formal news- or research-oriented interviewing, and genres in which generalizations are presented through hypothetical examples. They tend to use more explicit habitual morphological markers in narratives. In contrast, Kyrgyz do not seem to be changing the ways they use gnomic and generic aspect in proverbs. Proverbs have long been an important cultural focus in Turkic languages, and continue to be used in everyday speech to establish principles and explain change. Further ethnographic and linguistic research should refine these findings through investigation of how aspect forms are used in conversational narratives.

References

Aitpaeva, G. & A. Egemberdieva. (eds.). 2009a. *Ïsïk-köldögü ïyïk jerler: kasiet, zïyarat, önör.* Bishkek: Aigine.

Aitpaeva, G. & A. Egemberdieva. (eds.). 2009b. *Sacred sites of Ysyk-Köl: Spiritual power, pilgrimage, and art.* Bishkek: Aigine.

Babajanian, Babken V. 2009. *Decentralised governance and poverty reduction in Kyrgyzstan.* ESRC Research Working Paper. London: London School of Economics. https://www.esrc. ac.uk/my-esrc/grants/PTA-155-27-0012/outputs/Download/7d86ac89-07fe-4a23-ab33-c8ef0e22960f (accessed April 12, 2014).

Binnick, Robert. 2005. The markers of habitual aspect in English. *Journal of English Linguistics* 33(4). 339–369.

Binnick, Robert. 2006. Aspect and aspectuality. In Bas Aarts & April McMahon (eds.), *The handbook of English linguistics*, 244–268. Malden, MA: Blackwell.

Binnick, Robert. (ed.). 2012. *The Oxford handbook of tense and aspect.* Oxford: Oxford University Press.

Briggs, Charles L. 1985. Treasure tales and pedagogical discourse in *Mexicano* New Mexico. *Journal of American Folklore* 98(389). 287–314.

Briggs, Charles L. 1986. *Learning how to ask: A sociolinguistic appraisal of the role of the interview in social science research.* Cambridge: Cambridge University Press.

Briggs, Charles L. 2007. Anthropology, interviewing, and communicability in contemporary society. *Current Anthropology* 48(4). 551–580.

Comrie, Bernard. 1976. *Aspect: An introduction to the study of verbal aspect and related problems.* Cambridge: Cambridge University Press.

Croft, William. 2012. *Verbs: Aspect and causal structure.* Oxford: Oxford University Press.

Fina, Anna de & Alexandra Georgakopoulou. 2011. *Analyzing narrative: Discourse and sociolinguistic perspectives.* Cambridge: Cambridge University Press.

Friedrich, Paul. 1974. On aspect theory and Homeric aspect. Memoir 28. *International Journal of American Linguistics* 40(4, pt. 2). S1–S44.

Gumperz, John. 1999. On interactional sociolinguistic method. In Srikant Sarangi & Celia Roberts (eds.), *Talk, work and institutional order: Discourse in medical, mediation and management settings*, 453–471. Berlin: Walter de Gruyter.

Hatto, Arthur T. 1990. *The Manas of Wilhelm Radloff. Re-edited, newly translated and with commentary.* Wiesbaden: Otto Harrassowitz.

Hill, Jane H. & Judith T. Irvine. (eds.). 1993. *Responsibility and evidence in oral discourse.* Cambridge: Cambridge University Press.

Holk, André G. F. Van 1990. Aspect in textual deep structure. In Nils Thelin (ed.), *Verbal aspect in discourse*, 367–382. Amsterdam: John Benjamins.

Hopper, Paul J. 1979. Aspect and foregrounding in discourse. In Talmy Givón (ed.), *Discourse and syntax*, 213–41. New York: Academic Press.

Huskey, Eugene. 1995. The politics of language in Kyrgyzstan. *Nationalities Papers* 23(3). 549–572.

Ibraimova, Asel. 2009. *Legal and institutional framework for empowerment of rural communities in the Kyrgyz Republic.* Münster: LIT Verlag.

Imart, Guy. 1981. *Le kirghiz (turk d'Asie centrale soviétique). Description d'une langue de littérisation récente.* Aix-en-Provence: Publications Université de Provence.

Iudakhin, K.K. 1965. *Kirgizsko–russkii slovar'.* Moscow: Sovetskaia Etsiklopediia.

Jensen, Peter A. 1990. Narrative description or descriptive narration: problems of aspectuality in Čechov. In Nils Thelin (ed.), *Verbal aspect in discourse*, 383–409. Amsterdam: John Benjamins.

Johanson, Lars. 1971. *Aspekt im Türkischen: Vorstudien zu einer Beschreibung des türkeitürkischen Aspektsystems.* Uppsala, Sweden: Uppsala University dissertation.

Johanson, Lars. 1995. On Turkic converb clauses. In M. Haspelmath & E. König (eds.), *Converbs in cross-linguistic perspective. Structure and meaning of adverbial verb forms*, 313–347. Berlin: de Gruyter.

Johanson, Lars. 1996. Terminality operators and their hierarchical status. In B. Devriendt, L. Goossens & J. van der Auwera (eds.), *Complex structures: A functionalist perspective*, 229–58. Berlin: de Gruyter.

Johanson, Lars. 1999. Typological notes on aspect and actionality in Kipchak Turkic. In Werner Abraham & Leonid Kulikov (eds.), *Tense-aspect, transitivity and causativity*, 171–184. Amsterdam: John Benjamins.

Johanson, Lars. 2000. Viewpoint operators in European languages. In Östen Dahl (ed.), *Tense and aspect in the languages of Europe*, 27–187. Berlin: Mouton de Gruyter.

Johanson, Lars. 2002. *Structural factors in Turkic language contacts.* London: Curzon.

Johanson, Lars. 2003. Evidentiality in Turkic. In A. Aikhenvald & R. Dixon (eds.), *Studies in evidentiality*, 273–290. Amsterdam: John Benjamins.

Kirchner, Mark. 1998. Kirghiz. In Lars Johanson & Éva Csató (eds.), *Turkic languages*, 344–356. London: Routledge.

Korth, Britta. 2005. *Language attitudes towards Kyrgyz and Russian: Discourse, education and policy in post-Soviet Kyrgyzstan.* Bern: Peter Lang.

Labov, William. 1972. *Language in the inner city.* Philadelphia: University of Pennsylvania Press.

Labov, William. 2013. *The language of life and death: The transformation of experience in oral narrative.* Cambridge: Cambridge University Press.

Linde, Charlotte. 1986. Private stories in public discourse: Narrative analysis in the social sciences. *Poetics* 15(1). 183–202.

Light, Nathan. Under review. History, experience and narration: Emergent novelty and the double recounting of history. Svetlana Jacquesson (ed.), *History making in Central Asia.*

Norrick, Neal R. 2005. The dark side of tellability. *Narrative Inquiry* 15(2). 323–344.

Ochs, Elinor & Lisa Capps. 2009. *Living narrative: Creating lives in everyday storytelling.* Cambridge: Harvard University Press.

Orusbaev, Abdykadyr, Arto Mustajoki & Ekaterina Protassova. 2008. Multilingualism, Russian language and education in Kyrgyzstan. *International Journal of Bilingual Education and Bilingualism* 11(3–4). 476–500.

Polanyi, Livia. 1982. Linguistic and social constraints on storytelling. *Journal of Pragmatics* 6(5). 509–524.

Polanyi, Livia. 1985. *Telling the American story: A structural and cultural analysis of conversational storytelling.* Norwood, NJ: Ablex.

Prior, Dan. 2012. *The Šabdan Baatır Codex: Epic and the writing of northern Kirghiz History.* Leiden: Brill.

Richland, Justin B. 2005. "What are you going to do with the village's knowledge?" Talking tradition, talking law in Hopi tribal court. *Law & Society Review* 39(2). 235–272.

Richland, Justin B. 2010. Perpetuities against rules: Law, ethnography and the measuring of lives. *Law, Culture and the Humanities* 8(3). 433–447 [Print version dated 2012].

Riessman, Catherine K. 1990. Strategic uses of narrative in the presentation of self and illness: A research note. *Social Science & Medicine* 30(11). 1195–1200.

Riessman, Catherine K. 1991. Beyond reductionism: narrative genres in divorce accounts. *Journal of Narrative and Life History* 1(1). 41–68.

Sasse, Hans-Jürgen. 2002. Recent activity in the theory of aspect: Accomplishments, achievements, or just non-progressive state. *Linguistic Typology* 6(2). 199–271.

Shuman, Amy & Carol Bohmer. 2004. Representing trauma: Political asylum narrative. *Journal of American Folklore* 117(466). 394–414.

Silverstein, Michael. 1974. Dialectal developments in Chinookan tense-aspect systems: An areal-historical analysis. Memoir 29. *International Journal of American Linguistics* 40(4 pt. 2). S45–S99.

Silverstein, Michael. 1996. The secret life of texts. In Michael Silverstein & Greg Urban (eds.), *Natural histories of discourse*, 81–105. Chicago: University of Chicago Press.

Thelin, Nils. (ed.). 1990a. *Verbal aspect in discourse.* Amsterdam: John Benjamins.

Thelin, Nils. 1990b. On the concept of time: Prolegomena to a theory of aspect and tense in narrative discourse. In Nils Thelin (ed.), *Verbal aspect in discourse*, 91–129. Amsterdam: John Benjamins.

Vendler, Zeno. 1957. Verbs and times. *The Philosophical Review* 66(2). 143–160.

Elise S. Ahn and Antonia Jensen

4 Language Teaching in Turkmenistan: An Autoethnographic Journey

Abstract: Since becoming independent on October 26, 1991, Turkmenistan has had two presidents, Saparmurat Niyazov and its current president, Gurbanguly Berdimuhamedow. Under these two administrations, Turkmenistan's education system has undergone a number of drastic reforms affecting every aspect from its infrastructure, human resources, policies, curriculum, and program. And like the other former Soviet republics, the Turkmen government implemented a comprehensive language planning campaign in order to elevate the Turkmen language in four domains (status, corpus, acquisition, and prestige) vis-à-vis education. This chapter provides an overview of the Turkmenistani education system, the education-related language reforms and the various policies that create a conflicted picture regarding the government's broader long-term, socio-political aims through the lens of an English language lecturer that spent several years teaching in Turkmenistan. By taking an autoethnographic approach, this chapter also demonstrates how this method can be a means of engaging in research in politically sensitive environments.

Keywords: Turkmenistan; language change; autoethnography

1 Introduction

Since Turkmenistan gained independence in 1991, its education system has undergone a number of drastic reforms affecting every aspect, from its infrastructure, human resources and policies to its curriculum and programs. And like the other former Soviet republics, the Turkmen government implemented a comprehensive language planning campaign in order to elevate the Turkmen language vis-à-vis education. While this chapter brings together research that has been conducted on Turkmenistan, the aim of this chapter is two-fold. The first is to provide an overview of the Turkmen education system and the language and education-related policy changes which have been passed since 1991. The second is to explore the use of autoethnography as a method to understand language change in transition contexts. In language-related research, autoethnography is a relatively new approach to conducting research. The focus of this type of phenomenological research assumes that "to know the world is to be in the world" and that the "act of researching, questioning, theorizing is the intentional act of attaching ourselves to the world" (Van Manen 1990: 5).

Autoethnography can provide a vehicle through which a researcher and/or other participants can reflect upon and theorize what they experienced. Moreover, the use of autoethnography can elucidate the ways one's context is changing and the ways that different agents, e.g., educators, find their professional and personal identities challenged and restricted as they navigate their way through those situations. In this way, the focus of this chapter is to show the context in which language through education change is taking place in Turkmenistan vis-à-vis a milieu of contributing factors as seen through the autoethnographic account of one English language lecturer. By doing this, this chapter explores complex and dynamic socio-political contexts in a more nuanced way.

2 Background

Surrounded by Iran, Afghanistan and Uzbekistan, Turkmenistan is located in the western portion of Central Asia, occupying the far southwestern corner of the former Soviet Union (FSU). It has one of the largest natural gas reserves in the world, yet despite this, the majority of the people live in poverty. Between 2000 and 2006, the country's GDP grew by 500%. In 2005, its GDP was $3,838 USD. At the time, this was the second highest in Central Asia and the Caucasus after Kazakhstan (UNICEF 2008).

The total population is not definitively known and ranges from between 5.2 and 6.6 million people (Table 4.1). According to TIHR (2006), the population at the time of publication was roughly 6.8 million with an annual growth rate of 2.93%. UNICEF (2008) approximated that about 40% of the population is under the age of 15. Of the estimated five million, approximately 77% of the population is Turkmen, 9.2% Uzbek, 6.7% Russian (Observatory on Borderless Higher Education 2004).

Table 4.1: Estimated Population of Turkmenistan

Year	Population
2006 (official)	6,631,500
2005 (UNPF)	4,833,000
2005 (US Population Bureau)	5,200,000

Similar to the other Central Asian republics, in terms of population and demographic shifts, there was an exodus of ethnic Russians in the latter half of the

1990s. Another large migration from the country took place following the establishment of bilateral agreements in 2003 between Turkmenistan and the Russia Federation, which allowed for dual Russian-Turkmen citizenship (Observatory on Borderless Higher Education 2004), further contributing to the demographic shift. Regarding the titular nationality, under the Soviet Union, 92.9% of the 1,525,284 Soviet Turkmen lived in the Turkmen Soviet Socialist Republic (SSR), where they constituted about 66% of the total population.

Politically, unlike other parts of the FSU that had historical ties with Europe prior to the Soviet era (i.e., the European or Caucasian parts of the FSU), Turkmenistan was unfamiliar with a Western-style or party politics system. Consequently, upon independence, as Hinnemo (2003) notes, Turkmen intelligentsia did not appear to strive for a revival of some historic statehood. This resulted in some of the more unique characteristics of the Turkmen nation-state building project.

Since 1991, Turkmenistan has had two presidents, i.e., Saparmurat Niyazov (1991–2006), also called *Beyik Turkmenbashi* [The Great Leader of the Turkmen people], and its current president, Gurbanguly Berdimuhamedow (2006–present), Turkmenistan's self-appointed *Arkadag* [The Protector]. The unfamiliarity with a party political system combined with no pre-existing history with public political debate allowed Niyazov, as the last head of the Turkmen Communist Party, to transition into the presidency. He introduced a rotation system at all levels of government, creating a sense of constant change and transition, and limiting the processes that contribute toward the creation of institutional memory that could have led to long-term change. Niyazov maintained these old political mechanisms in order to stay in power but the "lack of public movements and the limited scale of Turkmen civic society made it easy for Niyazov to control his opponents" (Hinnemo 2003: 67). These residual mechanisms of the Soviet system provided and promoted national integration within Turkmenistan during those early years.

Also unique in this context was a lower degree of concern regarding ethnic conflict. As Hinnemo (2003: 64) notes, "The rather homogenous Turkmenistan, where the nominal population makes up almost 80% of all inhabitants, feared ethnic conflict less than most other republics."

2.1 Education infrastructure changes

At the time of independence, Turkmenistan had an education system that was typical of a Soviet state. However, a number of education reforms were instituted in the early years of the newly independent country via the *Bilim* program.

This program essentially dismantled the existing education system and replaced it with an education infrastructure that reflected the various notions that Niyazov had regarding education and the need for the development of a particular type of citizen, including the change to Turkmen medium of instruction (MOI) education. By the early 1990s, 100 secondary schools were closed while the actual number of students increased by 43% (TIHR 2006: 9). The number of vocational schools decreased by 80% but the number of universities more than doubled, going from six to 14. When the MOI was changed to Turkmen, it was non-Turkmen speaking teachers that were summarily dismissed (Clement 2008). Consequently, between changes in the curriculum and the MOI, a massive number of teachers were dismissed. Between 2006 and 2011, 10% of the overall teaching force was dismissed (TIHR 2006). The funding structure for schools was also changed; whereas previously, the government bore the brunt of education costs, the onus then shifted to local government. Tables 4.2 and 4.3 outline the way the education landscape has shifted since the Soviet era.

Table 4.2: Education Statistics Between 1975 and 2005 (Source: TIHR 2006)

Year	Level of schooling	# of institutions	# of students
1975	Secondary	1,800	700,000
	Vocational	44	177,000
	Secondary (specialty)	31	294,000
	University	6	311,000
1990	University	7	40,000
2004	Secondary	1,705	1,000,000
	Secondary (specialty)	15	
	University	16	

Table 4.3: Student: Teacher Ratio (Source: TIHR 2006)

Year	# of teachers	# of students	Note
Sept. 1, 2005	68,714*	1 million	100,000 new entrants; 1: 14.5 (Teacher: student ratio)

For teachers that continued working, their salaries ranged from 296,000 to 3,900,000 manats (approximately $125 USD) per month for 30 hours of work weekly. However, because of class sizes and the fact that frequently two teachers co-taught a class, teachers are more likely to receive $60 USD a month. This has resulted in many teachers moonlighting in other jobs (e.g., cleaning, selling goods at the market, or baking) and demanding bribes, especially since teachers are not only underpaid, they are also often paid two to three months late (Horak 2013; Sartor 2010; TIHR 2006).

In terms of general teacher quality, as TIHR (2006) notes that in the past, professional and continuous education were facilitated by older teachers that would share their experience with rookie teachers. However, professional development and lifelong learning has been discontinued because of lack of institutional support for teachers, including cancelling subscriptions to Russian language periodicals that focused on new methods of teaching because of a ban on foreign language periodicals (TIHR 2006). The lack of support for continued improvement in teacher practice, along with insufficient teacher salaries and demanding hours, have all contributed to the overall diminishing quality of education in Turkmenistan.

Other challenges that teachers and students face include: the regular and frequent interruptions of the school day to participate and congregate *en masse* at various venues and in stadiums for holidays or foreign visits, a practice that was started by Niyazov and maintained under Berdimuhamedov (Horak 2013; Sartor 2010); participation in seasonal activities like cotton harvesting; or *subotnik* activities [Saturday work]. While students are exempted from school, teachers are not. Further challenges to teaching and learning include: irregular or limited internet service, limited online resources that are available in Turkmen since the dominant accessible languages of the internet are English and Russian, and the lack of classroom supplies (Sartor 2010).

2.2 Change in the MOI

In addition to the structural changes in the education infrastructure, in its 1993 Law on Education, Turkmenistan also implemented language interventions in several other arenas, e.g., the language of public service, education, and the alphabet, as was the case with a number of FSU countries (Landau and Kellner-Heinkele 2011). A trilingual policy (i.e., Turkmen, Russian, and English) was established. Turkmen is the national language, Russian is the language of commerce, and English is seen as its global language. The 1993 education-related legislation changed the Turkmen language alphabet from Cyrillic to New Latin script (Clement 2008).[1]

---

[1] In the 20th century, Turkmenistan has experienced three major script changes. Prior to the 20th century, Turkmen had been written in Arabic script. Then in 1928, the Latin script was adopted. In 1940, Cyrillic became the orthography of the Turkmen language with a return back to the Latin script in 1993.

After the establishment of Turkmen as the official language of Turkmenistan, Turkmen became the sole MOI in both primary and secondary schools. Graduates were expected to pass their secondary school completion/university entrance exams in Turkmen. However, efforts to learn Turkmen were slowed down by the lack of teachers who could teach content area and language courses in Turkmen, along with a lack of textbooks (Landau and Kellner-Heinkele 2011; TIHR 2006). As an unintended consequence of this policy change, students who studied and memorized the new Turkmen Latin alphabet were unable to read Cyrillic subsequently, limiting their ability to access resources that were available only in Cyrillic Turkmen and/or Russian. At the time of its publication, TIHR (2006) reported that many schools were still using textbooks published in 1986. Consequently, teachers had to adjust and TIHR (2006) noted that many teachers began teaching Cyrillic to second graders in order to be able to use those textbooks. In a project called *Ene Dil* [native language], 136,000 copies of the language book were published and distributed in 2001. However, despite this, many Turkmen libraries had little or no written materials in Turkmen (Latin script) for lending (TIHR 2006).

Berdimuhamedov has stated that language education is a priority, which has broadened students' options to theoretically include classes in Russian, English and other languages. However, as Horak (2013) points out, in reality, only 30 Russian classes were available in 2011, allowing just 750–1,000 students out of 100,000 first graders to enroll in these classes. Moreover, while English has received symbolic and cursory substantive support from the government (it is now a compulsory subject from first to 11th and 12th grades), foreign government-sponsored programs like the US Peace Corps or English Language Fellows have been indefinitely suspended and even local education non-governmental organizations (NGOs) have undergone intense scrutiny.

Regarding the trilingual policy, critics of these policy changes argue that the government did not hold up its responsibility to implement the policy (TIHR 2006). Of the three languages, only Turkmen was comprehensively taught in the schools, with Russian and English language courses often being cancelled due to lack of teachers. What language classes are available are provided through private or elite schools or through private tutoring, further limiting those who have access to these languages of wider communication. Ostensibly, this also limits who has access to opportunities outside of Turkmenistan for work or school, effectively making both the languages gatekeepers to access to a wider range of employment opportunities (Sartor 2010).

This gate-keeping effect is greater among non-Turkmen minorities, e.g., Uzbek and Kazakh students, who had previously been allowed to attend minority language schools (Horak 2013). Not only are students required to learn Turkmen in school, since the national university entrance exams are in Turkmen, further limiting the opportunities available for non-Turkmen students (TIHR 2006).

What is puzzling is for university entrance, however, is that potential students have to take three exams. One of the written portions is in Russian but the interview is done in Turkmen (EC Report 2012). Given the scarcity of Russian language teachers and resources, the ideologically conflicted nature of the government's language policy and planning efforts amplifies the difficulties encountered by minority language speakers. Similarly, it is interesting to observe the paradoxical ideology that seems to have motivated the language and script changes. As Clement (2008: 177) points out, on the one hand, the language change was a way for the Turkmen government to "[clarify] a national identity more than their shared Turkicness". On the other hand, Niyazov often linked the script change to the idea of symbolically joining the international community, thus connecting language change with processes of modernization and development.

2.3 Curriculum changes

The Turkmen curriculum changes provide an intriguing glimpse into this particular context of Turkmen identity, but also challenge discussions regarding how nation-states go about developing a national imaginary (Anderson 2006). In the Turkmen case, "national" content (i.e., content that was related to historical Turkmen figures, writers, and poets like Berdy Kerbabaev, Rahim Esenov, Hydyr Deriaiev, and Nurmurad Saryhanov) was actually removed from the curriculum (TIHR 2006). While the Turkmenistani government's goal was still to replace the communist ideology from the curriculum, the alternative was not a grand narrative about the Turkmen state; rather, it was the development, reproduction and embellishment of Niyazov's own personality cult. Replacing the textbooks undergirded by communist ideology were a number of textbooks revolving around Niyazov himself, e.g., *History of Neutral Turkmenistan*, *Policy of Independence of Saparmurat Turkmenbashi the Great*, and a series of poems by Niyazov (TIHR 2006). The most significant articulation in this process being the publication and incorporation of the Niyazov's book, *Ruhnama*, into the national curriculum.

TIHR (2006) provides a number of examples of how the *Ruhnama* was incorporated into content textbooks. One example the report gives is that of a math problem which sets up the following problem, "[T]he chapter of the Turkmen nation of the sacred book Ruhnama consists of 60 pages and the chapter on the state of Turkmen 16 pages more. How many pages are there in the second chapter?" On the secondary school completion/university entrance exam, TIHR (2006) reported that 26 out of the 57 examination cards (i.e., exam prompts) referenced the *Ruhnama* or revolved *Ruhnama*-related ideological issues. And out of 100 essay exam topics for ninth graders, 66 were about Niyazov, his various literary works, and/or relatives (TIHR 2006).

All these policy and systemic changes have resulted in a state of institutional paralysis. Policy plans have been underfunded, understaffed, and undercut by a lack of technical support to inform the transition. Drastic cuts in the teaching staff, a change in the MOI, and the lack of relevant or contemporary reading materials consequently contributed greatly to the overall decline in the quality of the Turkmen education system (Sartor 2010). UNICEF (2008) also reported that schools are becoming increasingly overcrowded, and as the population continues to grow, are also becoming more and more deteriorated because of lack of funding. While there are some activities that are taking place in the NGO sector, much of that is limited or constrained by the restrictive political environment (Clement 2011; Dailey and Silova 2008).

3 Autoethnography as method

Since research is not conducted in a contextual vacuum, the absence or weakness of the rule of law can create challenging conditions for work and conducting research. As Belousov et al. (2007) note, where democracy is weak (or absent), ethical concerns are often made more challenging by the on-the-ground situation. Belousov et al. (2007) go on to discuss interviewing protocols in the Russian Federation and the role of informed consent. More theoretically, their work raises the question, should research be governed by research that can safely be conducted? Or to rephrase, does the benefit of doing the research outweigh the challenges? How do researchers then conduct ethically responsible research that is empirically based?

For these reasons, autoethnography can be used to challenge how a particular experience has been discussed and to give voice to the previously unheard. Autoethnography is a type of phenomenological research, where the focus of research is the lived experiences of people. Spry (2001: 710) defines this as "a self-narrative that critiques the situatedness of self with others in social contexts." Autoethnography "self-consciously explores the interplay of the interpersonal as its situated through a linguistic, historical or ethnographic explanation" (Chang 2008). Where theory informs practice or the structure of a particular research design to produce empirically-grounded research, phenomenological research privileges life stories over theory. As Van Manen (1990: 9) writes "Phenomenology asks 'What is this or that kind of experience like?'… it attempts to gain insightful descriptions of the way we experience the world pre-reflectively, without taxonomizing, classifying or abstracting it."

In the Turkmen context, using an autoethnographic approach provided a way to be able to reflect on socio-political change in Turkmenistan without negatively impacting others since autoethnography focuses on subjectivity, or as Ellis and Flaherty (1992: 1) define it, "human lived experience and the physical, political, and historical context of that experience." In this way, Spry (2001: 711) notes, "The researcher is the epistemological and ontological nexus upon which the research problem turns."

Despite the use of autoethnography as a form of qualitative inquiry, there is, however, some discomfort with it as being "not academic enough." As Ellis and Flaherty (1992) suggest, it is the inherently subjective, but sociologists (and more broadly social science researchers) feel uncomfortable when thinking or talking about subjectivity. Why? They posit that

> Subjectivity can be both unpleasant and dangerous; unpleasant because emotional, cognitive, and physical experiences frequently concern events that, in spite of their importance, are deemed inappropriate topics for polite society; dangerous because the workings of subjectivity seem to contradict so much of the rational-actor worldview on which mainstream sociology is premised. (Ellis and Flaherty 1992: 1)

This distinction however, between subjective and objective can attributed to the lingering influence of positivism among social scientists that engage in qualitative inquiry. If anything, it may be that the problem is not the subjectivity of the researcher who is conducting the work; rather, as Van Manen (1990) argues, the issue in phenomenological research is the reality that the researcher/writer knows too much about the subject. "Or, more accurately, the problem is that our 'common sense' pre-understandings, our suppositions, assumptions, and the existing bodies of scientific knowledge, predispose us to interpret the nature of the phenomena before we have even come grips with the significance" of the question (Van Manen 1990: 46). Here, Husserl's notion of bracketing is useful, i.e., to take hold of a phenomenon and then place it outside of one's knowledge about the phenomenon. This can be accomplished as a solo writer or in the context of a dialogue, as is done in the case of this chapter (Van Manen 1990; Frentz and Hocker 2000). For language researchers (or researchers who look at language-related issues and focus), autoethnography provides one way to be able to capture the complexity of language change situations. Wijayatilake (2012: 403), reflecting on her own milieu of experiences as a language professional, notes that "[B]y bringing autoethnography to the field of language education, I am recognising that in our field, too, there are emotional, complex and difficult situations to which traditional forms of inquiry fail to do justice."

An autoethnographic account is defined by its narrative structure because it should be both emotionally engaging and be able to "transform readers and transport them into a place where they are motivated to look at their own personally political identity construction" (Spry 2001: 713). Moreover, it should reflect a level of critical self-reflection between oneself, others, and the sociopolitical context in which it is situated. Similarly, Goodall (2000) suggests that a good ethnography (including autoethnography) should be dialogic, be affective (for the reader and the writer, and be self-reflexive. These are the criteria that formed the narrative underpinnings of this chapter.

4 Reflections of a language educator

The journey to writing this autoethnographic account of Toni's experience in Turkmenistan was a long one. As a segue into the autoethnography itself, we decided to provide excerpts of conversations that were held over e-mail and Skype between May 2013 and May 2014 in an attempt to provide a glimpse into forming this account and to highlight in particular the ethical struggles that both writers grappled with. As Adams (2008: 181) points out in writing this type of work, it "motivates us to discern who we might hurt or silence in telling stories as well as whose stories we do not (and may not ever) hear. An ethical life writer is someone who responsibly reflects on these issues, not someone who irresponsibly rambles about life's difficulties."

4.1 The project preparation process

As this book project began to form, it became evident that in a book about language change(s) in post-Soviet Central Asia, Turkmenistan was glaringly absent. However, upon doing further research, it became clear that this was because researchers looking at this context were limited. Through a mutual colleague, Toni's name was raised as a potential contributor because of her experience in the country.

The conversation started with Toni receiving and responding to an invitation to contribute a chapter to this volume.

> Dear Elise, I hope you can count me in on this project.... I am having conversations with people here in an attempt to resolve the dilemma here between being frank, truthful and honest in my perceptions and reflections of things here and the need to protect [others]...
>
> These two constraints, keeping safe the trust I have earned and the opportunity to go home to a free and open society, are at cross-purposes with my need to speak out and talk about the elephant in the room. It is not just about freedom of press, academic freedom, and professional integrity; it is also about potential violation of trust and regard for relationships...
>
> Please advise how to tread these sensitive waters; also how to utilize and integrate my survey data. (TJ, e-mail, 24 May 2013)

After a few brief responses back and forth and starting to draft a more "traditional" research paper, Toni came to the conclusion that she would have to withdraw from the project, writing

> I write this with deep regret. Unfortunately, I have to withdraw from your project... Writing the actual story, the plain, unadorned truth, with verified facts and statistics, is and would be offensive to the authorities... I have come to this conclusion only after talking to a wide range people. (TJ, e-mail, 1 June 2013)

After reflecting on the complexity of the actual situation, the real-world implications of this project, and the ethical nature of doing research in restrictive environments, Elise responded as follows.

> Hi Toni: Sorry for the delay – I've been thinking about your situation, which is why I haven't written back. I totally understand the constraints of being in this context... I was wondering if it'd be possible to Skype and bounce some ideas around – seeing if there are other ways of approaching this chapter that won't jeopardize your colleagues or [other commitments that you have]? (EA, e-mail, 13 June 2013)

The Skype appointment took place about seven weeks later on 21 August 2013 when we were both back in the US.

> Dear Elise: I enjoyed the chance to speak with you the other day because I now have the feeling that I am writing for a "real person"! It also clarified the ethical issues in my mind, kind of parsing them out and helping me to prioritize them. Now I feel as if there really is a possibility for me to get this chapter included in your book. (TJ, e-mail, 22 August 2013).

During this conversation, we began discussing the possibility of writing an autoethnography rather than using the surveys and interviews that Toni had conducted. After reading about the method, Toni wrote

> Hi Elise, As I was saving [the articles] for deeper reading later and reading just the abstracts, I was feeling a growing sense of exciting "buzz" within me, because this kind of writing is perfect for what I want to say!!!... I have never before heard of this form of research writing... I have begun writing my own, and now I am happily reading and writing in my "zone" again! (TJ, e-mail, 4 September 2013)

Upon submitting an initial draft, Toni wrote "I think [writing this as an auto-ethnography] may solve some of my issues of confidentiality that we discussed" (e-mail, 30 September 2013). The contribution underwent review and was sent back and forth a few more times for revision. After the second review, Elise sent back some comments and questions for further revision.

> Hi Toni: Hope things are going well! Here are some comments and questions regarding your chapter... Overall, the chapter is interesting and has a lot of potential... However it feels unfocused. Even if you are looking at language change (or using autoethnography), the vignettes need to have a theme that ties them together. Right now, the anecdotes feel a bit disconnected.
>
> Along those lines, maybe pick a theme and allow that to run through? Some themes might be a focus on students, teaching, teachers, institutional culture... [but] whatever theme you pick, provide the relevant concrete details.
>
> One question that came to our minds while we were reading your chapter was "Where is the agency in this context? Despite the system, how do teachers and students navigate the system?" Second, what is the difference between "what should be" and "what is"? Is there a difference? If so, why? (EA, e-mail, 3 December 2013)

After a few more weeks of e-mail discussion, we decided to approach writing this paper collaboratively by adopting a dialogic and narrative structure similar to the one utilized by Ellis and Bochner (2006) as well as Frentz and Hocker (2010). We did this in order to provide a glimpse into this work-in-progress in order to show the struggle and issues that emerged in the course of conceptual-izing what type of research activity would provide insight into this particular context (TJ, e-mail, 17 December 2013). But we also wanted to avoid a self-indulgent (but perhaps cathartic) exercise in intellectual navel-gazing, which proved to be challenging given the criteria for a "good" autoethnography as laid out by Spry (2001) and Goodall (2000). In the end, we decided to provide background information that is publicly available in the first part of this chapter to situate the autoethnograpic account of Toni's various teaching experiences with the intention of showing one life lived in the context of others (Goodall 2000).

4.2 Reflections: Toni's Journey

The English language in Turkmenistan is shrouded by conflicted feelings. Politically, there is a measured, cautious view toward English, what it represents, and what role exactly it should play in their society. These feelings are situated in different historical experiences with English, seen by traditionalists as a modern-day Trojan horse that will hasten the deterioration of the its society by traditionalists, or as the way forward by progressives. This ambivalence toward English is what underpinned particularly my second experience teaching English in Turkmenistan.

My thoughts of the role of English in Turkmen society changed over time since first teaching there in 2006. Some of these changes were simply due to the passage of time, but others came as the result of living through two very different teaching experiences in Turkmenistan. For this reason, my reflections for this chapter revolved around the following questions: As a teacher of English in Turkmenistan, what changes did I observe in Turkmen society toward the role of English language? How did those changes in their attitude toward English impact me as a teacher on a personal level?

Because I could not have derived my ideas and perceptions here without the help of many kind and generous individuals that I have met in country, I want to acknowledge their vital role and vast contributions. None of these words would be possible without them and memories of their voices are embedded in every idea that I express here as they spoke to me despite their reservations about their personal safety and job security. This is because in Turkmenistan, it is dangerous to express opinions which strays from the official discourse(s). For this reason, I have disguised individual identities by creating composites of people that I have met over the course of seven years. By doing this, I have tried to stay true to my experiences but protect others.

4.1.1 The first fling: The early 2000s

My first trip in Turkmenistan was filled with a wide variety of English-promoting activities. I taught in a local higher education institution (HEI). Housed in a 75-year old cluster of Soviet-style stucco buildings, it served more than 900 students each year who were studying one of any of the seven languages taught there. Many of the students were planning to become English teachers back in their villages, or translators or interpreters in the city. Enthusiastic, the students were happy and eager to learn.

Aside from my primary full-time work assignment as an English teacher in this institute, I was also engaged in numerous and varied secondary activities. A few of those include giving extra classes for the broader community on topics ranging from leadership to cooking, evaluating scholarship applications, proctoring English exams at the United Nations' local office, providing occasional private English lessons, and co-directing summer camps for teachers. Those days were exciting, heady, and extremely gratifying on both a personal and professional level.

I felt the Turkmen love for everything English. The dean of my institute put me on local Turkmen TV on two occasions to publicly promote English, as well as the role of groups like the US Peace Corps in Turkmenistan. Students applauded me even as I walked into class, and there was a high demand for private tutoring. I turned down countless wedding invitations, as well as evening meals at teachers' homes (often their chance to practice "real" English). The students I encountered in the market were excited with simple things like talking about fruits and vegetables with me. I had no trouble assembling students for extra classes in their spare time. They flocked to those, as well as the English classes and events at the operating NGOs in Turkmenistan. Teens volunteered for weekend trash pickups at the nearby river just for the chance to hang out and chat English. Teachers from around the country competed fiercely to be included in the summer immersion camps that my teacher friends and I directed. Turkmen teens, professionals, and academics vied to be accepted to study English abroad. There was even talk about the establishment of a US-Turkmen University. English occupied a very happy, privileged and generous place in the Turkmen community in those days. In hindsight, that first stint was one long happy love affair with this unique desert country.

4.1.2 The second sojourn

After returning to the States, I was later given another chance to teach in Turkmenistan. I did not hesitate. Of course I'd go! But this second experience would be a profoundly different experience. Although I entered into this second stint with a light heart an eager spirit, I left the country 10 months later feeling sad, and distressed that I was sad, yet relieved to have escaped. I also felt vaguely bewildered, not truly comprehending the full depth of my experience and different accompanying emotions.

Since my first stint, Ashgabat, the capital city, had changed remarkably. Evidence of its rapid economic growth was evident throughout the city. Even locals regularly got lost while driving because there were so many new streets and unfamiliar buildings. It was visually disorienting. Sparkling stainless steel stoplights sorted out traffic jams in which BMWs and Lexuses idled side-by-side with old Russian Ladas. Shelves in markets were stocked with imported goods, e.g., fresh oranges and frozen chicken from the USA, cheeses and chocolates from Italy, dried fruits and dairy products from neighboring Iran, and clothing and household goods from China. While these changes initially delighted me, they later faded away in importance in the cloud of my growing despair.

To capture my feelings, I composed a poem. The three verses of this poem reflect the three stages of my emotions and writing it helped me articulate and reflect on the cascade of grief surrounding this second tour. Verse one describes simple, unabashed love for Turkmenistan.

Oh, Turkmenistan!
Your deserts vast and quiet echoing
poets' voices ancient, ever vital.
Your camels stately, softly padding,
reviving traditions bold and bright.
Your manners patient, never hurrying
give sufficient time to every human.
Your families richly welcoming
with faces handsome, full of hope.
Your warm embraces melding
past and present, an undivided feast.

For this second stint, I was placed at several HEIs. My assignments were to serve the institutions not only as an instructor of English, but as an English mentor-teacher trainer, to provide resources and to advance the quality of English instruction in any way I saw fit. Initially, my plan was to visit each institution, assess their needs, and then make suggestions how they can best utilize my abilities and assets. Remembering the joy I felt teaching at the institute five years before, I was excited.

I entered the modern facilities of one institution, secretly thrilled as I took the initial tour. The facilities were modern and sparkling clean. The classrooms were equipped with smart boards, there were computer/listening labs and I was provided a PC for my personal use. What a contrast to my former institute of eight years ago, housed in a 75-year old cluster of buildings with classrooms that had treacherous potholes in the floors and often lacked a functioning chalk-board. To me, it seemed that the state of the buildings at this HEI showed a high regard for the importance of education. Who would not be impressed with these changes? However, as I would come to understand, in this new world, the over-arching, crucial fact to keep in mind was that appearances were not just important, they were (and are) the end goal, i.e., form over function. This underpins the vast sums of petro-dollars spent that have been spent to make Ashgabat a showplace for foreigners and this HEI was one of those showplaces.

Not long after I began my teaching duties, I discovered that if the Turkmenistani authorities could give the appearance of providing a "first-class" education, then that was all that matters. For example, students talked about their frustration with the lack of books, confirming that they had no text for my classes except an old, digitized version of a Russian-English book. Someone had photocopied an old textbook from Moscow and provided it to the staff and students. Most students, however, could not understand it since their native language was Turkmen (a requirement for entrance to the HEI). I found the book nearly incomprehensible myself; it was far too lexically dense to be accessible to students. The book's topics were outdated, it was dependent on grammar-translation method, and it did not help students develop any communicative competence. A student wondered how the president could purchase a multi-million yacht on the Caspian Sea but was unable to provide basic English language textbooks in schools. They had been frequently told how fortunate they were to be at this particular HEI and yet they questioned what exactly were they receiving at this institution? What did it mean to receive a "world-class education"? Moreover, the government stated that students were (and are) entitled to free higher education and yet, their families had to gather $50,000 USD to pay a bribe to graduate. Both the students and I felt various disconnects between the discourse and the realities of being at this HEI.

These are just a few examples of the contradictions that I faced in the early days of this assignment. I continued having trouble reconciling the clash between the words I heard and the realities I witnessed. I soon discovered many more discrepancies that made teaching English an exercise in absurdity and meaninglessness. They made me question whether the government really wanted people to learn English, or simply wanted to give the appearance of teaching and learning it. For example, I was advised to keep a lesson plan with me at all times while teaching. This lesson plan was not of what I was actually teaching, but the one according to the official curriculum just in case the rector or dean drops in to observe my class. This meant writing two plans for each lesson, the real one and the "fake" one that matched the curriculum.

Similarly, I was told to complete the class register on a monthly basis with all the days and meetings I had with all the groups I taught (not actual class dates but the official ones), and include the topics of the lessons I taught – again, not the topics I actually taught but the topics from the official curriculum.

So I filled out this register every month with all the topics that I supposedly taught and the days we presumably met. This document was the basis for calculating my salary (as well as all the other teachers). As a side note, the first time I did this, I made the egregious mistake of using a black ballpoint pen. I had to rewrite it all in blue ink since blue ink is used for all originals.

Just write it and forget it, I am told and then you'll be paid. OK, OK! I am going crazy trying to understand this form of record keeping. I am just copying one document into another. What a waste of teacher time and talent! Copying, copying, mindless copying!

I spent a great deal of time to doing purposeless paperwork. I became unconvinced that senior administrators genuinely cared whether their students learn English. More broadly, these lesson-writing charades were supposed to hide the fact that the majority of students at this institution had little or no English language proficiency, despite many years of classes.

At the end of each term, many students worried about exams. In this incidence, I was told to create an English test. I created an exam that included assessments of all the language skills and some contextualized grammar that was covered that semester. Because it was an extensive exam, scoring the exam took a long time. However, I felt that the test would provide an accurate sense of what students had learned throughout the semester. When my co-teacher reviewed the scores, he disregarded my scores, and following directions from senior management, he re-scored students in order to punish some students with low scores. These students who received point penalties committed different, unrelated violations throughout the semester, e.g., wearing clothes that broke the dress code or had extended absences from class without a pre-approved excuse. But on the last day of class, I was told to announce the final grades, which, in the end, were practically identical to the previous term's grades. This only fueled my growing sense that course outcomes had nothing to do with actuality, but were pre-determined by some combination of politics, personalities, and corruption.

Why did they ask for a test if they had no intention of using the results? What is the point?

The English curriculum from one year to the next was interchangeable, and I witnessed colleagues simply copying and pasting it from one year to the next. I guess this did not matter, since regardless, it was not being taught. The smart boards did not function as smart boards, but sat mostly unused. The institute did not provide easy access to the Internet for either students or teachers.

Teachers spent a lot of hours at the institute; they were required to be on the campus six full days a week regardless of their teaching load. Early in the winter, I tried to organize a teachers' club, which could be a space for teachers to learn from each other and discuss different challenges they were experiencing in the classroom. Colleagues had previously expressed that they too wanted more of this informal conversational time, so we set up a time and location that was compatible for all. I posted a sign in the staff room announcing our weekly meeting with the approval of the department head. But in the end, the attendance was sparse. Teachers could not attend because they had other "meetings," had to fulfil other commitments which the department head had required of them, were sick, or were called away. At some point, I also learned that the institute also had an active English club for students that I was never invited to or officially had been made aware of. These two incidents were perplexing to me and stood in contrast to my situation seven-years prior. Because I was the only native speaker of English with whom most students and teachers had ever interacted, one would think the HEI would make every effort to keep me engaged, but this was not the case. In the end, I felt terribly alone and isolated, while wondering at the same time if I had committed some un-mentionable cultural gaffe.

At the other institution where I was assigned, the experience was both similar and different. On the first day, I was ushered into the chilly, ancient and dingy basement that housed this institution. I was engaged here in order to work with graduate students and teachers, with the same goals as at the first institution; that was, to be an English resource in any way I could be. I conducted an informal needs survey on the first meeting with students. They were enthusiastic and told me they wanted to know more about academic writing. *Great! Maybe I will be able to teach here!* These students seemed to be quite different from the undergrads at the first institution. At this institution, they were working professionals in a variety of occupations, including doctors, lawyers, scientists and some teachers. They were quite bright and eager, and I was more hopeful here.

The relationships I developed at this second location, however, also became a perplexing source of contradictory statements and behaviors. In the beginning, I was welcomed profusely. I was assigned to the largest and most modern class-room in the basement. But no matter what teaching/learning strategy I employed throughout the semester, I could rarely get consistent attendance, nor could I get any written work in class or homework completed. My colleagues said this was normal, that students were busy with their lives, and that I should just keep on with what I was doing. At the end of the fall semester, only six students attended regularly and just two had marginally fulfilled the requirements of my course.

Then at the departmental new year's eve party, an administrator told a joke in English. The punch line of the joke poked fun at Americans' reputation for not learning second languages. I felt nonplussed since I was the only American present at the party. I decided at the time to consider this event as an example of poor judgment; however, it felt as if I were being given a message, i.e., *we don't want you here.*

Later, my classroom was closed and sealed off with crime scene tape. I received no explanation despite my inquiries. Did it have to do with the remodeling project that was going on throughout the institution? And how was this renovation connected to the fact that only signs related to US government funded programs (e.g., USAID) had been removed? Other teachers offered to let me use their classrooms. Consequently, from day to day, my students never knew where we were going to meet. With the advent of spring and warm weather, we sometimes met outside in the sunshine, and later we moved to a small cafe adjacent to the institution. Realizing at this point that my writing class had morphed into a conversation club, I felt that meeting in a congenial setting where we could sip tea and chat made this setting perfect for us.

I eventually discussed this solution with my local supervisor at this institution. She was horrified and immediately arranged a meeting with a departmental administrator. We met, and instead of providing an explanation regarding what was happening or how to appropriately respond to some of the challenges I experienced in the classroom, I received an hour-long lecture about how Turkmen teachers have always been highly respected throughout history, and how they intended to accord me the same respect. During this meeting, I increasingly felt I was being vaguely scolded. I was then ushered into an empty classroom that she would let me use. My few remaining students and I entered a dirty, musty room full of broken desks and chairs. When we opened the window to aerate the room, the sound of traffic made conversation impossible. We could neither sit nor talk.

At this point, I decided to cancel my class six weeks early. These students could take a bus and join another English conversation club I was conducting outside the institution. I hoped at that point that my relationship with this second institution was finished, because they were obviously finished with me. I contacted my program supervisor and after informing her of my intention to quit and my reasons why, I was given the green light.

All in all, things definitely felt less friendly to me this second time around. The once fertile ground for English in Turkmenistan felt barren and indubitably less hospitable toward this American.

4.1.3 Verse two: Crazy making

I am feeling alone. Who is in my world with me? My head is going to explode!
Will someone please talk with me? Tell me what is real? What is true?
Did everyone in the world but me get together and decide to change things?
I'm scared. I feel betrayed by everyone and everything.

The second verse of my poem grieves over what I had observed in my second stint.

Oh, Turkmenistan!
Don't make me crazy with your smile
when you cannot lie to me!
And how can you forget yourself
and then deny forgetting?
I believed you when you said you loved,
but now I feel deceived about
What is real and what is not,
I beg of you, just say it right out loud!
Don't make me hate your silence
and confusing incarnations.

Was I just a "feather in the cap" of the institution they could put out there when they needed some window-dressing prestige to impress some foreign visitor? This was a likely explanation in a country obsessed with appearances. Or was I merely another miscellaneous cog, the "foreign expert type" in an HEI that has the form of a university but functions like aimless organization?

Turkmen teachers live, work, and manage their lives under conditions American teachers would consider intolerable. In educational institutions, teachers work long shifts, six days a week. They are often given tasks that are unrelated to teaching, e.g., translating government documents or fulfilling administrative tasks for others. Oftentimes, there are no printers or paper available for teachers to print things out. The use of the Internet at schools is either limited or simply unavailable.

Teachers are not only acutely aware of the lack of support, they often feel powerless to do anything about it. This sense of powerlessness breeds a sense of resignation or "institutional repression." I have witnessed this among many Turkmen teachers, and experienced it first-hand. Turkmen teachers cannot leave their country freely to participate in education opportunities of their choice.

They cannot access online educational opportunities for themselves or their students. They cannot freely participate in local US embassy-sponsored educational activities, nor allow their students to do the same. They cannot participate in curriculum and materials choices for their students. They cannot choose how best to advance professionally in their field. They cannot organize to advocate for their profession. They cannot decide which activities should fill the hours they must spend at their work sites. They have to show up for work six days a week, 10 hours a day, and hope they are not called at the last minute to chaperone the student dormitory until 11PM.

4.1.4 Verse three: The end

I came to the end of my year in Turkmenistan feeling like I was a source of embarrassment at the institutions where I had been placed because by working in-country, I had become acquainted first hand with the devastating effects of the poor Turkmen education system on its "Lost Generation" and the hypocrisy of its reform efforts.[2]

Evidence of a new moneyed and apparently privileged class is pervasive in Ashgabat. Luxury and imported cars abound. Even the police drive a modern fleet of Mercedes sedans. Name brand goods line supermarket shelves. Ashgabat was even included in the *Guinness Book of World Records* for having the largest concentration of white marble-lined buildings. Yet, despite the numerous new, multi-storied, white marble-faced buildings going up in the capital, there remains the question of what happens behind their walls. Education in Turkmenistan in one sense appears to be an exercise in appearances, a charade as deceptive as the marble facades that line the capital's streets that house the entire enterprise. And yet, what is clear is the fact that the government clearly has the resources needed to move forward.

---

2 A number of teachers both inside and outside the institutions where I worked mentioned Turkmenistan's "Lost Generation." This refers to the generations of students who finished secondary school after only nine years, as was the limit for many years during President Niyazov's term. This limit effectively prevented Turkmenistan students from qualifying for university programs abroad, thus slowing the "brain drain." Graduates then were required to either work or enter the military for two years before qualifying for any higher education in Turkmenistan

Berdimuhammedov later reinstated 10 years of secondary education after taking office in 2007, and recently increased it again to 12 years (Dovletti 2009; "In Turkmenistan" 2009). But the students that I encountered at these institutions were those of the "lost generation". I was sad because they are Turkmenistan's future, and from my colleagues, I felt like I witnessed a deep collective shame about what these students had experienced.

Oh, Turkmenistan!
Your brown and lovely visage shimmers
under flashing cottonwoods.
But can your hooded eyes reveal your heart,
while blinking slowly, flat and blank?
Still worse, your heart should wither when
your dreams grow up abandoned.
Oh, how could you, I cry, I cry?
Bereft of truthful memory you say?
I vow I'll never forget today forever
the tomorrows you've surrendered.
Oh, Turkmenistan, someday you will remember!

4.2 Discussion

Through writing this chapter, some of the questions that helped guide the reflection process included: How is social change experienced in the life of an experienced educator? What insights does this bring to bear regarding language change contexts? How does one's lived experience show the complexity of the context in which they are working? And perhaps more broadly, what is life like to be a foreign educator in this particular context?

This final product emerged out of the process of months of online discussions regarding methods, the nature of data and research, ethical concerns, and the commitment to want to share a personal narrative. Van Manen (1990: 77) discusses this, writing that "[T]he insight into the essence of a phenomenon involves a process of reflectively appropriating, of clarifying, and of making explicit the structure of meaning of the lived experience." This was done by focusing on a phenomenological question as seen above and by examining different themes that emerged in the previous section. In phenomenological type research, themes "are not objects or generalizations. They are more like knots in the web of our experiences, around which certain lived experiences are spun and thus lived through as meaningful wholes" (Van Manen 1990: 90). In this chapter, the two major themes that emerged out of the discussions and the account involved the ideas of dissonance and teaching as performance.

4.2.1 Dissonance

Dissonance provides the autoethnographer with the opportunity to reflect. Castell and Bryson (1997: 1) note that dissonance that can take place with the "often contradictory implications of theoretical debates concerning identity politics/essentialism juxtaposed with the embodied actualities of producing, negotiating, performing, and troubling differences in educational contexts." The narrative of Toni's second trip was full of dissonance. What the government says, what is actually practiced. What supervisors tell teachers, and what they actually do. What program coordinators are told, what volunteers experience. This tension or contradiction between what is said and what actually is, which is most clearly demonstrated in the experience of having two sets of lesson plans, i.e., one in case someone comes to check on the teacher and the actual lesson plans that are taught by the teacher, which is a common practice throughout education systems in many post-Soviet countries.

When looking at the earlier e-mail dialogue between Toni and Elise and then the narrative, it was the dissonant points, e.g., ethical issues, perspectives, perspective on the education system, that were the points that were collaboratively thought through and interpreted. In this sense, they helped provide a thread of coherence through which these different experiences could be organized (Van Manen 1990). Agar (1994) calls what we are calling points of dissonance as "rich points" referring to those points in a conversation or an exchange where one realizes they do not know what is going on. He writes that upon hitting these moments one can respond in several ways. One can "wonder why you don't understand, wonder if some other language culture isn't in play... [but] If you wonder, at that moment and later as well, you've taken on culture, not as something that 'those people' have, but rather as a space between you and them, one that you're involved in as well, one that can be overcome" (Agar 1994: 106).

In this chapter, these rich or dissonant points reflect the uneven way that socio-political change is taking place in Turkmenistan. They challenge the assumption that nation-state building processes (particularly in FSU countries) are taking place seamlessly or satisfactorily. At the same time, they do capture these changes through the experiences of an American English language teacher in this context. And while there are some similarities as Hiro (2009) and others point out, Toni's experience does highlight some of the particularities of the Turkmen case.

4.2.2 Teaching as performance

Related to this theme of dissonance, or lack of connection between aspiration and actuality, is seeing teaching as performance. Alexander (2003) discusses this in a paper comparing the performative aspect of teaching to drag, where he asserts that the classroom can be seen as a particularly culturally situated site in which teachers are performers and teaching is perfomative.

Langellier (1999: 127) defines performance as describing "a certain type of particularly involved and dramatized oral narrative. Of special importance is how performance contributes to the evaluative function of personal narrative – the 'so what? How is this interesting? Who's interested in this/whose interest is this?' Similar to Langellier (1999), Diamond (1996) states that when thinking about a performance itself raises important questions. She writes

> Certainly powerful questions posed by theater representation – questions of subjectivity (who is speaking/acting?), location (in what sites/spaces), audience (who is watching?), commodification (who is in control?), conventionality (how are meanings produced?), politics (what ideological or social positions are being reinforced or contested?) – are embedded in the bodies and acts of performers. To study performance is not to focus on completed forms, but to become aware of performance as itself a contested space, where meanings and desires are generated, occluded, and of course multiply interpreted. (Diamond 1996: 4)

Studying performance as performativity is "to become aware of performance itself as a contested space, where meanings and desires are generated, occluded, and of course multiply interpreted" (Diamond 1996: 4). For Langellier (199: 129), looking at performativity "articulates and situates the personal narrative within the forces of discourse, the institutionalized networks of power relations... which constitute subject positions and order context; and performance implies the transgresssive desire of agency and action."

Thinking about teaching as performance and then thinking about the performativity of teaching provides an interesting perspective to look at Toni's experience in Turkmenistan. If the classroom is a culturally situated site, and the teacher a performer, who was she performing for? Who was the audience? Presumably, the primary audience in a classroom is arguably the students, with different networks then being linked to different performative aspects of occupying the space of both teacher and foreigner. Yet, it seemed that institutionally, there were a number of obstacles blocking the audience's "view". Not providing institutional support, administration, teaching approaches, and logistics are subversive attempts to diminish the expected performative role of a foreign teacher. The question this raises then is, who then is the actual intended audience here?

Arguably, the stage is much bigger than the classroom where the intended audiences are the different international organizations that the Turkmen government forges alliances with. On the one hand, by hosting people like Toni, the government demonstrates its ostensible commitment to "development", "Western-ization", and "democratization". On the other hand, by not providing the infra-structure and institutional support that would allow people like Toni to actually teach, undermines those commitments, something which countries like the USA are far too often complicit in and complacent with due to their own political agendas. But as Diamond (1996: 5) argues, "Performativity, I would suggest, must be rooted in the materiality and historical density of performance" which becomes more evident in Toni's narrative.

5 Conclusion

Spry (2001: 712) notes, autoethnographic texts (and more broadly, autoethogra-phies) "reveal the fractures, sutures, and seams of self-interacting with others in the context of researching lived experience". This chapter attempts to provide the reader with a brief introduction to Turkmenistan as illustrated through the lived experience of one English language teacher during two separate trips. What Toni's experiences, as well as the dialogues that ensued, demonstrate is what Spry (2001) talks about regarding the fractures or dissonant notes that arise when people interact with each other, particularly in different socio-political-cultural contexts. But as Denzin (1992: 25) writes, "The tale being told should reflect back on, be entangled in, and critique this current historical moment and its discontents."

Langellier (1999: 140) posits, "Performing and studying personal narrative is a way of grasping the world. If, in postmodern times, we are 'getting a life' through telling our stories and consuming others' stories in increasingly ritualistic and public ways, the future of personal narrative performance will be shaped by continuing to critically question how it embodies cultural conflict about experience and identity and renders it discussable." And while it is uncertain how others may respond to this chapter or approach in the field of sociolin-guistics or the sociology of language, we ourselves acknowledge that despite its limitations, autoethnography in language research can help us gain insight through and into the lived experiences of others.

References

Adams, Tony E. 2008. A review of narrative ethics. *Qualitative Inqury* 14(2). 175–194. DOI: 10.1177/1077800407304417.

Agar, Michael. 1994. *Language shock: Understanding the culture of conversation.* New York: William Morrow/Quill.

Alexander, Bryant K. 2003. (Re)visioning the ethnographic site: Interpretive ethnography as a method of pedagogical reflexivity and scholarly production. *Qualitative Inquiry* 9(2003). 416–441. DOI: 10.1177/1077800403009003006

Anderson, Leon. 2006. Analytic autoethnography. *Journal of Contemporary Ethnography* 35. 373–395. DOI: 10.1177/0891241605280449

Clement, Victoria. 2008. Emblems of independence: script choice in post-Soviet Turkmenistan. *International Journal of the Sociology of Language* 192(2008). 171–185.

Clement, Victoria. 2011. Grassroots educational initiatives in Turkmenistan. In Iveta Silova (ed.), *Globalization on the margins. Education and postsocialist transformations in Central Asia*, 345–361. Charlotte, NC: Information Age Publishing.

Dailey, Erika & Iveta Silova. 2008. Invisible and surrogate education. Filling educational gaps in Turkmenistan. In Iveta Silova & Gita Steiner-Khamsi (eds.), *How NGOs react. Globalization and education reform in the Caucasus, Central Asia, and Mongolia*, 211–229. Bloomfield, CT: Kumarian Press.

Castell, Suzanne de & Mary Bryson. 1997. Introduction: Identity, authority, narativity. In Suzanne de Castell & Mary Bryson (eds.), *Radical in‹ter›ventions: Identity, politics and difference in educational* praxis, 1–11. New York: State University of New York Press.

Denzin, Norman. 1992. The many faces of emotionality. Reading persona. In Carolyn S. Ellis & Michael G. Flaherty (eds.), *Investigating subjectivity: Research on lived experience*, 17–30. Newbury Park: Sage.

Diamond, Elin. 1996. Introduction. In Elin Diamond (ed.), *Performance and cultural politics*, 1–12. New York: Routledge.

Dovletti, Nazar. 2009. Turkmenistan adopts new education law. *Central Asia Online*. http://centralasiaonline.com/en_GB/articles/caii/features/2009/08/31/feature-02 (accessed January 2014).

Ellis, Carolyn S. & Arthur P. Bochner. 2006. Analyzing analytic autoethnography: An autopsy. *Journal of Contemporary Ethnography* 35. 429–449. DOI: 10.1177/0891241606286979

Ellis, Carolyn S. & Michael G. Flaherty. 1992. Introduction. In Carolyn S. Ellis & Michael G. Flaherty (eds.), *Investigating subjectivity: Research on lived experience*, 1–13. Newbury Park, CA: Sage.

European Commission. 2012. Higher education in Turkmenistan. Report published by the National Tempus Office Turkmenistan (July 2012). http://eacea.ec.europa.eu/tempus/participating_countries/turkmenistan_en.php (accessed on June 12, 2014).

Frentz, Thomas S. & Joyce L. Hocker. 2010. Layered reflections on a written story through real-time conversations. *Qualitative Inquiry* 16(8). 621–629. DOI: 10.1177/1077800410374037

Goodall, H. Lloyd. 2000. *Writing the new ethnography*. New York: Alta Mira Press.

Hinnemo, Torgny. 2003. The blocked road to Turkmen democracy. In Birgit N. Schlyter (ed.), *Prospects for democracy in Central Asia*, Vol. 15, 59–68. Papers presented at a conference in Istanbul, 1–3 June 2003. Swedish Research Institute in Istanbul Transactions.

Horak, Slavomír. 2013, September 1. Educational reforms in Turkmenistan: Good framework, bad content? *Central Asia Policy Brief*, 11(September 2013). http://centralasiaprogram.org/central-asia-policy-brief-no-11-september-2013/ (accessed January 2014).

In Turkmenistan, the state standards of education. (2012, January 2012). *Turkmenistan.ru, Internet Gazet*. http://www.Turkmenistan.ru/ru/articles/36954.html (accessed January 2014).

Landau, Jacob & Barbara Kellner-Heinkele. 2011. Turkmenistan. In Jacob Landau & Barbara Kellner-Heinkele (eds.), *Language politics in contemporary Central Asia*, 151–172. London: I.B. Tauris.

Langellier, Kristin M. 1999. Personal narrative, performance, performativity: Two or three things I know for sure. *Text and Performance Quarterly* 19(1999), 125–144.

Observatory on Borderless Higher Education. May 2004. Turkmenistan rejects foreign higher education degrees: what are the consequences of de-internationalisation? http://www.obhe.ac.uk/documents/search?region_id=&theme_id=&year=All+Years&keywords=&author=&document_type_id=2&search=Search&pageID=14 (accessed January 2014).

Roberts, Sean P. 2012. Research in challenging environments: the case of Russia's managed democracy. *Qualitative Research* 133(3), 337–351. DOI: 10.1177/1468794112451039

Sartor, Valerie. 2010. Teaching English in Turkmenistan. *English Today*, 26(4), 29–36.

Spry, Tami. 2001. Performing autoethnography: An embodied methodological praxis. *Qualitative Inquiry* 7(6), 706–732.

Turkmen Institute for Human Rights [TIHR]. 2006. Education in Turkmenistan. http://www.chrono-tm.org/photos/2560683175898658.pdf (accessed January 2014).

UNICEF. 2008. Country profile: Education in Turkmenistan. *UNESCO EFT Global Monitoring Report*. http://www.unicef.org/ceecis/Turkmenistan.pdf (accessed January 2014).

Van Manen, Max. 1990. *Researching lived experience*. London, Canada: State University of New York.

Wijayatilake, Claire. 2012. An autoethnographic exploration of my professional experiences as teacher trainer and principal at two international schools in Sri Lanka. *Language Teaching* 45(3), 403–405. DOI: 10.1017/S0261444812000122.

I Language and Nation-State Building

Juldyz Smagulova

5 The Re-Acquisition of Kazakh in Kazakhstan: Achievements and Challenges

Abstract: This chapter focuses on the re-acquisition of Kazakh in Russian-dominant urban areas in Kazakhstan. It analyzes developments in Kazakh-language education and their impact on the revitalization of Kazakh. My approach is analogous to other research on multilingualism and language in education in bilingual contexts which are grounded in poststructuralist and critical theory (Gal 1998; Heller 1999; Tollefson 1991, 1995). This chapter first outlines the wider sociolinguistic and historical context by identifying factors that led to the drop in Kazakh-medium school enrollment and language shift from Kazakh to Russian in urban areas the late 1960s and native language revitalization efforts after Kazakhstan became independent in 1991. This is then followed by the report of findings from a mass-survey (2,555 respondents) on the reported proficiency and use of Kazakh across different age groups and description of ethnographic interviews and observations at Russian-dominant urban homes and a Kazakh-language school.

Keywords: Kazakh; language revitalization; language education policy

1 The Kazakh language in education: A brief history

Formal education of Kazakhs and education in the Kazakh language were first introduced during the Tsarist era after it became the part of the Russian Empire. In the beginning of the 18th century, Kazakhs were fighting among themselves, were at major war with the Zhungars while also fighting with Yaik and Siberian Cossacks, Bashkirs, Kalmyks, Sarts, Uzbeks, Bukhara and Kokand khanates. Tribes were rapidly losing land and pastures. For this reason Abulkhair, the khan of the Small Horde, was forced to seek military protection of the Russian Empire.[1] The agreement on political subordination was sealed in 1731. This was the beginning of the long process of the Kazakh tribes' inclusion into the Russian

---

1 Even today Kazakhs identify themselves with a particular tribe within a particular Horde (or *Zhuz*), i.e., Small, Middle or Great.

Empire. Some tribes followed Abulkhair's example and voluntarily signed agreements with the Empire, while others were conquered. The last tribes to be defeated and incorporated into the Russian Empire were the Zhetysu and Tashkent tribes (1863–1867).

The imperial Russian administration took a range of actions to incorporate the newly subjugated Kazakhs into the Empire and implemented a number of administrative-political reforms which were ultimately aimed at transferring political, military, economic, and legislative power from numerous Kazakh khans and lords to centralized governmental bodies. By 1882, the institute of khans was abolished and Kazakh lands were consolidated within three main territorial-administrative divisions under the military administration: Turkistan, Orenburg, and West-Siberian region.[2]

The creation of a centralized system of government was only one aspect of the ultimate project of achieving uniformity of political and cultural structures across the Empire. Achieving political and cultural homogeneity across the Russian Empire was implicitly aimed at turning the "savages" of "Asiatic Russia" into the citizens of the state. This task was viewed to be possible only through linguistic and religious assimilation (Batunsky 1990), and therefore the local population was obligated to study Russian (Pavlenko 2006) in Russian schools as an alternative to traditional *medresses*, i.e., Muslim religious schools, and to offset the growing influence of Islam in the Steppe. A more mundane purpose for teaching Russian to locals was to satisfy the bureaucratic apparatus' need for more clerks and translators.[3]

By the end of the 19th century, 162 Russian-Kazakh bilingual schools offered instruction to 3,560 boys and 962 girls (Pavlenko 2011: 342). These schools for non-Christian and non-ethnic Russians (*inorodtsy*) were following a "natural approach" developed by a Christian missionary and Turkologist, Nikolay Il'minsky (1822–1891). It was based on two fundamental principles, i.e., that children had to start school in their native languages before switching to Russian and that they also had to be taught by local teachers. As Pavlenko (2013: 655) observed "The 1870 decree sanctioned transitional bilingual education for these learners that began in the pupils' native languages (often transcribed in Cyrillic) and then shifted to Russian, with the native language used as an aid and studied as a subject."

---

2 The Kazakh khans and sultans were granted hereditary nobility and were equalized in privileges with Russian nobility. This meant that they were given land ownership rights, and their children received access to Russian universities and military academies.

3 The first school for Kazakhs was opened in Orenburg in 1850 and was exclusively aimed to prepare local cadre for administrative work. Initially, the education was in Russian and Tatar (Dzhumagulov 1975).

Since the implementation of such a policy required the development of teaching materials in Kazakh, the unintended consequent of creating a bilingual education system was the adoption of vernacular Kazakh for both educational and literary purposes. Ibray Altynsarin, the first Kazakh educator and a student of Il'minsky, wrote several textbooks in the Cyrillic-based Kazakh alphabet, including *Kazakh Grammar* and the famous *Киргизская Хрестоматияг* [Kirgiz Anthology] in 1875, which are often regarded as the beginning of the Kazakh language teaching and literature tradition.[4,5]

However, the combination of the Kazakhs' nomadic lifestyle as well as their suspicion toward these Russian schools and the Christian religion impeded the process. By the end of the 19th century only about one percent of Kazakh children were attending schools (Masanov et al. 2001), while almost all the ethnic Russian settlers were schooled and literate (Isayev 1979). Despite negligible school attendance by locals, these initial developments played significant role in the formation of an educated class, Kazakh-Russian bilinguals, and Kazakh as a language of education.

During the revolutionary struggle of the early 1900s, education became an area of further contestation since each of the aforementioned educational models represented particular ideological stances of different social groups in pursuit for domination. Some, mainly Russian missionaries, were advocating for Russian-medium schools, which they saw as a tool of both linguistic and religious assimilation. Religious Muslim groups, particularly Tatars, who "strove for control over their nomadic kinsmen, not only in commerce but also in education and cultural life" (Zenkovsky 1953: 311) were backing traditional religious medresses. Kazakh liberals were in favor of secular Kazakh-medium schools and mass literacy, because for them, the existence of a national language was a prerequisite for making legitimate claims for cultural distinctiveness and national self-determination. In a program address in the *Kazakh* newspaper, Baitursunov proclaimed, "To preserve our independence, we should put all our efforts and resources to increase educational and cultural level, for that we must develop literature in our mother tongue. It must not be forgotten that only those people who speak their own language and have literature in that language have rights to claim independence" (cited from Rysbekova 2010: 1). However, at the same

---

4 Until 1925, Kazakhs were misnamed as Kirgiz and Kirgiz-Kaisak to differentiate them from Russian Cossacks.

5 Ibrahim Altynsarin (1841–1889) is credited as a founder of public Kazakh schools and Kazakh literature. While working as a school inspector, he opened four types of schools, i.e., a school for girls, agricultural, technical and teacher training colleges. Altynsarin himself was a graduate of the first Orenburg Kazakh school.

time, the latter recognized the emancipatory power of the Russian language and continually promoted proficiency in Russian in order to gain access to the achievements of European science and culture. These main identity projects and corresponding ideological approaches, pro-Turkic, pro-Islamic, pro-Kazakh, and pro-western, would surface repeatedly during later discussions on national policies and state-building, on the polemics of alphabets, processes of corpus planning, and the educational curriculum.

The October Revolution of 1917 brought Kazakhstan political identity. It became a distinct politico-administrative entity first in 1920 as an autonomous region within the Russian Federation, and then in 1936 as a separate republic. The 1918 decree "On National Minority Schools", along with other language management measures (e.g., developing new alphabets, standardization and modernization of local languages, and status planning of local languages) laid out the provisions for setting up schooling in local languages (Pavlenko 2013) including Kazakh. On the wave of these new national policies, Kazakhstan was able to drastically reshape the social, political, and cultural institutions, create national cadres, and establish a national educational system and mass media – all of which further contributed to the development of the Kazakhs as a nation and Kazakh subsequently as a national language.

During this early Soviet period the number of schools and pupils increased dramatically as seen in Table 5.1. The raise was especially noticeable after 1925 when the Soviet government introduced free compulsory primary education.

Table 5.1: Schools and Enrollment in Kazakhstan (1911–1937)[6]

	1911	1920	1931	1927
Total number of schools	1,246	3,748	7,110	7,731
Number of Kazakh schools	350			
Total number of pupils	66,000	217,861	600,000	929,000
Number of Kazakh pupils	6,100			312,700

Note that in the academic year of 1925–26, only 12% of Kazakh children and 39.1% of Russian children of school age attended school. The lower proportion of Kazakhs in the student population was mainly due to the fact that in the early 1920s a mere quarter of Kazakhs led a sedentary lifestyle – the majority of the population was still nomadic. By 1931–1932, these numbers increased with 72.7% of Kazakh and 92.0% of Russian children were involved in the educational process. By 1937, 96% of all school-aged children attended schools with 45% of Kazakh students being identified as female.

---

6 Sources: Khasanov (1976) and Mirzoyan (1937)

One major difficulty Kazakhstan had to overcome in the 1920–1930s was the lack of Kazakh schools, teachers, and textbooks. In 1921, the new government organized a special committee in *Narkompros* (*Narodnyj Kommissariat Prosveshcheniya* – People Committee of Education – a precursor of the future Soviet Ministry of Education and Sciences). Its main objective was to build an educational system, which included the development of Kazakh language textbooks and teaching materials. In 1927 alone, the new government published more than 575,000 copies of 30 different textbooks in Kazakh. In 1930, the state provided people with 590,000 textbooks. Later, large quantities of textbooks were produced and distributed in the regions, e.g., 400,000 reading textbooks; 475,000 alphabet primers; and 300,000 elementary math textbooks (Suleimenov and Bisenov 1967, cited from Khasanov 1976: 38). To prepare the national teaching cadres in the late 1920s, the state also created 13 pedagogical vocational schools and colleges that trained teachers in 15 different specializations. Notably, almost all of these institutions had Kazakh language-medium departments training teachers for Kazakh schools as well (Khasanov 1976).

One of the greatest achievements of this period was the elimination of illiteracy. In just seven years, from 1919 to 1926, the literacy rate increased from 2% to 22.5%.[7] Despite several alphabet changes, i.e., the Arabic alphabet reform (1924) and then back to Latin (1929), by 1939, the literacy rate was at 83.6% (Shokamanov 2001).

The institutionalization of Kazakh-language education subsequently led to Kazakh being established as both the standard and official language, as well as a language for print media. At the same time however, with various advances in education, publishing and research, the role of Russian increased as well. Due to the lack of Kazakh-speaking teachers and instructors, the language of instruction in early Kazakh schools and universities was often Russian. For example, the first Kazakh institute of higher education, the Kazakh Pedagogical Institute, which opened in 1924 in Tashkent, had to offer most of the classes in Russian because initially its faculty consisted of Russian speaking instructors and professors (Khasanov 1976: 116). Consequently, Kazakhs who were educated in those early schools became Kazakh-Russian bilinguals.

---

7 Olcott (1995) notes that rapid increases in literacy rates were obtained because of the Kazakhs' familiarity with and attraction to the Arabic alphabet. Yet another facilitating factor was the reform of the writing system by Akhmet Baitursunov in 1924. The Arabic script used for Kazakh prior to that time was poorly adapted to the phonetic system of the language – only 16 letters had independent symbols, the other 12 used various diacritical marks to distinguish them from each other, there were only three symbols for all vowels, and there were several variants of the same letter.

Despite the briefness of the *korenizatsiya* [nativization] period during the Soviet era, this process played a key role in transforming the Kazakh national identity. The major outcomes of this period included: the emergence of Kazakhstan as a distinct political entity, the strengthening ethnic identity of Kazakh, and the rise of Kazakh as a standard national language, which was then further developed to be used in political and educational institutions. However, in the late 1930s, the *korenizatsiya* policy was replaced by a new policy which was aimed at Russification. A number of measures were undertaken to increase proficiency in Russian among various local populations throughout the Soviet republics. In 1938, Russian was declared an obligatory subject in all non-Russian schools (Suleimenova 1997). In 1955, the obligatory teaching of Kazakh as a subject in Russian-medium school was cancelled (Suleimenova 1997: 225).

After the 1958–1959 Educational Reform, which enabled free parental choice regarding their children's language of education, it was no longer assumed that children must be taught in their native languages. While the total enrollment in Kazakh-language schools in Kazakhstan after the 1958–1959 Reform slightly increased (Pavlenko 2013), the change of policy had rather devastating effect in urban areas. In many cities where the economic, political and demographic power of Russian-speakers contributed to the prestige of Russian, in order to succeed it was required to learn Russian and act like Russian-speakers. Moreover, in the Kazakh SSR context, the disparity in prestige and functional distribution of Kazakh and Russian led to disparity in educational attainments in these two languages. Most communicative domains (and corresponding educational institutions) which were considered strategically important by the Communist party, e.g., the army, transport, the police, national security, state planning, industry, banking, statistics, engineering, science, mass-media and publishing, were almost exclusively Russian-medium. Choices regarding institutes of higher education and professional training for post-graduate study in Kazakh were limited to education, humanities, arts, and agriculture.

The inequality in power distribution and in potential education attainment in Kazakh and Russian sealed the fate of Kazakh-language schools in urban areas. Even though Kazakh had become institutionalized and the Kazakh-language education was available from primary school to university, because of the aforementioned reasons, there was little interest among urban parents in educating children in Kazakh. At the same time, in urban Kazakh families, Kazakh was also being displaced as the home language by Russian. The peak in this type of this shift in family language practices was observed between the 1960s and 1980s, when an increasing number of Kazakh parents adopted Russian as the language of child-rearing. Massive language shift in urban areas lead to the formation of a whole Russian monolingual generation or, at best, passive bilinguals. By the time members of this Russian-speaking and Russian-language educated group had reached adulthood, the Soviet Union collapsed – and they became parents of the first post-Soviet generation and faced the dilemma of choosing the language of education for their children, i.e., to maintain Russian or re-acquire Kazakh.

2 Kazakh-language education today

Since the establishment of independent Kazakhstan's language planning laws, the main focus of these Kazakh language acquisition policies was children since, needless to say, Russian-speaking adults regardless of their ethnic background were reluctant to put effort into learning the language. The other reason for focusing language revival efforts on the education sector might be the fact that in a centralized state like Kazakhstan, the government has full control over schooling and other educational institutions. This means that state bodies (i.e., the Ministry of Education and Sciences and local municipal Education departments) are in complete charge of curriculum and textbook development, as well as teacher training, budget, and testing.

This type of centralized control may explain why the changes in the education system with regards to Kazakh and "Kazakhization" were swift and drastic in comparison to other social areas. Changes in the educational sphere could be observed in a various forms, e.g., the re-establishment of schooling in Kazakh, making Kazakh a required subject in Russian-medium schools, the inclusion of a language component in the national standardized test (which serves both as a school exit and university entrance exam), the development of linguistically, culturally, and politically appropriate curriculum materials and textbooks (e.g., teaching the rewritten History of Kazakhstan instead of the History of the Soviet Union), as well as the increased number of hours for teaching Kazakh and Kazakh literature and reduction of the number of hours allocated for teaching Russian and Russian literature. These and many other changes, e.g., making schoolchildren learn the new anthem in Kazakh and ensuring that school events like the annual school opening ceremony and concerts in Russian-language schools are bilingual, have drastically impacted the educational context.

Along with these top-down changes, there has been an amplified grass-root support of Kazakh-language education. The enrollment in Kazakh-language schools across the country has increased rapidly since 1989, while the enrollment in Russian-language schools has decreased. Between the 1988–89 and 2006–2007 academic years, the share of schoolchildren enrolled in Kazakh-language schools nearly doubled from 30.7% to 59.3% (Altynbekova 2010;

Государственная программа развития образования 2005). The number of Kazakh-medium schools increased by 781 from 1991 to 2007 (Kuzakov 2007). Currently about 80% of Kazakh children attend Kazakh-medium schools (Kuzakov 2007) in comparison to 1991, when number was 34.4% (UNDP 1992).

Nevertheless, in urban areas, Russian-language schools are still prevalent since almost 80% of Kazakh schools are located in rural areas (*Концепция расширения сферы применения государственного языка* 2006). In 2009, the number of students enrolled in Russian medium-schools across Kazakhstan was 1.9 times higher in urban areas than in rural regions (Altynbekova 2010). For example, in Almaty, the biggest city in Kazakhstan with a population of about two million, about half of all schoolchildren attend Kazakh-medium schools. After a swift rise of Kazakh-medium schools during the previous three decades from virtually non-existent (two schools in the 1980s) to 50 Kazakh-medium schools and more than 60 mixed schools (where Kazakh-language, Russian language or other medium of instruction classes share the same building) in 2011, the growth has seem to slow down. As Table 5.2 shows, from 2008 to 2012 the share of children studying in Kazakh increased from 41% to 44.5%. The analysis of the Almaty school data suggests that this growth is mainly due to inclusion of the former rural (and thus Kazakh-speaking areas) into the Almaty municipality and also because of internal migration from rural areas to the city. The rate of enrollment of children from Russian-speaking homes in Kazakh-language school has remained relatively the same.

Table 5.2: Almaty School Enrollment by LOI[8]

LOI	2008		2009		2011		2012	
Kazakh	64,999	41.0%	68,157	42.6%	64,144	43.7%	70,954	44.5%
Russian	91,112	57.6%	89,532	55.9%	86,709	54.8%	85,827	53.9%
Uighur	2,114	1.3%	2,125	1.3%	2,190	1.4%	2,318	1.45%
German	233	0.1%	221	0.1%	217	0.14%	212	0.13%
Total	158,458		160,035		158,260		159,311	

In summary, a strong language policy and parental support has turned education into a key and a potent agent of change contributing to Kazakh language revitalization. As the survey data described in the next section demonstrates, these factors have contributed to a considerable increase in Kazakh language proficiency among young people. The survey also shows that this new generation, who went through schooling in post-Soviet Kazakhstan, is more loyal to the state, and is more likely to subscribe to the Kazakhization ideology.

---

8 Source: Official site of Almaty city (2011, 2014)

3 Data

This chapter draws on survey data and ethnographic observations conducted both at homes and schools. The survey took place between November 2005 and February 2007. The data was gathered by convenience sampling in schools, universities, workplaces (e.g., kindergartens, government offices, shops, industries and construction sites) and among families located in both rural and urban areas throughout the different regions of Kazakhstan. The survey drew from several earlier surveys conducted in Kazakhstan such as Rivers (2003), Masanov (2002), Laitin (1998), and Son (1999). The self-report questionnaire contained 46 closed-ended questions and two open-ended questions. The questions left open were about ethnicity and ethnic language (mother tongue). The survey measured self-assessed proficiency in Kazakh and Russian, reported language use in a range of contexts such as family, friendship circle, school and the workplace, and language beliefs.

The sample consisted of 2,555 respondents of different ethnic background, age, gender, place of residence (urban/rural), and socio-economic class. There were 1,548 female respondents (68.6%) and 703 male respondents (31.2%). Urban residents represented 54% of the sample (1,220 respondents) and rural represented 43.9% (991 respondents) of the sample.

Table 5.3: Ethnic Composition of the Sample

Ethnic group	Number of respondents	
Kazakhs	1,022	(45.3%)
Russians	527	(23.4%)
Turks	351	(15.6%)
Slavs	86	(3.8%)
Others	267	(11.8%)

The respondents ranged from 16 to 80 years old. For analytical purposes the sample was divided into four age groups. The first cohort includes respondents who were 23 years old or younger, the second and third cohorts were respondents ages 24 to 35 and 36 to 55, and the fourth cohort consisted of those who were older than 55.[9] These age groups corresponded with their employment status. The first group consisted of students, the second group were young

---

9 The numbers do not add up to 2,555 because ethnicity was not specified for missing two, age was not specified for missing 12, gender was not specified to missing four, place of residence was not specified for missing 44 (1.7%), and income was not specified for missing 123 (5.5%).

adults entering the job market, the third group were the respondents at the middle of their careers, and the last group were retired or about to retire (Table 5.4). The sample was then divided into five income groups (Table 5.5).

Table 5.4: Age Structure of the Sample

Age group	Number of respondents	
<23	886	(39.3%)
23–35	602	(26.7%)
36–55	588	(26%)
>55	167	(7.4%)

Table 5.5: Income Structure of the Sample

Monthly income	Number of respondents	
<50 dollars	395	(17.5%)
50–100 dollars	700	(31%)
100–300 dollars	702	(31.1%)
300–500 dollars	202	(9.0%)
>500 dollars	133	(5.9%)

The survey data was complemented by ethnographic interviews and observations which were conducted among three urban families in Almaty conducted from October 2007 to February 2008. In these ethnically Kazakh families, the parents had no or limited proficiency in Kazakh and Russian was their home language. Yet they were involved in the process of language revival in that their children were all enrolled in Kazakh-medium schools. I had also observed one of the participant children (a nine year boy) at his school for two months. The school is located in one of the oldest and prestigious districts so called *Золотой квадрат* [The Golden Block]. Because of high property prices, there are few new immigrants that settle in that area (e.g., migrants from rural areas) in comparison to other municipal tax districts. The goal of the ethnographic study was to understand how maintenance of Russian and the revival of Kazakh are accomplished in everyday language practice.

4 Achievements

The survey data suggests that language shift to Russian among Kazakh has halted; in fact, we might be observing Kazakh language revival. There were several findings in the survey pointing to school as a key source of Kazakh revitalization, e.g., the increased enrollment in Kazakh-medium schools, increasing reported proficiency in Kazakh among the youngest respondents, higher levels of reported use of Kazakh in schools in comparison to other public domains, and more positive attitudes toward Kazakhization among the youngest respondents.

4.1 Enrolment in Kazakh-medium schools

Both the survey results and the official statistics show dramatic increase in enrolment in Kazakh-language schools. Three times more respondents from the youngest group reported attending a Kazakh school in comparison to the group representing the generation of their parents. Table 5.6 summarizes the reports on language of education at school sorted by age and rural/urban residency. These numbers seemed to reflect a fundamental reassessment of the value of Kazakh within socio-economic changes in the country.

Table 5.6: Schooling in Kazakh by Urban and Rural Kazakhs

<23		23–35		35–55		>55	
Urban	Rural	Urban	Rural	Urban	Rural	Urban	Rural
218	222	73	74	43	110	33	38
(45.2%)	(57.6%)	(21.3%)	(30.4%)	(14.3%)	(39.7%)	(37.5%)	(47.8%)

However, in the dataset, the choice of language of schooling ran along income lines. According to the survey data, only 16.1% of young urban Kazakhs in the wealthiest group reported attending Kazakh-medium schools; in contrast, 42.3% of the young urban Kazakhs in the poorest group reported that they studied in Kazakh. This difference between more and less economically powerful groups suggests that the choice of language of education, and thus language preferences in general, are indeed linked to social stratification. Russian is a choice of Kazakhs with greater access to wealth and social capital.

The respondents were also asked to assess the market value of Kazakh by agreeing or disagreeing with the following statement "Do you agree that Kazakh has potential economic benefits for children (grandchildren)?" The results are presented in Table 5.7.

The results showed that the majority of the respondents believed in the potential economic returns of Kazakh language proficiency. At the same time, we can observe that the higher the income level, the less people are likely to agree with the statement.

Table 5.7: Kazakh: Perceived Economic Benefits for Children

	Agree		Disagree		Don't know	
<$50	306	(77.5%)	28	(7.1%)	45	(11.4%)
$50–100	492	(70.3%)	48	(6.9%)	97	(13.9%)
$100–300	491	(69.9%)	40	(5.7%)	80	(11.4%)
$300–500	141	(69.8%)	13	(6.4%)	24	(11.9%)
>$500	87	(65.4%)	16	(12.0%)	12	(9.0%)
Total	1617	(71.7%)	153	(6.8%)	267	(11.8%)

4.2 Age difference in reported language proficiency

The survey results demonstrated that the youngest respondents who started schooling after introduction of Kazakhization language policies were also more likely to claim fluent proficiency in Kazakh than the respondents of the middle-age who went through schooling during the Soviet era. Furthermore, the youngest respondents were less likely to claim proficiency in Russian in comparison to the older respondents. Table 5.8 summarize reports on oral fluency in Kazakh and Russian by age and place of residence.

Table 5.8: Reported Oral Proficiency in Kazakh and Russian by Urban and Rural Kazakhs (%).

		<23	23–35	36–55	>55
Kazakh language	Urban	77.0	60.2	66.2	87.5
	Rural	95.6	87.2	89.4	100.0
Russian language	Urban	66.8	88.0	89.6	100.0
	Rural	28.8	52.7	62.9	87.0

The data points to a language shift trend reversal. Urban ethnic Kazakhs ages 23 and older were more likely to claim proficiency in Russian than in Kazakh, while the opposite was true for urban ethnic Kazakhs younger than 23. Older respondents were more likely to be bilingual Kazakh/Russian speakers than their younger counterparts. Attention should be drawn to the abrupt drop in reported proficiency in Russian by the youngest respondents, especially among rural informants, i.e., less than 70% of young urban Kazakhs claimed fluency in Russian compared to 100% among the eldest group.

To cross-validate the self-assessment data with actual language use, the respondents were offered questionnaires in two languages to choose from, Kazakh or Russian. As expected, the actual use of Kazakh was lower than self-reported proficiency. While 70.5% of Kazakhs claimed that they could write fluently, only 55% actually filled the questionnaire out in Kazakh. This discrepancy was smaller among the youngest respondents: 66.0% of them selected question-naires in Kazakh (64.8% claimed fluent writing skills) in comparison to 38.7% among the respondents older than 55 years old (68.9% reported writing fluency). From this it could be inferred that younger respondents tended to underestimate their language abilities while older respondents seem to overrate them.

4.3 Use of Kazakh

The analysis of data on reported language use demonstrated that among partic-ipants, Russian remained the prevailing language in most public domains and was the language choice of more affluent speakers. The rural/urban division was also a factor influencing the language distribution, i.e., urban residents are less likely to use Kazakh. At the same time, the findings hinted at changes in language conventions in favor of Kazakh, as young Kazakhs were more likely to claim using Kazakh for wider variety of functions. Table 5.9 shows the results on the reported use of Kazakh and Russian by age from the whole sample.

Table 5.9: Reported Language Use by Age (%)

	Kazakh language only				Russian language only			
	<23	**24–35**	**36–55**	**>55**	**<23**	**24–35**	**36–55**	**>55**
Interaction in school	29.5	17.8	18.0	7.8	28.2	42.0	44.4	52.1
Interaction at work	15.2	13.5	12.6	7.8	23.7	36.7	45.2	56.3
Interaction in state offices	15.0	8.8	11.9	6.6	46.7	47.2	48.6	55.7
Interaction in banks	12.1	6.6	8.5	5.4	43.8	51.8	49.7	62.3
Interaction with friends	24.0	16.1	15.6	9.0	33.0	40.0	42.3	52.7
Listening to radio	15.1	6.8	10.5	7.8	38.8	44.5	43.2	46.7
Watching TV	12.4	4.8	8.3	2.4	35.2	36.6	40.0	46.1
Reading newspapers	19.6	9.1	10.0	6.0	35.0	45.0	50.5	60.5
Reading non-academic texts	25.4	12.3	13.3	6.6	35.7	45.0	50.7	62.3
Reading academic texts	22.0	10.6	11.2	7.2	40.3	45.7	46.9	52.7

Additionally, the youngest respondents were more likely to claim that they spoke Kazakh at school than the respondents from the older cohorts. Corre-spondingly, teachers were most likely to claim to use Kazakh at work. Almost a quarter of teachers reported that they use Kazakh at work; in comparison, only 4.3% of people involved in services reported using Kazakh at work. So, the school appears to be the domain that was most conducive to the use of Kazakh.

4.4 Changes in language attitudes

The role of the education system appears to be instrumental in the re-acquisition of Kazakh by the younger generation. Moreover, it also seems to be linked to changes in views on Kazakh and its role in society. The youngest respondents were those who have received their education post-1991 when schools and universities introduced a new Kazakhstani curriculum and textbooks as mentioned earlier. So, it should not be surprising that after years of being exposed to Kazakhization ideologies, younger respondents demonstrated more loyalty and tolerance to the idea of the monolingual Kazakh state.

Table 5.10: Attitudes to Kazakh as the Sole State Language by Age, Ethnicity, and Residence (%)

		<23	23–35	35–55	>55
Kazakhs	Urban	71.4	53.7	63.6	75.0
	Rural	83.6	77.7	82.8	73.9
Russians	Urban	16.5	17.9	9.0	9.8
	Rural	13.0	8.3	9.4	9.6

In general, the survey findings suggest that the state's intervention in education (i.e., re-establishing Kazakh-medium schools, developing curriculum changes and introducing Kazakh language class as a required subject in Russian-language schools) has effectively led to Kazakh revitalization and shaping a more positive stance towards Kazakh among the first post-Soviet generation.

The findings show that reported competence in Kazakh and its use are on the rise as seen among younger respondents. The survey data on cross-generational, urban/rural, and income variability permits us to conclude that Kazakh is gaining social prestige. Nearly all respondents subscribed to the notion of Kazakh as a symbol of a new independent Kazakhstan and perceived it as a must-know language for upward social mobility. Most telling in this respect were the reports on prospective language of education and perceived economic proceeds for children from the knowledge of Kazakh. The majority of respondents reported that they were interested in educating their children in Kazakh and they saw Kazakh language proficiency as linked to better economic chances for their children.

5 Challenges

Despite the measurable success of Kazakhization policies, however, the survey data also detected issues that signal complications and contradictions in the revival movement.

5.1 Kazakh lacks appeal to socially powerful middle-class urban Kazakhs

The survey results showed that there were a considerable residential and class differences in school enrolment choices. Urban Kazakhs were less likely to enroll their children in Kazakh-language schools and were also less likely to have attended such schools themselves. Wealthier Kazakhs were less likely to speak Kazakh fluently, use Kazakh at work, and find Kazakh valuable. It appears that for this social group, education in Kazakh lacks the "competitive edge" (Reynolds, Bellin and ab Ieuan 1998, cited from Jones and Martin-Jones 2004: 49) that education in Russian and English might offer. This implies that socially powerful urban middle-class Kazakhs are among those who are most ambivalent to the current language policy and the Kazakhization ideology. When asked about the latest sociolinguistic changes in the country, urban Russian-speaking parents' responses were similar to the views of the majority of the survey respondents. They agreed that in the future the knowledge of Kazakh might improve their children's changes of social advancement. One participant noted,

> Now a lot (is) said about that Kazakhs should know Kazakh and so on. And it is not like there is pressure. It is like a pendulum swung in the other direction and if before it was good to know Russian, now it is even better if you know Kazakh... In other words, there is a stereotype. Now it is socially approved to know Kazakh... (P1, personal communication, February 2007)

Despite this view, parents often express an opinion that the recent sociolinguistic changes are more in the heads of people with little affect on their everyday lives. "[My husband] thinks that there is a growing need in knowing Kazakh. But I don't see how Kazakh could be needed. I personally don't need Kazakh in my everyday life" one participant shared (P2, personal communication). When asked why they decided to educate children in Kazakh, all of the interviewees emphasized distinctly instrumental motivation of their choice. For example,

> Learning Kazakh for me is only linked to social advancement. I am not interested in politics. I am not much interested in culture and something like that. In other words, I want my children to have an adequate education so that, to put it blatantly, they could move upwards socially. So that in the future it does not impede (.) Say, if they for some reason they decide to stay in Kazakhstan and decide to work in the government or somewhere else where it requires more Kazakh, business correspondence (.) so that it does not hinder them. (P1, personal communication, February 2007)

Notably, many parents do not see their children pursuing a career in the government sector where knowledge of Kazakh is perceived to be essential. Instead, they expect that they would study abroad and work for international companies.

Another participant noted, "Will kids need Kazakh in the future? We are aimed at western education, so not. Maybe only for identity. Our kids will be more cosmopolitan. If you know for sure that kids will live in this country, work in government structures, then they better learn Kazakh" (P3, personal communication, December 2007).

It seems reasonable to infer that the decision by these parents to send their children to a Kazakh-medium school does not imply commitment to language revival. In these cases, there appeared to be a very weak link between ethnic identity and language. For them, Kazakh, like Russian or English, was a form of linguistic capital that could allow their children to gain access to a wider job market and improve their life chances.

5.2 Lack of natural intergenerational transmission of Kazakh in urban families.

Three findings strongly imply that language reproduction is taking place outside of the urban home, and instead in schools. Firstly, while only 60% of urban Kazakhs in the youngest age group reported Kazakh as their home language, 77% of them claimed fluent proficiency in Kazakh. Secondly, the younger respondents were more likely to claim fluency in Kazakh than their older counterparts. Finally, the survey data discovered a curious inconsistency in reported oral and literacy skills among the youngest respondents, who claimed that they read and write in Kazakh better than they speak and understand oral speech in Kazakh, suggesting the schooling effect, a greater exposure to the written text than to a natural spontaneous conversation. All these suggest that we might be dealing with Kazakh re-acquisition without much support at home. The figures on Kazakh school enrolment in urban areas further backs that interpretation.

The case of Amir (a nine year old boy, fourth grade attending a Kazakh-medium school) illustrates this point. Despite five years of schooling in a Kazakh-medium school, he avoided speaking in Kazakh whenever possible. The recording of his sessions with a private tutor, who was hired by his parents to help him with school work, showed asymmetrical language choices, e.g., the tutor speaks in Kazakh and the boy persistently talks in Russian. My observations led me to believe that the problem may not just be resulting from language practices at home where he received virtually no support for his Kazakh, but also from language practices at school. Even in the Kazakh-language school he attended, Amir had very little opportunity to interact in Kazakh. Amir's Kazakh in school was limited to short responses, i.e., a sentence or two, to his teacher's questions during the lessons. Outside of the classroom he spoke Russian, as was common among most of the students, and would switch to Kazakh only during the lessons or in the presence of teachers who were known for their strict language policing.

5.3 Russian remains the dominant language of public domains

Kazakhstani language policy practitioners and the general public see Kazakh-language schooling as "a powerful agent of revitalization" (Huss 2008: 76) and perceive children, the first generation growing up in independent Kazakhstan, to be at the forefront of the revitalization efforts. However, both the quantitative and ethnographic data included in this chapter show that despite years of schooling in Kazakh, for many children, Russian remains their dominant choice of communication. Even Kazakh-language schools are not the monolingual spaces the state, teachers and parents want them to be. The case of Saule (a 10-year old girl, fifth grade attending a Kazakh-medium school) suggests that children's proficiency in Russia improves dramatically when they start the middle school and their peer network expands. Indeed observations in the school revealed that during the breaks between lesson and outside of classrooms children interacted mainly in Russian. Moreover, the older children were more likely to speak Russian among themselves and less likely to be policed by teachers.

6 Conclusion

On the one hand, Kazakhstan's language revitalization policy has been successful. This is seen in the fact that language shift from Russian to Kazakh appears to be halted and the percentage of Kazakh speakers among the younger generation is rising primarily due to education reforms. On the other hand, the findings from the survey and ethnographic interviews show that the critical-for-language-revival goal of reinstatement of natural intergenerational transmission at urban home and establishment of Kazakh as a primary choice of urban interaction has more distance to cover.

However, the Kazakhstani case allows us to address some fundamental questions: What is the role of school in language revival? How effective is schooling in minority language in producing fluent speakers and active users? The ethnographic observations certainly raise questions about the impact of schooling in Kazakh on the changing of language practices outside of the classroom. It calls for closer investigation of the role of schooling in Kazakh in relation to a language shift reversal in urban areas. As Huss (2008: 76) argues "the school might succeed in producing pupils with second language skills in the endangered language, but the problem remains how to go further and increase the number of pupils with high enough competence to maintain the language in the long run and, at best, to transmit it to their own children".

Moreover, the findings imply that while macro-level policy initiatives have impacted institutions that implement the various reforms, they have limited direct impact on micro-levels of everyday talk. This suggests that the language planning agencies need to reconsider their understanding of language policy as large-scale governmental top-down activities only. For language revival of Kazakh to be fully realized, language planning must include activities focusing on the micro-level constraining factors.

References

Altynbekova, Olga. 2010. *Языковые сдвиги в образовательном пространстве Казахстана* [Linguistic shifts in Kazakhstan's education space]. In Eleonora Suleimenova (ed.), *Динамика языковой ситуации в Казахстане* [The dynamics of the language situation in Kazakhstan], 295–341. Almaty: Lingua.

Batunsky, Mark. 1990. Islam and Russian culture in the first half of the 19th century. *Central Asian Survey* 9(4). 1–27.

Gal, Susan. 1998. Multiplicity and contention among language ideologies: A commentary. In Bambi Schieffelin, Kathryn Woolard & Paul Kroskrity (eds.), *Language ideologies: Practice and theory*, 317–331. Oxford: Oxford University Press.

Heller, Monica. 1999. *Linguistic minorities and modernity*. London: Longman.

Heller, Monica & Marilyn Martin-Jones (eds.). 2001. *Voices of authority: Education and linguistic difference*. Westport: Ablex.

Huss, Leena. 2008. Researching language loss and revitalization. In Kendall King & Nancy Hornberger (eds.), *Encyclopedia of language and education*, Vol. 10 [Research Methods in Language and Education], 2nd edn., 69–81. New York: Springer.

Isayev, Magomet. 1979. *Языковое строительство в СССР* [Language planning in the USSR]. Moscow: Nauka.

Khasanov, Bakhytzhan. 1976. *Языки народов Казахстана и их взаимодействие* [Languages of the people of Kazakhstan and their infraction]. Almaty: Nauka.

Kuzakov, Marat. 2007, August 6. *Триединство языковой политики* [Tri-unity of language policy]. Мегаполис 30(345). http://www.megapolis.kz/show_article.php?art_id=6325 (accessed on 9 October, 2007).

Laitin, David. 1998. *Identity in formation, the Russian-speaking populations in the near abroad*. Ithaca: Cornell University Press.

Masanov, Nurbolat. 2002. Perception of ethnic and all-national identity in Kazakhstan. Nurbulat Masanov, Erlan Karin, Andrei Chebotarev & Natsuko Oka (eds.). *IDE-JETRO Middle East Series* 51. http://www.ide.go.jp/English/Publish/Download/Mes/51.html (accessed on 10 December, 2007).

Masanov, N., Zh. Abylkhozhin, I. Yeropheeva, A. Alekseenko, & G. Baratova. 2001. *История Казахстана: Народы и культуры* [The history of Kazakhstan: Peoples and cultures]. Almaty: Daik-Press.

Mirzoyan, Levon. 2002 [1937]. *О проекте Конституции Казахской ССР* [On the project of the Kazakh SSR Constitution]. In E. Yertysbayev (ed.), *Антология социально-политической мысли Казахстана* [An anthology of historic-political though in Kazakhstan from ancient times until today], 443–450. Almaty: Institute of Development of Kazakhstan.

Olcott, Martha Brill. 1995. *The Kazakhs*. Stanford: Hoover Institution Press.

Pavlenko, Aneta. 2013. Language management in the Russian Empire, Soviet Union, and post-Soviet countries. In Robert Bayley, Richard Cameron & Ceil Lucas (eds.). *The Oxford handbook of sociolinguistics*, 651–679. Oxford: Oxford University Press.

Pavlenko, Aneta. 2011. Linguistic russification in the Russian Empire: Peasants into Russians? *Russian Linguistics* 35. 331–350.

Rivers, William. 2003. *Factors influencing attitudes and behaviors towards language use among Kazakhstani university-level students*. Bryn Mawr, PA: Bryn Mawr College dissertation.

Rysbekova, Saltanat. 2010. *Роль институтов просвещения и образования в социальной модернизации казахского социума в 30-ые гг. XX в.* [The role of the institutes of education in social modernization of the Kazakh society in the 30s of the XX century]. http://conf.rudn.ru/unesco/materials/1sec/rysbekova.pdf (accessed on 10 July 2011).

Shokamanov, Yuriy. 2001. *Тенденции человеческого развития в Казахстане* [Trends in human development in Kazakhstan]. Almaty: Agency of Statistics of Republic of Kazakhstan.

Son, Svetlana. 1999. *Социолингвистический анализ функционирования коремар и русского языка в корейской диаспоре Казахстана* [Sociolinguistic analysis of the function of Kore Mar and Russian in the Korean diaspora in Kazakhstan]. Almaty: Qazaq Universitety.

Suleimenov, R. & Kh. Bisenov. 1967. *Социалистический путь культурного прогресса отсталых народов. (История строительства советской культуры Казахстана 1917–1965 гг.)* [Socialist way of cultural progress for backward people (History of building of Kazakhstan Soviet culture 1917–1965)]. Almaty: Nauka.

Suleimenova, Eleonora (ed.). 1997. *Языковая политика в Казахстане (1921–1997): Сборник документов* [Language policy in Kazakhstan (1921–1997): A collection of documents]. Almaty: Qazaq University.

Tollefson, James W. 1991. *Planning language, planning inequality: Language policy in the community*. London: Longman.

Tollefson, James W. (ed.). 1995. *Power and inequality in language education*. Cambridge: Cambridge University Press.

United Nations Development Program [UNDP]. 1992. Kazakhstan: Report on Human Development. Almaty: UNDP.

Zenkovsky, Serge. 1953. A century of Tatar Revival. *American Slavic and East European Review* 12. 303–318.

Концепция расширения сферы применения государственного языка [Principles of extension of the spheres state language use]. 2006. Astana: Ministry of Information and Culture of the Republic of Kazakhstan.

Государственная программа развития образования в Республике Казахстан на 2005–2010 годы [State program of development of education in the Republic of Kazakhstan from 2005–2010]. 2005. http://ru.government.kz/resources/docs/doc8 (accessed on 10 December 2007).

Maganat Shegebayev

6 Corpus Building in Kazakhstan: An Examination of the Terminology Development in the Oil and Gas Sector

Abstract: This chapter aims to contribute to the understanding of how corpus building, in the midst of a larger language planning context, is emerging in Kazakh and Russian languages in Kazakhstan on the example of oil and gas technical terminology. The oil and gas industry of Kazakhstan, a dynamically developing and exceptionally diverse sector of the national economy, is marked by the presence of numerous multinational companies working together with local ones; and is a cultural crossroads where issues of translation and interpretation of technical terminology and creation of new vocabulary are particularly essential. A number of talks, observations and interviews have established needs around the issue of corpus building and its current day realities and challenges.

Keywords: corpus building; language planning; Kazakhstan; terminology development

1 Introduction

Issues related to translation in technical fields to and from English have become increasingly important in areas like the oil and gas industry. This is particularly true in countries like Kazakhstan or Russia, where the natural resources sector plays an important part in the national economy.[1] However, while professional translation forums and in industry issues related to translation (e.g., how to interpret or understand a particular term or expression or how to avoid misunderstanding and miscommunication when dealing with professional technical

---

1 As noted in the *Oil & Gas Journal*, the oil reserves of Russia right after the breakup of the Soviet Union and in the Tyumen province alone produced 100.74 billion barrels, compared to 96.36 billion in Iraq, 95.63 billion in Kuwait and 88.33 billion in Iran. Russia inherited 85% of all explored Soviet oil resources, Kazakhstan (nine percent), Azerbaijan and Turkmenistan (approximately two percent), and all others (less than two percent) ("Russian reserves terminology", 1992).

jargon) have been heatedly debated, this is just gaining some attention in academic circles.

Examples of common English expressions in oil and gas vary depending on the purpose. They may include expressions or idioms like "being in the doghouse," "killing a well," "go-devil," or "Christmas tree". These are relatively simple or more generally familiar ones. However, when it concerns more complex vocabulary or expressions, lack of familiarity with the idiomatic meanings might result in some ambiguity and/or misinterpretation. Therefore, in addition to the overall expansion of English and changes it brings, Spolsky (2004: 90) suggests that "these changes, not so much linguistic as economic, technological, political, social, religious and structural, are where we need to look for underlying causes" to understand the challenges that the spread of English entails particularly in broader language change contexts. In addition, it should be noted here that the linguistic landscape in Kazakhstan reflects two main policy priorities. First, language policies reflect the government's efforts to establish Kazakh both symbolically and functionally as a fully-fledged state language in all fields, including business. However, second, the policies reflect a simultaneous commodification of English and Russian for pragmatic reasons. These trends reflect the interchangeable utilization of three languages in addition to the way that terminology building also affects other areas such as corporate culture, internal and external business communication patterns, professional development and others.

2 Background

According to the *Lingvistica* translation bureau's website info on the specifics of translating technical terminology from English in the oil and gas industry, incorrect translations may lead to serious operational consequences ("*Osobennosti perevoda tehnicheskih terminov*", 2009). Those consequences may negatively impact the reputation and market positioning of a company. Therefore, companies (and particularly ones that operate internationally), realize that the concordance of terminology lies in understanding its full meaning. This is why they are involved in terminological work, in order to avoid misunderstanding by having a more accurate and coherent operating lexicon. Many companies develop terminological databases, which contain not only highly specialized vocabulary related to a particular industry but also some in-house corporate acronyms or abbreviations and the terminology that is unique to itself and not necessarily commonly used.

However, as the *Lingvistica* website also points out, currently, the most challenging area in technical translation is the oil and gas terminology. Since this is a key industry in many economies, therein lies a lucrative opportunity for many translation agencies. The oil and gas terminology can borrow vocabulary with the same definitions from adjacent industries, such as engineering, chemistry, geology, insurance, etc. This is why expressions such as "to drill a well on the field" may be understood differently depending on what field it belongs to. However, agencies should be aware of the nuances of the languages they have to deal with and know the subject matter well. The biggest challenge is that terminology is sometimes produced by people who may have different proficiency levels in one of the different languages involved, i.e., the target or recipient languages. Consequently, according to *Lingvistica*, one of the solutions to tackle such problems is for companies to develop their own adapted terminological database.

Similarly, prominent Russian translator and researcher, Maslovskiy (n.d.), as well as Shalyt (2007a, 2007b), posit that technical translation challenges should be handled only by specially prepared experts, who (1) know the subject well, (2) are proficient in working languages, and (3) are able to explicate the translated matter. However, according to Maslovsky (n.d.), an additional challenge is to avoid loan translation which may give no clear meaning. For example, the English word "zooming" in Russian has been literally transliterated as *зуминг* (zooming), which would inevitably be misunderstood or not understood by the vast majority of Russian language speakers. Overall, Maslovsky (n.d.) describes the situation regarding technical translation as being dire, observing:

> To say that scientific-technical translation in Russia today is in depression is to say nothing. Though bookshop shelves are crammed with various terribly expensive scientific-technical translated literature (especially on IT), the quality of these products is often found to be so confusing that the competent reader has to reconstruct mentally with the help of his or her own intuition the source text which was completely spoiled by the negligent translator. Slapdash translation in technical sphere unfortunately becomes a customary standard.

Another Russian expert in technical translation, Grabovskiy (2005), claims that the Russian language technical translation market was estimated at approximately $100 million USD at the time of publication. While this was behind many other industries, it was catching up steadily. Grabovsky (2005) also confirmed the need for high quality translation similar to Maslovsky (n.d.). Additionally, he emphasized the role of quality assurance in translation. He expressed his concern that it was becoming more and more difficult to find a good translator or interpreter. There were many reasons to that trend. First, Grabovskiy (2005) argues, human resources for this kind of job were exhausted.

Second, technical translators were underpaid and the overall social status of the job was low. And third, perhaps most importantly, many employers did not understand that translation job was like a creative work of arts which requires a lot of time and effort to master. Other authors, such as Chester (2010), in many ways, agree with those statements.[2] Although there is new technology to assist, this technology is still a tool not a solution; therefore continuous learning and developing professionally are deeply embedded into the nature of translation job.

Similarly, Shalyt (2007a, 2007b) discusses the nuances in translation that are sometimes hard to catch and that there is a widespread misinterpretation of technical vocabulary. Like the others, Shalyt (2007a, 2007b) points out that there is an additional problem of staffing owing to insufficient human resources, i.e., the most common case is that people who are in translation do not have relevant technical background. The only chance for them to succeed is if there were a specific manual devised by the experienced translators and editors to use. Shalyt illustrates this by providing the example of his own company, which deals with staff training and development.

It should be noted however, that issues in technical translation are not unique to Russian or Kazakh. Heidenberg (2005) writes about translation challenges between English and German. Buckley (2002) discussed the Portuguese and English case and she also makes the observation that humor and multiple meanings are particularly difficult to communicate. As a result, she devised her own dictionary of terms and unique expressions common at the oilfields. Learning from this example, to upgrade his or her qualifications, it may be that a translator should do in-depth study and field research to overcome the challenges. As Buckley (2002) notes, "just as the perfect fitting of all components on a gigantic platform is necessary, the accurate use of technical terms is also vital for the safe exchange of knowledge and the success of operations". Similarly, Stacy (1998) describes the specifics of translation between English and Spanish. A humorous example which Stacy (1998) mentions is the word *guaya* from an oil field in Venezuela. It actually took some time and effort to figure out that this word was a distorted version of the English word "wire"

---

2 As Chester (2010) observed, "Becoming a technical translator is not an easy job, as it needs to have a thorough knowledge of the materials in the specific fields. A translator needs to have formal education and vast experience in the specific field of technical industry. A translator needs to be familiar with technical jargons of both the languages. Otherwise, proper conceptual interpretation of the documents will not be possible. A single wrong usage can alter the entire meaning of the article."

which had been locally adapted based on a southern North American pronunciation. This was because most of the oil workers in Venezuela came from either Texas or Louisiana. Moreover, apart from differences between English and Spanish, there are differences even between Venezuelan and Mexican variants of Spanish, where the divergence in oilfield vocabulary was sometimes as high as 60%. Stacy (1998), proceeding from his personal experience of translating at oilfields concludes thusly,

> My respect for translation continues to grow. It is humbling to admit that simply knowing a couple of languages and having a passing knowledge of a subject area are only the beginning requirements. Translators must also command an immense vocabulary and know how to write well. Even so, truly good translations are the result of several years of concentrated experience. There is simply no other way to acquire familiarity with the inevitable subsets of language, regionalisms, subject matter and styles that are involved. The nature of the translation process guarantees a humble attitude and a never-ending learning experience.

3 Theoretical framework

Corpus building is an interesting lens to examine the ways Kazakhstan's linguistic landscape is changing as a result of a number of different processes including new language planning and policies that have been produced and economic development. The focus of this chapter is examining how new terminologies get created and are developed in this specific area of technical translation. This is important for several reasons. First, there has not been much research in this area on that particular topic. Second, because of the need for natural resources, specifically for oil and gas, there will be more and more international companies (and by extension, languages) involved in the industry; therefore, all parties should be aware that miscommunication and misunderstanding may have a detrimental effect on their activities. As one representative of a local hydrocarbon company shared in their interview, their geophysical prospecting of a potential oilfield once extended beyond the limits set by the government owing, as the interviewee stated, to the "misinterpretation of some key technical terms". As a result, the company's license (at the time) was about to be suspended and punitive sanctions were going to be applied for a breach of terms.

Thus, informed by Cooper (1989)'s framework regarding language policy and planning, looking at this particular sector, I identified the main actors, i.e., the professional translators, the conditions under which actors operate. Consequently, the project showed how different companies' and their employees' behaviors are influenced by adopted language practices and how they formulate the terminological problems and challenges and tackle them.

4 Methodology

The preliminary talks and agreements represented the views of between five to seven companies (depending on the degree of involvement), which were a combination of both local and international. The companies were from various geographical locations within Kazakhstan including the city of Almaty. The companies were from small and medium-size of over 1,000+ employees to large national corporations. On average, they had been operating for 10 years and they also varied by type, i.e., joint-stock companies to private ownership. The companies' main areas of specialization included: prospecting and exploring, oil and gas extraction, drilling, transporting and concurrent services within the natural resources sector. During the initial stages of this project, representatives of these companies participated in data collection process, which was conducted by means of surveys, questionnaires and personal interviews.

The overall plan of the study required on-site visits to the targeted oil and gas companies at their headquarters, branches, and operative mining fields. These trips mainly took place in the fall of 2010, and then in the spring and summer of 2011.

The main idea behind the planned trips and data collection was to explore the challenges that translators and interpreters in natural resources companies experience when dealing with the specific industry-related terminology that has to be developed or translated into Russian and/or Kazakh from English. Since the main linguistic source of the industry-specific terminology and vocabulary is English, the investigation focused on, first of all, development and then on the interpretation and comprehension of these terms. The research also explored whether technical translation or specific terminology presented any major obstacles to the companies' overall performance. What sorts of miscommunication occur? Does any damage (e.g., fiscal, legal or reputational) result from this language blockage and mistranslation? How are these translation challenges then handled?

Access to these companies was gained mainly through personal contacts and networking (or, in some cases, even through negotiation and consequent agreement to share findings of this research with corporate employees). In all other cases, the attempt to approach some translation agencies and companies more formally, i.e., by calling or meeting them to solicit their consent in conducting research, proved to be unsuccessful. Overall, it took a lot of effort to explain the purpose of the research and, especially, to get the parties to agree to cooperate or release information. It should also be noted that confidentiality was a major issue that had to be negotiated. It took another effort to assure the

Table 6.1: Respondents' Company Profiles

	R1	R2	R3	R4	R5	R6	R7	R8	R9
1. Which field of business does your company operate in?	Prospecting & exploring, extraction & mining, drilling, transporting	Prospecting & exploring, extraction & mining, drilling	Extraction	Prospecting & exploring, extraction & mining, drilling, transport.	Services	Extracting and mining, transport., processing	Prospecting & exploring, extraction, drilling	Extraction	Extraction
2. How many employees does your company have on its payroll?	Over 1,000	Over 1,000	251–1,000	Over 1,000	Over 1,000	Over 1,000	Over 1,000	251–1,000	Over 1,000
3. How long has your company been in business?	Over 10 yrs	From 7 to 10 yrs	Over 10 yrs	Over 10 yrs	Over 10 yrs	Over 10 yrs	Over 10 yrs	Over 10 yrs	Over 10 yrs
4. What is your company's ownership type?	Joint venture	Foreign	Private	–	National	National/Foreign	Foreign	Private	Foreign

interviewees, mainly professional translators and their supervisors, all together over 20 people, that no information source or name would be released without a prior agreement.[3]

The project's main data collection instruments were via in-depth interviews and questionnaires. The interview questions for respondents focused on the following:
– How long and in what capacity they dealt with field-specific technical vocabulary;
– Their main site of operation is (e.g. at the oilfields, main offices, etc.);
– How the new terminologies or explanations were created or developed, if they were not available in dictionaries;
– Typical challenges faced while dealing with technical terms; and
– How challenges were overcome.

Due to possible language issues, the questions for the interviews were designed in English, Russian and Kazakh languages (with the possibility of reverse translation of the questions and responses to ensure more accuracy). In total, 23 interviews were conducted. The interviews were mainly unstructured (open-ended) and carried out conversationally. It should also be noted that apart from meeting in person, three interviews happened over the telephone, and two via Skype.

The questionnaires were sent out electronically. They consisted of the two main parts. The first section asked the respondents to answer several questions regarding their company for background information. The second part asked about the respondent's experience in dealing with technical translation, the challenges (e.g., in terms of language or resources) that they face through their work and how they handle new terminology. The questionnaires included unstructured questions, which offered an opportunity to deviate in any direction during the interviews regarding the issue. In total, 50 questionnaires were distributed electronically or hand-delivered, out of which nine were received completed. Thus, the more in-depth qualitative part of this research was elicited via unstructured interviews[4].

Since the target population was somewhat unknown, this research project was mainly an exploratory study focusing on examining the nature of the issue. As mentioned before, the corporate sample selected for this research project was both local and foreign owned enterprises. The participant sample from which

3 Because of confidentiality agreements, the author is unable to disclose the names of project participants and companies they represent.
4 See Appendix A for the interview responses table.

the respondents/interviewees selected were from middle and upper level employees from these companies who had been involved in translation business in their professional careers. It was a non-probability sampling because the particular members of the target population were mainly selected based on personal judgment or convenience. Due to the unfamiliarity with the potential participants, I also utilized two survey collection techniques: (1) judgment (or purposive) sampling and (2) snowball sampling. Purposive sampling was chosen because there were some necessary characteristics which were required of the sample members. Snowball sampling was chosen because the original intention was to find additional respondents based on the information provided by the respondents.

Because this study was exploratory it had a number of limitations, e.g., it did not generate conclusive evidence requiring future follow-up research. In addition, the current research project was a cross-sectional study of companies with different ownership status and various forms of organization. The survey respondents exclusively represented companies operating within the Republic of Kazakhstan. Additionally, this study had some inherent limitations stemming from the specificity of the topic and the realities of the industry. These limitations periodically challenged the process of data collection. As it was mentioned earlier, companies did not always agree to release information regarding their operations or allow outsiders to participate in company activities, such as meetings or negotiations. In some places, company regulations stipulate that their employees are not allowed to participate in any project carried outside their company. This severely limited the size of the sample, the approximation of information, and the utilization of other data sources.

Additionally, coordinating a project across a wide geographic area such as the territory of Kazakhstan was a challenge in itself. In order to explain the goals of the study to potential participants and to involve them, multiple trips had to be made to meet people in person and schedule time slots in their busy working schedules for this project's activities. Much coordination was required to bridge the gaps in communication across far distances. Therefore, limited data sources and methodological challenges plus real-world time constraints may have also influenced the project outcomes.

However, to fulfill its primary objectives and to collect the needed data, several field research trips were made to the regions, particularly southern, western and central parts of the country, where the companies and their branches are located. After the initial stages of field research were carried out thereby establishing the realities of the industry, each company representative, typically a specialist with extensive technical and/or appropriate linguistic background translating for their companies the industry-related documentation, e.g., petroleum equipment maintenance manuals, oilfield safety instructions, various technical descriptions, project technical specifications, engineering blueprints, international oil and gas standards, was invited to participate in a more in-depth study. Thus the field research activities established a firm network of a small, but highly-capable, group of professionals, including seven people of various specializations but who had dealt extensively in their professional careers with the technical translation and thus gained vast knowledge in it. Some of these professionals have formal educational background in philology and languages; the others have trained themselves to become proficient translators as a part of their other main duties. Their average experience in translation was seven years and their main sites of operation vary from oilfields and regional branches across Kazakhstan and headquarters in Almaty and Astana. They actively contributed to this research study by giving their ideas and advice, by active cooperation, and more importantly, by sharing their sample vocabulary entries and their expertise in developing technical terminology for comparison and analysis.

5 Findings

This research project focused on understanding the challenges of dealing with and developing technical terminology in the oil and gas industry specifically in the Kazakhstani context, which has been experiencing a substantial growth in the last two decades. Throughout the research, different examples and cases have been drawn to understand the effect that corpus building brings to companies. Since the scope of the issue is very wide, the primary attention was given to the importance of technical translation and terminology development and what it entails. Thus through numerous interviews, questionnaire responses, observations and studying the relevant literature, there has been established a topicality of developing new technical language in general and specific terminology in particular.

The overall field research yielded some results and the following quick facts have been identified after the preliminary overview of findings. Firstly, from a broader language utilization point of view, many companies in Kazakhstan use at least two or three languages for their day-to-day operations, which, in some ways, fit the definition Kaplan and Baldauf (1997: 217) use regarding a multilingual community but in a corporate context.

The languages used may vary depending on the purpose and means of communication. Misunderstanding and miscommunication, subsequent upon the vagueness in meaning or lack of information, were identified as major challenges

Table 6.2: Official and Working Languages of Respondents' Companies

Respondents	Company Language Policies
R1	Kazakh; Russian; English
R2	English; Russian
R3	Russian; Kazakh
R4	Russian; English; Kazakh
R5	Kazakh (official); Russian (working); English
R6	English; Russian; Kazakh
R7	Kazakh; Russian; English
R8	Russian; Kazakh
R9	Russian; English

for multilingual companies and this was especially essential relevant regarding technical and legal translations.

One interviewed head of a local company which deals with geological exploration of oil and gas reserves, emphasized that incorrectly translated documentation (which happens mainly due to the lack of specialized vocabulary) may seriously hinder the working process, as well as overall business communication, and even bring about some fiscal or reputational damage to a company (personal communication, October 25, 2010). It should be mentioned here that a lot of similar examples have been drawn in the related literature as well.

The majority of respondents noted that there was a constant need in updated specialized technical vocabulary and acronyms for the oil and gas operations. This need presumably proceeds from the specifics of the industry characterized by the presence of multilingual and multicultural environment. Another challenge, according to the translators, was that the technical vocabulary was getting more diverse and complicated with the rapid development of technology (especially related to engineering or mining) and overall scientific progress; hence, new skills and knowledge are required from people dealing with technical translation and interpretation. These new demands, therefore, should lead to an increase in training and professional development activities.

More focused and thorough analyses of the data collected revealed some subsidiary yet interesting findings. First, while most of corpus building in oil and gas was happening in the Russian language, there was still a diverse range in how languages were used. Kazakh, Russian and English were each utilized in the different companies' everyday functions but for specific uses. For instance, the overall pattern was that Kazakh would be used more for dealing with the government bodies and local authorities and for the official documentation. This was in comparison to Russian, which was used for business communication

Table 6.3: Language Utilization in Respondents' Companies

Respondents	Language	Domains
R1		No response
R2	English	Day-to-day communication, business correspondence, meetings, record-keeping, PR & marketing, decision-making
	Russian	Day-to-day communication, business correspondence, services, annual report, PR & marketing, decision-making
R3	Russian/Kazakh	Everyday communication, business correspondence, meetings, customer service, reports, record-keeping and documenting, PR & Marketing, decision-making
	English	Business correspondence with stockholders
R4	Russian	Everyday communication, business correspondence, meetings, customer services, reports, record-keeping and documenting, PR & Marketing, decision-making
	Kazakh	Rendering services to clients, record-keeping and documenting
	English	Business correspondence, meetings, customer service, reports, record-keeping and documenting, PR & Marketing, decision-making
R5	Russian	Everyday communication with local companies, meetings, rendering services to clients, annual reports, record-keeping & documentation, PR & marketing, decision-making
	Kazakh	With local authorities, rendering services to clients, annual reports, PR & marketing
	English	International business communication, annual reports
R6	English	Business correspondence
	English, Russian, Kazakh	Day-to-day communication
	English, Russian	Meetings, record-keeping, PR & marketing, decision-making
R7	Russian	Everyday communication
	Russian, Kazakh	Annual reports, record-keeping & documentation, PR & marketing, decision-making
	English, Russian	Business correspondence, meetings, customer services, decision-making
R8	Russian, Kazakh	Everyday communication, business correspondence, meetings, customer service, reports, record-keeping and documenting, PR & Marketing, decision-making
R9	Russian	Everyday communication
	Russian, English	Business correspondence, meetings, customer services, reports, record-keeping and documenting, PR & marketing, decision-making

with local partners and in internal reports. Then English was used for communicating with overseas business partners and decision-making.

Second, despite the plethory of different Internet-based and technology-assisted software, e.g., specialized websites for technical translation like *Multitran* (a multiple language on-line dictionary of around 8 million entries, with the option of adding new words by users), numerous specialized oil and gas dictionaries, and company vocabulary manuals, respondents still indicated that information on new technical vocabulary (particularly in Russian and Kazakh) was still insufficient. As a result, terminological gaps still exist, especially regarding newly appearing technological devices, equipment and machinery. Any new terminology has to be re-checked and matched to ensure its correct meaning. Other challenges include new word compounds and outdated (obsolete) words. Therefore each translated document requires a lot proofreading and careful editing, which is adding to the regular load in terms of time and effort, according to the translators interviewed.

6 Concluding thoughts

The processes of meaning development by translators themselves do not typically follow any pattern and vary depending on the task and the level of term complexity. For instance, in case something is a spare part of a machine, the translator refers to the machine's blueprint, then seeks an explanation from a worker who operates that machine, which often happened right on the oilfields. After getting a detailed picture of how the spare part functions and consulting with dictionaries and technical manuals, the translator then would develop an equivalent which would then go into a Word or Excel format sheet for future reference. In another instance, a translator may refer to specialized websites and forums like *Multitran* to seek advice from fellow translators who may be situated in any part of the world. However, in this case there is a greater degree of receiving erroneous (though numerous) interpretations and thus follow-up checks are necessary. Less experienced translators may tend to rely on machine translations or producing homonymic patterns e.g., *канализация* (canalization), *резервуар* (reservoir), *репетиция* (repetition), *оперировать* (to operate) or *митинг* (meeting). [5,6]

---

5 This refers to false-friends or words that sound the same in both languages but have different meanings.
6 However, this practice could be misleading or simply wrong because of the nuances in meaning or language subtleties; when, for instance, the machine does not see the difference between correctly spelled yet differently contextualized "message" and "massage".

If we look into some other common oil and gas terminology, further interesting patterns of terms creation could be discovered. For instance, it can be inferred that English language technical terms are created by associations that could be made about a particular piece of equipment, tool, action or type of work. A vivid example would be "graveyard tour", which refers to working a night shift at an oilrig. In some on-line sources, this is translated as *ночная смена на буровой вышке которая начинается в полночь*, which literally means "a night shift at an oil derrick which starts at midnight". This leads one to the following conclusions. Firstly, there is not yet a similar "compact" Russian equivalent. And secondly, in such cases when translating from English, translators may have to come up with a broad and long explanation to explain the meaning of the whole concept. Another interesting example is "go-devil", which is translated into Russian as *скребок для чистки внутренности трубы от нефтяных отложений*, i.e., "a scraper to clean up accumulated solid debris within an oil pipe", which is essentially the literal description of the process. Thus if there were a methodology of creating and developing such condensed oil and gas terminology (e.g., "wildcat" or "doghouse") or specific acronyms (e.g., BOPD [barrels of oil per day] or SEFDU [self elevating floating drilling unit]) in Russian and especially in Kazakh, this might lead to much more efficiency in delivering the meaning of a particular term thereby contributing to an overall higher output of a company working in a diverse geographic setting and employing linguistically diverse staff members.

It should also be mentioned that the personal language skills and educational background of an interpreter is a significant factor to take into consideration, according to the project respondents. This is because the quality of translation is consistent with the amount of research and involvement that an individual does in his or her area. Professional development of any kind is a lifelong learning process, and it is also quite common among interpreters to exchange specific dictionaries or notes on related professional vocabulary. Surprisingly, even location may help broaden substantially the level of expertise in terminology since from the interpreters assigned to central units and headquarters it is expected more than from their fellow colleagues in the remote oilfields.

Overall, there is a huge potential for further research in studying how terminology, within a broader issue of the country's language planning and specifically in corpus building in Kazakh, Russian and other languages, develops in other key industries as well, beyond just the oil and gas sector. In Kazakhstan this type of research can be done, for instance, in the agricultural sector, uranium industry, aerospace, international tourism and hospitality (especially, on the threshold of EXPO-2017 international exhibition in Astana). Other promising fields are also experiencing the increase in international cooperation and the rising need for various technical terminologies. These trends together with the research findings show that the language change is happening in Kazakhstan and companies are responding to it. The exploration and unification of corpus building processes will inevitably result in better understanding and communication, in better productivity and higher output, as well as demonstrating the pragmatic, everyday realities in language change contexts.

References

Buckley, Márcia. 2002. How to avoid landing in the "doghouse" when dealing with oil and gas terminology. *TranslationDictionary.com.* http://www.translationdirectory.com/article1050. htm (accessed 19 January 2011).

Chester, Kathleen. 2010. Technical translation: brings the global technology under one roof. http://ezinearticles.com/?Technical-Translation:-Brings-The-Global-Technology-Under-One-Roof&id=5488860 (accessed 23 January 2011).

Cooper, Robert L. 1989. *Language planning and social change.* Cambridge: Cambridge University Press.

Grabovskiy, Viktor N. 2005. *Blesk i nischeta tehnicheskogo perevoda v Rossii* [The shine and misery of technical translation in Russia]. http://langinfo.ru/index.php?sect_id=64 (accessed 22 January 2011).

Heidenberg, Charles. 2005. Diesel engines: a brief overview. http://www.proz.com/translation-articles/articles/165/1/Diesel-Engines%3A-A-Brief-Overview (accessed 16 January 2011).

Kaplan, Robert B., & Baldauf, Richard B. 1997. *Language planning from practice to theory.* Clevedon: Multilingual Matters.

Maslovskiy, Evgeniy. (n.d.). *Aktualnye problemy nauchno-tehnicheskogo perevoda* [Topical problems of scientific and technical translation]. http://www.lingvoda.ru/transforum/articles/maslovskya1.asp (accessed 17 January 2011).

Osobennosti perevoda tehnicheskih terminov s angliyskogo yazyka na primere neftegazovoy otrasli [The specifics of translating technical terminology from English in the oil and gas industry]. 2009, August 7. *Lingvistica.* http://www.lingvistica.ru/articles/4.html (accessed 21 January 2011).

Russian reserves terminology becoming clearer. 1992. *Oil & Gas Journal* 90(40). 102. ABI/INFORM Global Document ID: 697881 (accessed July 20, 2011 from).

Shalyt, Izrail. 2007a. *Kachestvo perevoda tehnicheskoi dokumentacii* [Translation quality of technical documentation]. http://www.trworkshop.net/lib/articles/qualityintent.pdf (accessed 16 January 2011).

Shalyt, Izrail. 2007b. *Teoriya tehnicheskogo perevoda- obuchenie perevodu tehnicheskoy dokumentacii* [The theory of technical translation- teaching technical documentation translation]. http://www.trpub.ru/art-etud-transl.html (accessed 17 January 2011).

Spolsky, Bernard. 2004. *Language policy.* Cambridge: Cambridge University Press.

Stacy, Charles. 1998. Overcoming the odds. *Translation Journal.* http://translationjournal.net/journal//09prof.htm (accessed 18 January 2011).

Stephen A. Bahry

7 Societal Multilingualism and Personal Plurilingualism in Pamir Tajikistan's Complex Language Ecology

Abstract: This chapter looks at societal multilingualism and personal plurilingualism in the Pamir region of Tajikistan through a linguistic ecology lens. While Central Asia is itself a region distinguished by a high degree of multilingualism, the Mountainous Badakhshan Autonomous Province (MBAP) in the Pamir Mountains is one of the most linguistically diverse areas within this already linguistically complex region. This chapter reviews information from a range of sources to produce an exploratory descriptive synthesis of this complex language ecology and to suggest implications of this synthesis for research on language use and language policy in support of societal multilingualism and personal plurilingualism in MBAP, Tajikistan and Central Asia.

Keywords: Pamiri; Mountainous Badakhshan Autonomous Province; Tajikistan; language ecology; bi-, multi-, and plurilingualism

1 Introduction

While Central Asia is a region characterized by a high degree of multilingualism, Mountainous Badakhshan Autonomous Province (MBAP) in the Pamir Mountains of Tajikistan is the quintessential example of how complex one language ecology within this region can be. This chapter reviews information from multiple sources in order to produce an exploratory descriptive synthesis of this complex language ecology.[1] MBAP can be divided geographically into West and East Pamir. West Pamir is bordered on the west by the Panj River that runs south to north separating the Pamir Mountains of Tajikistan from the Hindu Kush Mountains of Afghanistan, while also serving to divide Tajikistan's Badakhshan province from Afghanistan's Badakhshan province.

---

1 While the studies that were surveyed themselves do not utilize an explicit language ecology perspective, the aim of this project was to provide a descriptive overview by drawing from numerous studies.

East Pamir consists of a high mountain plateau, sometimes called the "Roof of the World". The Tian Shan Mountains create East Pamir's eastern border, which separate MBAP from the Xinjiang Uyghur Autonomous Region, China. The Wakhan Corridor, a narrow finger of Afghanistan territory that separates MBAP from the Karakoram Mountains of Pakistan's northern territories, forms MBAP's southern border.

Tributaries of the Panj run east to west from the Pamir heights to the Panj River with each river running through narrow valleys divided from each other by a high mountain ridge. Almost each of these valleys is home to a separate Pamiri language: from north to south, there are the Vanji (extinct), Yazgulami (endangered), Khufi, Rushani, Bartangi, Roshorvi, Shughni, Ishkoshimi, and Wakhi languages (see Figure 7.1).[2] East Pamir is home to Kyrgyz speakers (Karabaev 2011; Niyozov 2001; Mostowlansky 2012; Zholdoshalieva 2010) with a population in MBAP of 10,949, or five percent of the provincial total in 2010 (Republic of Tajikistan Statistics Agency 2012). Within west Pamir, Pamiri languages are traditionally learned as first languages and used in familiar domains as community languages, while in Murghab district this true of Kyrgyz as well as Pamiri languages.[3]

---

[2] These languages are transliterated into English in multiple ways, largely according to whether it is attempting to reproduce original pronunciation, is an English transliteration of a Persian, Tajik, or Russian transliteration. Thus we can find: *Yazgulami, Yazghulemi, Yazghulami, Iazgulyami; Rushani, Roshani; Sarikoli, Sarykoli; Shughni, Shugni, Shughnani, Shugnani; Ishkashimi, Eshkashemi, Wakhi, Vakhii*. This chapter maintains original spelling in references and citations, but otherwise uses the first of each set, following UNESCO usage. See Moseley (2010) for more detailed information. Wakhi language communities are also found across the border in Afghanistan, Pakistan and China, while Shughni, Rushani and Ishkoshimi are found across the Panj River in Badakhshan, Afghanistan, and Sarikoli are found across the border in Tashkurgan, Xinjiang, China

[3] Speakers of Pamiri languages are found in some parts of the East Pamiri Murgab district of MBAP, in Dushanbe (Tajikistan's capital), and in the Vakhsh Valley (Khatlon district), where whole villages were resettled in the 1950s under the Soviet regime. Pamiri languages are also spoken outside of Tajikistan as community languages in the Badakhshan province of Afghanistan (Bahry 2013; Kieffer 1983; Owens 2007), Pakistan's northern areas (Backstrom 1992; Rahman 2006), and in Tashkurgan County, Xinjiang Uyghur Autonomous Region, China (Gao 1985; Luo and Zhao 2004). Additionally, speakers of Pamiri languages are also found in other regions of Tajikistan, throughout Central Asia and other former Soviet Union (FSU) countries, and internationally, due to temporary labor migration, cross-border trading, and permanent emigration (Clément 2011; Marsden 2012; Niyozov and Shamatov 2006; Olimova and Bosc 2003).

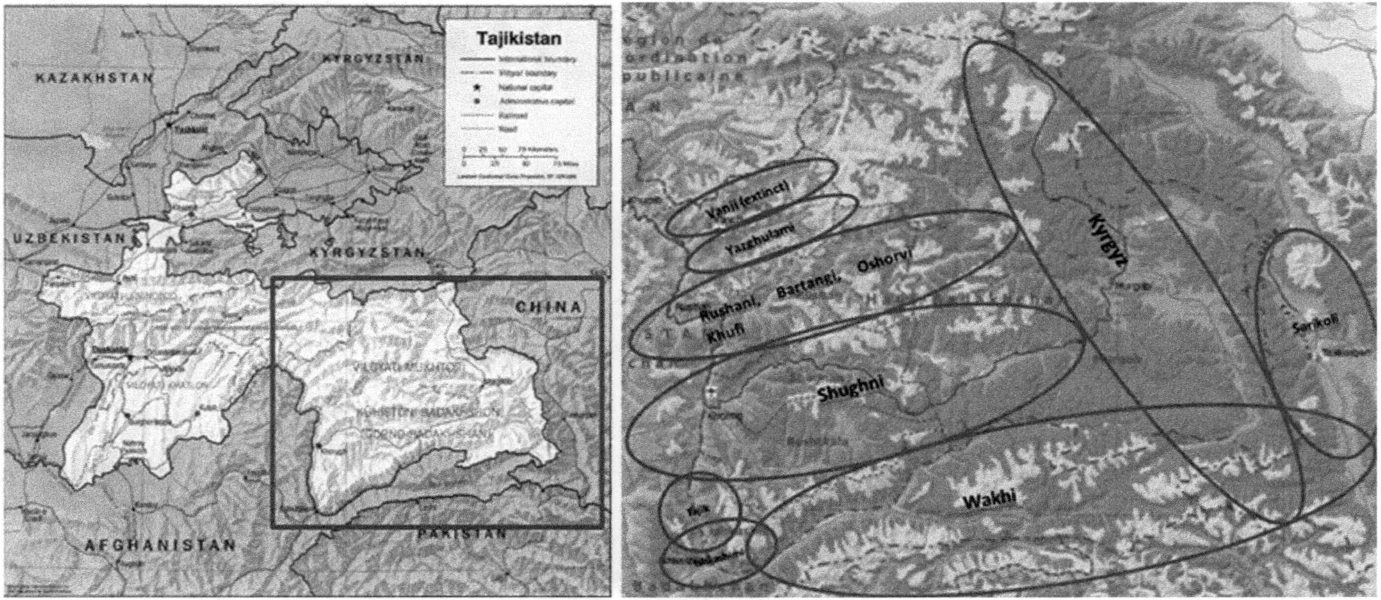

Figure 7.1: Languages of the Pamir Mountains and Plateau, Mountainous Badakshan Autonomous Province, Tajikistan
Adapted from public domain maps courtesy of University of Texas Austin, Perry-Castañeda Map Collection and Wikimedia Commons.

There are some areas in MBAP where a local vernacular form of Tajik now is the community language, e.g., in the Vanj district, where Tajik replaced the extinct Vanji Pamiri language over a century ago. In addition, there are individual villages on the right bank (Tajikistan side) of the Panj River between Khorugh and Ishkoshim and the town of Ishkoshim where Tajik is the dominant language (Rastorgueva 1964; Rozenfel'd 1964; Müller et al. 2005a).[4]

1.1 Historical background

Like other FSU countries, Tajikistan inherited a system that was both ideologically and administratively shaped by the Soviet system, where language was a key criterion in the delimitation of official nationalities. Thus, the all-Union language census reported the number of each nationality for whom their "native language" (*rodnoi iazyk*) was (a) the language of their own nationality, (b) Russian, or (c) other. Tajikistan's post-independence censuses have similarly asked respondents whether their "mother tongue" (*zaboni modari* in Tajik) falls into one of the following four categories: (a) language of one's own nationality, (b) Tajik, (c) Russian or (d) other.[5] Post-independence censuses have also asked whether respondents "freely know" (in Tajik); or "freely command" (in Russia) as a second language the language of their own ethnicity, Tajik, Russian or another language.

Despite the presence of language-related questions on censuses both during the Soviet and post-Soviet periods, estimating the numbers of speakers of Pamiri languages is rather difficult due to the nature of the classification of nationality and language during both periods. During the early Soviet period, speakers of Pamiri languages were considered a sub-ethnicity and recorded in the census as such, and data on speakers of these languages was gathered Subsequently, they have been counted as Tajik, and Tajikistan's census still does not record individual Pamiri languages (Roy 2007: 70). Table 7.1 is a compilation of the various available figures and estimates for the number of speakers of each language.

---

4 Khorugh is a transliteration of the Tajik name; Khorog is a transliteration of the Russian name; its Pamiri name, Kharagh rarely appears in print. This chapter uses the official Tajik name, Khorugh, except in the English "Khorog English Language Program", which follows Russian usage.

5 The reliability of statistics on "native language"/"mother tongue" has been called into question as a measure of actual language proficiency/use. Some have argued that statistics represent more accurately the degree of identification with the language of their nationality (Silver 1975).

Table 7.1: Estimated Numbers of Pamiri Communities of MBAP

Language	1939/40s	1980–90s	after 2000
Yazgulami	2,000	2,000	3–4,000 (2001); 3,000–3,500 (2003)
Rushani	5,300	18,000	40,000–45,000 (2003)
Khufi		2,380	
Bartangi	3,700	2,425	5,000–6,000 (2003)
Roshorvi		1,950	
Shughni	18,600	57,500	70,000–75,000 (2003)
Ishkashimi			3–4,000 (2001); 1,000–1,500 (2003)
Wakhi	4,500	17–18,000	20,000 (2001); 20,000–25,000 (2003)

Sources: Elnazarov (2007) and Margus et al. (2001)

Beyond these first languages/community languages, there are a number of additional languages that are used in Tajikistan for various reasons, e.g., to function as a lingua franca or language of wider communication (LWC) or for use in a specialized domains like administration, economic affairs, education, science and technology. Classical Persian/Tajik was traditionally used for higher knowledge transfer activities, particularly in spheres related to religion, while education today has been conducted mostly in standard modern Tajik, Kyrgyz and Russian. Before independence, higher education was available in Tajik and Russian in Dushanbe, and for Kyrgyz speakers, in the Kyrgyz language in the Kyrgyz SSR. In the last years of Soviet Tajikistan, there were more open complaints about the use of Russian in place of Tajik in many domains and many calls were more often made for the additional use of Pamiri languages in domains such as education (Elnazarov 2004; Jamshedov 1991).

After the civil war in 1991, a university was opened in the MBAP administrative centre, Khorugh, in which the language of instruction (LOI) continued to be Tajik and Russian. What was unique about this situation was that this Tajik and Russian LOI institution was surrounded by a Shughni language community, where some administrative/technical functions are carried out in the province in Tajik and/or Russian but the general LWC is Shughni.

2 Conceptual framework: Language ecology

While the linguistic diversity in MBAP, Tajikistan, Badakhshan Province, Afghanistan, and neighbouring areas in Pakistan and Xinjiang, China is well known, little work has attempted to deal with the ensemble of languages and language use in the region as a whole. The scope of the region's multilingualism and personal plurilingualism provides a sharp challenge to attempts to deal with the linguistic phenomena in the Pamir region. Accordingly, this chapter turns to language ecology as a conceptual framework which is intended to accommodate a broad range of linguistic, geographic and social phenomena. Following Voegelin and Voegelin (1964), all languages and language varieties found within and adjoining MBAP are considered in this chapter. Then, adopting Haugen (1972), detailed consideration is given to the various users of the languages and varieties of language chosen for different social uses. Ferguson's (1959) notion of diglossia and the specialization of language varieties into high status (H) and low status (L) uses, and Fishman's (1967) extension to combine diglossia and bilingualism, further elucidate four language contexts, i.e., those with both diglossia and bilingualism (D+, B+), neither (D–, B–), and either diglossia (D+, B–) or bilingualism (D–, B+) are present. This approach adds to the conceptual sophistication and utility without overcomplicating affairs. Of course, the addition of one more language increases considerably the number of theoretically possible cases. By examining this region through this lens (or these lenses), this chapter attempts to capture and engage with this linguistically complex context in a more dynamic and rich way.

3 Methodology

This chapter reviews research published in Russian and English about the Pamiri language ecology in order to assess to what degree the research provides information on the place of language(s) or language varieties and the practices of speakers in this context. The outcome of this attempt, a tentative portrait of the ecological relations between languages and the extent and types of plurilingualism, is a preliminary step in producing a descriptively adequate account of the multiple languages and literacies currently found in MBAP and its environs.

Explanatory adequacy regarding the phenomena observed depends first on the quality and completeness of the account of the language ecology and dynamics of its multiple language and literacy practices. A review of existing research by an outsider to the ecology cannot claim completeness and quality of description and an insider's insights. However, in such a complex ecology, no insider experiences the whole continuum of language varieties and practices. Moreover, an outside perspective may nevertheless stimulate a fruitful dialogue of research, theory, policy and practice with each other (Cummins 2000: 1–7). This chapter concludes with a discussion of tentative implications of the ecological view of languages and literacies in MBAP, tasks for future research, and the relevance of language ecology to policy formation, implementation, assessment and review, and education.

4 Research on the languages of the Pamir language ecology

4.1 Soviet scholarship on the languages of MBAP

Early Soviet policies focused on developing the writing systems and literature in the unwritten vernacular Pamiri languages of MBAP. This approach was related to the idea of reaching the masses through vernacular literacy (Figure 7.2). After 1936 however, the use of written Pamiri languages was forbidden. From the 1950s to the 1970s, a number of studies by Soviet linguists appeared on the languages of MBAP on Tajik dialects (Rastorogueva 1964; Rozenfel'd 1964), and various Pamiri languages, such as Yazgulami (Edelman 1966), Rushani, Khufi (Sokolova 1959), Bartangi (Sokolova 1960), Shughni (Zarubin 1960), and Wakhi (Gryunberg and Steblin-Kamenskii 1976; Pakhalina 1975).

These works were largely confined to descriptive and structural analyses of each language variety. Some comparison with neighboring Pamiri language varieties was made, mainly with the purpose of classifying varieties into groups, e.g., debating whether Rushani and Shughni should be considered dialects of a single language or independent languages. The varieties that were studied were considered as relatively static entities, i.e., social variation in language forms, bidialectism, or bilingualism were little discussed.

Rabbit and Hedgehog

A rabbit saw a hedgehog and told him: Your thorny coat is too ugly. Why do you wear it? The hedgehog responded: yes this is not beautiful. But this ugly coat of mine has saved me from the claws of wolves and dogs. But are you saying that if your dress is soft and white, it can serve you this much or not? The Rabbit took a heartfelt breath, did not say anything more and left.

Where does the rabbit live?

Where does the hedgehog live?

Figure 7.2: Example of a Shughni primer from the 1930s in Romanized script
Source: Zarubin (1960); translation by Sarfaroz Niyazov

Soviet scholarship on bilingualism focused on asymmetrical national-Russian bilingualism, examining the degree the non-Russian nationalities knew Russian (Guboglo 1984), ignoring Russian-national bilingualism, and failing to explore why so few Russophones in other SSRs learned the local languages. Further restricting this area of research was the fact that such scholarship focused on languages of officially recognized nationalities. This meant that speakers of Pamiri languages in MBAP were not distinguished from other Tajiks. During the last days of Soviet rule, new language laws were passed in the Central Asian SSRs making the titular language of each republic the state language, suggesting an opening of a space for examination of bilingualism and multilingualism in the USSR, and a seeming greater tolerance for discussion of languages besides the titular languages. During this period, for example, a suggestion was made for trilingual education in MBAP schools using Pamiri, Tajik, and Russian as languages of instruction (LOI) (Jamshedov 1991).

4.2 Post-Soviet research on the language ecology of MBAP

After the fall of the USSR, Soviet-trained scholars of Central Asian languages participated in a UNESCO project where they discussed Central Asian multilingualism in much broader terms than previously. This meant that, in addition to local-Russian bilingualism, research could also include Russian-local bilingualism, local-local bilingualism, and local-local-Russian trilingualism. The edited book providing an overview of this dialogue included chapters on languages of interethnic communication in Central Asia (Baskakov 1996a), the Republic of Tajikistan (Baskakov 1996b), and in MBAP (Šombezoda 1996; Wurm 1996). This move from focusing on local-Russian bilingualism to a broader discussion of languages of interethnic communication in these chapters was indicative of a major shift from a prescriptivist view on language to a more descriptive one that considered the variety of languages which could play this role. Noted in the volume was that within MBAP, there are three major LWCs, i.e., Shughni, Tajik and Russian.

At that time, Baskakov (1996b) suggested that the use of Pamiri languages in Tajikistan was shrinking in the face of competition from Tajik and Russian. Šombezoda (1996) in contrast claimed that knowledge of Russian among Pamiri communities of MBAP was actually greater than among Tajik-speakers in other provinces of Tajikistan, but did not note any tendency of shift to Tajik or Russian as primary community language. Indeed, she pointed out that, in addition to the use of Tajik and Russian as languages of interethnic communication in MBAP, Shughni sometimes played a role of local lingua franca for communication between various Pamir language communities. Šombezoda also noted the existence of mixed Ishkashimi-Tajik and Wakhi-Tajik speech in MBAP.

Among the issues that have emerged in post-Soviet language research is the question of language vitality and language endangerment. Official statistical mechanisms stopped collecting questions of language use in 1939 (Landau and Kellner-Heinkele 2012). As a result, the estimates of numbers of speakers are produced based on the population statistics by district; from there, conclusions about language speakers (and by extension, language vitality) are drawn. For example, Elnazarov (2010) treats endangerment as a combined function of relative number of speakers, official status of the languages and existence of a written form of the language. By these criteria, all Pamiri languages can be considered endangered since none of them have any official status or approved script, and even those languages with the greatest number of speakers, i.e., Wakhi and Shughni with an estimated 70,000 and 100,000 respectively (including speakers across the border in Afghanistan, China and/or Pakistan), have relatively few speakers. Endangerment is greatest for the Ishkashimi language, now restricted to one or two villages in the face of in-migration of Tajik speakers from neighboring Ghoron district. Similarly, the Shughni language is also apparently retreating from Ghoron in favor of Tajik (Edelman and Dodykhudoeva 2009a, 2009b; Hojibekov 2010). More recently, local scholars of Pamiri languages have advocated for some enhanced official status for Pamiri languages as a written language, creating and seeking approval of, for example, a Cyrillic alphabet derived from the Tajik alphabet (D. Karamshoev, personal communication October, 6, 2003; see Figure 7.3).

Хуг̌нӯни Зив̌
Алифбо

Аа А̄а̄ Бб Вв В̌в̌ Гг Дд Д̌д̌ Ее Ээ Жж Зз З̌з̌ Ии Ӣӣ Йй Кк Лл Мм Нн Оо Пп Рр Сс Тт Т̌т̌ Уу Ӯӯ Ӯ̊ӯ̊ Фф Хх Х̌х̌ Цц Чч Шш Г̌г̌ Ққ Чч Хх

Figure 7.3: Proposed Shughni alphabet
Source: Wennberg, Franz. (n.d.) *Shugnani.* http://www.afro.uu.se/forskning/iranforsk/ Franzbilder/shughnani.htm (accessed 30 July 2003).

4.3 The status quo regarding local language vitality in MBAP

Clifton (2005) provides several case studies regarding the smaller ethno-linguistic groups in Tajikistan, most of which focus on the Pamiri languages of MBAP and their relations with and to Tajik and Russian and in some cases, to each other.

The overall book project was particularly concerned about the possibility of language shift from local languages to Tajik and investigated the domains of use of three languages in each case, i.e., one local language and the two LWCs (Tajik and Russian). However, it should be noted that the team did not investigate the Kyrgyz language in East Pamir, nor did it include questions about the most recent LWC to enter the language ecology, English. The case studies followed similar methods, but those approaches were not completely replicated, which limits the comparativeness of the studies.

Müller et al. (2005a) surveyed the use of the Shughni, Tajik and Russian languages by domain and classified their use by language strength in each domain as dominant, secondary, or not used. In the chapter, the quantitative survey results were presented in tabular form, which makes the language vitality and social spaces in which the languages were used difficult to visualize. However, when transformed into graphic form, the space and niches in the ecology occupied by each language become much more evident. Certain domains are "niche" domains occupied by one language; others are shared domains, where more than one language is present, and sometimes more than one can be strong (Figure 7.4).

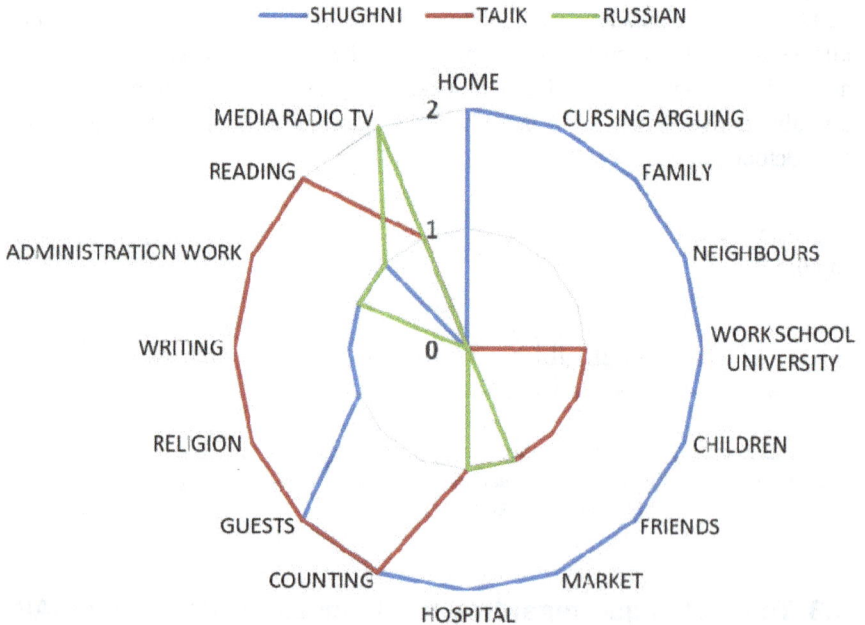

Figure 7.4: Language choice and domains among Shughni speakers
Note: dominant use = 2, weak use = 1, not used = 0. Source: prepared by author from Müller et al. (2005a: 165)

From Figure 7.4, we can more clearly see the local language ecology as a social and linguistic space. Speaking metaphorically, certain functional domains seem, as in a biological ecology, to be linguistic niches. This can be seen in the case of several domains centered on communication with intimates in which Shughni is the exclusive language (e.g., cursing, family, neighbors), Russian is the exclusive language (e.g., radio and TV), and others are hierarchical zones where one language is predominant over one or more, e.g., Shughni is predominant over both Tajik and Russian in communication at the hospital while in other symbiotic spaces, languages are equally strong like the case of both Tajik and Shughni being used with guests depending on where the guests come from.

Extending Fishman (1967), it seems that there is a dynamic trilingualism evidenced in this context, with some domains reserved for one language, while in others two languages, and still others, three languages are used, e.g., in public spaces like markets and hospitals. It is hard to be sure whether to term this language ecology diglossic or triglossic; there seems a clear separation into L and H language uses and domains into two levels, L and H, as laid out by Ferguson. However, as seen in Figure 7.4, there is one L language, Shughni and two H languages, Tajik and Russian, with Tajik used in most H domains, Russian in broadcast media, and Tajik and Russian both used as H languages for reading as well as in administration and the hospital.[6]

The remaining chapters similarly examine language vitality and multilingualism of other Pamiri languages, i.e., Rushani, Khufi, Bartangi, and Roshorvi (Abbess et al. 2005), Yazgulami (Tiessen et al. 2005), Ishkashimi (Müller et al. 2005b), and in a follow-up publication, Wakhi (Müller et al. 2008). All of the chapters observed the vitality of Pamiri language use in L domains as community and home languages. This was true even in the case of Ishkashimi, which is only spoken in Tajikistan in two villages. The Ishkashimi communities studied reported a large number of mothers, native speakers of Wakhi or Tajik from outside the community, who had learned Ishkashimi and spoke it with their children. Proficiency in Tajik among children was acquired in school and was reportedly greater among children whose parents are proficient in Tajik.

---

6 The figure and section above refers to language uses within the Shughni language community of the Shughnan and Roshtqala districts and the provincial capital of Khorugh. However, the language ecology of Khorugh is more complex. As the provincial centre, it attracts non-Shughnis who go there temporarily for work, or study at the university. The data suggest that within Khorugh, Shughni has become the LWC among Shughni and long-term residents from other parts of MBAP for L uses. For those from other parts of Tajikistan, other parts of Central Asia and FSU, Tajik and Russian function as LWCs respectively.

Abbess et al. (2005) examined the status of Rushani and its dialects, i.e., Khufi, Bartangi, and Roshorvi, which are community languages in the next valley north of Khorugh and the Shughni-speaking area. The authors found a high degree of vitality of these languages with almost exclusive use in L functions. While Tajik language was used as language of instruction in schools, the chapter found varying levels of Tajik proficiency according to distance from the district centre and the Panj river. In addition, the oldest and the youngest in the community were the least proficient in Tajik, with many children not knowing Tajik at all when beginning school. Indeed, Rushani was used as supplementary language of instruction in early grades. The chapter also found that Russian proficiency was less than Tajik proficiency; yet, over 50% reported stronger ability to read Russian than Tajik. Men old enough to have served in the Soviet military and those who had travelled outside Tajikistan for work also reported higher proficiency in Russian. A limited amount of popular literature written in Rushani is published in newspapers. The chapter had little to say about Rushani-Shughni bilingualism (or bidialectism), and how Rushani speakers communicated with Shughni speakers, particularly when visiting, working or studying in Khorugh, the Shughni-dominant capital of MBAP. It is unclear from the findings whether Rushani and Shughni are sufficiently close for passive bilingualism (Rushani and Shughni speakers each used their own language in addressing the other or modify their speech to more closely approximate Shughni), or whether Rushani speakers in contact with Shughni speakers use Shughni rather than Rushani, as seems that Shughni is a regional lingua franca (Wurm 1996).

Tiessen et al. (2005) found that the Yazgulami language is vital as both a home and community language. As in other districts, Tajik was learned as LOI in school, as well as through broader cultural and linguistic exposure via travel outside the valley. However, it should be noted that people's travel patterns were different in this community from Rushan. There was no public transportation to other districts. But the distance to Vanj (the district centre) where a MBAP variety of Tajik is spoken, is less, and so, travel to Vanj was reported as more frequent than to Khorugh, consequently leading to a greater contact with Tajik outside school than in the previous districts discussed. In addition, while Yazgulam's Pamiri language resembles other Pamiri languages, residents of this district are Sunni Muslims, in contrast to most Pamiris, who are Ismaili Muslims. As a result, in Yazgulam, wives from outside the district are Tajik-speaking Sunnis from Vanj and other districts. The chapter found that children from families with one parent who is a native speaker of Tajik have higher Tajik proficiency. While over a century ago conversion of the population of Vanj from the Ismaili to the Sunni interpretation of Islam was associated with language shift from the Vanji to Tajik, the similar conversion of Yazgulamis has not seen Tajik make significant inroads as a community or home language in Yazgulam.

Müller et al. (2005b) also examined the case of Ishkashimi, a language spoken in two villages neighbouring the town of Ishkashim. Despite the small number of speakers of Ishkashimi in Tajikistan in comparison with other Pamiri languages of MBAP, the vitality of the language is relatively high.[7] In Ryn, a homogeneous Ishkashimi village, Ishkashimi is the language of daily communication. Similar to the previous case, mothers from outside the village who are Tajik or Wakhi speakers seemed to all acquire Ishkashimi and used it in communication with their children. Müller et al. (2008) also looked at three communities where Wakhi is spoken, i.e., a homogenous Wakhi village, a mixed population but Wakhi-dominant village, and the Tajik-dominant town of Ishkashim. In the first two contexts, Wakhi was used as the home language and language of daily communication, while in the Tajik-dominant context of Ishkashim, Wakhi was used primarily in the home. Moreover, in one Wakhi home which was studied, the oldest generation used Wakhi with each other and Wakhi with some Tajik with the younger generations; then, the younger generations used mainly Wakhi with the older generation and mainly Tajik with some Wakhi amongst each other.

From these studies, the predominance of Tajik for H language uses and its use as sole official LOI does not seem to be associated with language shift to Tajik as a home language or language of daily communication. Intergenerational language shift to Tajik seems to happen only in centers where there is a significant proportion of the population for whom Tajik is the home language and language of daily communication. Clifton (2010) refers to a continued situation of this sort with languages specializing by domain within a community as "stable multilingualism", which he argues is currently the prevailing situation in MBAP. The bilingualism and diglossia of the region with Tajik the major language for H uses seems to be stable as well. Moreover, these studies also found that Tajik was the predominant language for reading and writing, with Russian used to some extent for reading.

In Pamiri-speaking contexts, Tajik as schools' LOI has been supplemented by informal oral explanation in Pamiri languages. Associated with this was the limited development of written materials in Pamiri languages to develop mother tongue literacy and to assist understanding, especially among rural children with little to no Tajik proficiency. Nevertheless, there is mixed level of support or resistance from parents and government for the use of written Pamiri languages in schools, and very little information as to how prevalent use of oral

---

7 Beck (2012) looks at Ishkashimi and another Pamiri language, Sanglechi in Badakhshan province of Afghanistan, and reports that Ishkashimi is spoken in six villages outside the town of Ishkashim.

and/or written L1 is and what effect it may have on children's education and the language ecology of MBAP. Some fear that development of written forms of these languages could lead to demands for greater autonomy of the province or even separatism among MBAP residents. The research in this edited volume suggests that if members of other different communities, such as Rushani or Wakhi, have access to Shughni, Tajik and Russian as LWCs, then they have access to at least four languages, i.e., their community language and three LWCs. Unfortunately, these chapters are quite brief, and do not provide detailed data or their sources. Nevertheless, these chapters are suggestive of a much higher degree of social multilingualism and varying degrees of individual pluri-lingualism than was suggested by earlier scholarship with its various limitations as discussed earlier.

Still unexplored are questions like: how do Yazgulami-speakers communi-cate with Rushani-speakers, the closest Pamiri language geographically, spoken one valley to the south? Do they accommodate towards each other's languages? Does one of them serve as local lingua franca? Are Shughni, Tajik, or Russian chosen as LWC? The same points apply to Rushani-Shughni, Shughni-Ishkashimi, and Ishkashimi-Wakhi languages which are spoken in contiguous districts.

Each of these cases examined the vertical relationship between a local lan-guage and one or two H languages that function as languages of wider com-munication, and taken as a whole can be considered an examination of the vertical language ecology dynamics of MBAP. Nevertheless, the entire language ecology is not examined, for the interrelationships between Pamiri languages and their speakers do not fall within the scope of the study, nor does the Kyrgyz language. A more complete ecological account would have to take into con-sideration these horizontal aspects of the language ecology, such as the inter-relationship between Rushani and Shughni, for example, and of Kyrgyz with Tajik, Russian and Pamiri languages. This also leaves unexamined the question of mutual intelligibility among Pamiri languages.

4.2.2 The language ecology in the Murgab District (MBAP), Tajikistan

As noted earlier, information on Kyrgyz language and its relation with Pamiri languages, Tajik and Russian in the MBAP, Murgab, where the Kyrgyz-speaking population is dominant is scarce. Speakers of Pamiri primary languages who grow up in Murgab may become proficient in oral Kyrgyz without studying Kyrgyz in school (personal field notes, 1998). Niyozov (2001) examined a Tajik-medium school in Murgab district and found that some Kyrgyz students whose families wished their children to learn Tajik and/or who were dissatisfied with education in the Kyrgyz-medium school were attending the Tajik-medium school. Karabaev and Ahn in this volume, also examine different experiences within Kyrgyz LOI schools in this region.

Despite the limited research, it seems that there are numerous challenges regarding the education of Kyrgyz-speaking students in MBAP. For example, contemporary textbooks have not yet been prepared in Kyrgyz language. As a result, pre-independence Kyrgyz language teaching materials from Soviet Kyrgyzstan are used for instruction in most subjects. There are no textbooks in Tajik language education that are intended for Kyrgyz students. Instead, there are cases where Kyrgyz-speaking students are taught with a bilingual textbook developed for teaching Tajik to Uzbek-speaking students in western Tajikistan. While Kyrgyz and Uzbek are both Turkic languages, the differences between the languages do present problems for both students and teachers. One teacher, who is ethnically Tajik, observed that

> It is really difficult to teach Tajik language for Kyrgyz children with Uzbek language text-books. (1) the textbook content is difficult which is designed for children who already know Tajik language, for example, for grade 2, book starts with sentence analysis while Kyrgyz children cannot read the sentences in Tajik language and (2) it is in Uzbek language that makes more problematic. The vocabulary translations are given in Tajik, Russian, and Uzbek languages. Primary class children do not understand both Russian and Uzbek trans-lations. I try to find and use Kyrgyz translation. (Karabaev 2011: 65)

The limited number of empirical studies examining school-based learning of Tajik among Kyrgyz-speakers of Murgab, provides a glimpse into this particular context. How this translates into Tajik use outside schools is little known, as is the nature of Pamiri-Kyrgyz-Tajik-Russian plurilingualism.

4.2.3 The Rushani-Shughni-Dari/Tajik language ecology in Badakhshan, Afghanistan

Showing another layer of complexity in the broader region, Beck (2013) looked at the case of a Rushani-speaking community in Badakhshan, Afghanistan, which is situated across the Panj River from the Rushani-speaking areas of MBAP, Tajikistan. Beck focused on the question of the desirability and feasibility of using Rushani as a language of instruction in basic education for this com-munity. This study looked at the receptive and productive use of Shughni and

Dari/Tajik by Rushani speakers and by doing so, was attempting to take into account both the vertical and horizontal intra-Pamiri dimensions of language use and language attitudes. Local opinion stated that Rushani speakers can understand Shughni but that Shughni speakers do not understand Rushani. The study found that those who frequented local bazaars where the Shughni language is predominant had more exposure to the Shughni language and claimed strong receptive understanding. It seems that in the bazaar, reciprocal passive bilingualism was developed where Shughni speakers would speak Shughni and their Rushani counterparts responded in Rushani.

Beck (2013) also attempted to test to what extent the comprehension by Rushani speakers of Shughni was learned through exposure or was facilitated by the similarity of the related language varieties. Rushani speakers were given comprehension tests of Shughni. They were then classified by the degree of their exposure to Shughni, ranging from those women who did not leave the community and had not been exposed to Shughni to males who often attended markets in Shughni-speaking areas and conducted business with Shughni speaking interlocutors. Beck found that men generally had higher Shughni comprehension than women, but that no-one had lower than 60% comprehension of Shughni narrative discourse. When looking at different degrees of contact with Shughni (the lowest degree of contact = 1, highest = 4), Beck found mean comprehension among those with the lowest degree of contact to be 77%, more contact (2) to be 85%, higher levels of contact (3) to be 95% and the highest amount of contact (4) to be 94%. Beck explained this relatively high comprehension as due to an interaction of lexical similarity and high exposure to Shughni. Lexical similarity to Dari/Tajik and Shughni was calculated based on a word list adapted from the 200-word Swadesh list typically used in such comparisons, finding low lexical similarity with Dari/Tajik ranging from 30–36% (263), and very high lexical similarity with Shughni, ranging from 74–84% (264).

Education also may have played a role, since local teachers in Rushani-speaking villages themselves were often Shughni-speakers. For example, Shughni-speaking teachers in MBAP studied by Niyozov (2001) often supplemented lessons in Tajik with explanations in local language. Iti s possible that teachers in Rushani-villages might also have explained Dari lessons to Rushani-speaking children in Shughni not Rushani. When asked about the most suitable language of instruction for their children's basic education, the first choice of parents was Rushani, with Shughni their second choice, and both local languages were preferred to Dari/Tajik. Nonetheless, parents expressed support for their children's learning and using Dari/Tajik, but opposed its use as the primary LOI in early grades.

5 Areas for future research

5.1 The impact of the entrance of English into the Pamiri language ecology

In general, Pamiris have an identifiable accent in Tajik and are seen as having a lower standard of Tajik than people from Tajik-speaking areas, and some claim that teachers discriminated against them in Tajik-language sections in universities in Dushanbe. However, during the Soviet period, study in special Russian language sections in schools was believed to provide higher Russian proficiency and higher quality education. Because of these differences in terms of language prestige, a student from MBAP in the capital could trump perceptions of "weaker" Tajik by playing the Russian "card", if they had as strong or stronger Russian than L1 Tajik speakers (Niyozov 2001).

Today, because international organizations which are active in Tajikistan and MBAP often have English as their working language, the possibility of playing the English "card" has become a reality. These organizations require local English-speaking staff, and in response to this need, the University of Khorog English Language Program was opened in collaboration with the Aga Khan Development Network and was funded by the Canadian International Development Agency. Many of the graduates of this program and the university's English department have found employment as English teachers in schools, at the university, and as staff of international organizations. At the same time private schools have opened with multiple LOIs (Tajik, Russian and English). Thus, while since independence the academic and economic rewards of learning Russian have been somewhat lessened, opportunities and incentives to study and learn English have correspondingly increased. At least in Khorugh, there are now three languages functioning as H varieties used for administration: Tajik, Russian, and English, while Shughni remains the dominant language used in non-official public spaces, e.g., bazaars, bus stations, etc. (personal field notes, 1998).

5.2 The role of technology, the Internet and script reform in impacting MBAP's language ecology

Jamshedov (1991) publically advocated the use of Pamir languages in basic education and Karamshoev designed a Cyrillic alphabet for Shughni and advocated its official adoption for many years (Müller et al. 2005a). But it has been noted that generally Pamiri languages are unwritten and consequently have no scripts.

However, this is perhaps an understatement. It has always been possible for speakers of Pamiri languages who are literate in some other language to use these known scripts and apply them to writing in non-codified languages. Unfortunately, there is very little information on this question since it has not fallen within the research agenda of those investigating Pamiri languages and bilingualism in the region. Little attention has been devoted to the development in the 1920s of a Romanized script for Pamir languages or the use of either Romanized or Cyrillic script for the writing and publication of stories, poems and songs beyond the work of specialists in language and folklore who have compiled oral narratives transcribed in a modified IPA. Nevertheless, several studies have shown that there is much use of Pamir languages in basic education, e.g., Niyozov (2001) found spontaneous initiatives among teachers to extend the use of Pamiri languages when this supported understanding and communication.

Similarly, much spontaneous individual innovation is evident in the use of multiple languages and multiple scripts in internet environments where language users have autonomous choice in which language(s) and script(s) they use. For example, in one online university guest book former students left messages in Tajik, Russian and English with Tajik and Russian both written sometimes in Cyrillic and sometimes in a spontaneous Romanization. Even more interestingly, written messages in Romanized Shughni, a non-codified language, were also observed. It is interesting to speculate as internet access spreads beyond the university whether written communication in Pamiri languages will similarly spread with a bottom-up standardization process of language and spelling develop through interaction and mutual adaptation. One example of this possibility is the increasing use in MBAP of Pamiri languages in the H domain of university classroom instruction, where they have been used as supplemental instructional languages in the teaching of English as a Foreign Language as a way of explaining the English language more clearly than in Tajik or Russian (Olimnazarova 2012).

6 Conclusion

There is much need for more research on the language ecology. However, taking a bird's eye view of research that has been conducted, findings point to the presence of stable social multilingualism and personal plurilingualism such that small unwritten languages continue their vitality, despite the power of the state behind Russian and Tajik (USSR) and the Tajikistani government and the

Tajik language (see Table 7.2). Thus the challenge remains for research to develop descriptively rich accounts of the language ecology in these complex settings that highlight the uniqueness of these contexts and capture the dynamic ways in which languages (and language communities) continue to change and adopt to new socio-political-cultural realities.

Table 7.2: Languages and Domains of Use in MBAP's Language Ecology

Level	Language(s)	Comments
International	English	LWC in offices of international NGOs
Russia & Central Asia	Russian	LWC with outsiders from other republics of FSU; also used widely for administrative/technical/specialist work, for example, in medical field
Tajikistan	Tajik	LWC for those from other parts of Tajikistan; Tajik-speaking districts of MBAP; H language in many domains, such as education
Khorugh	Shughni	LWC for non Shughni living/working/studying in Khorugh; Passive or active bilingualism unclear
Local	Kyrgyz, Tajik dialect, Pamiri Languages	Passive or active bilingualism? Symmetrical or asymmetrical bilingualism? Koineization of Rushani-Shughni? Vitality of Ishkashimi and Yazgulami? Contact phenomena? Language shift?

From a research and policy perspective, this has several implications. First, on the level of descriptive adequacy of research, not enough rigorous published knowledge exists about the nature and extent of societal multilingualism and personal plurilingualism in MBAP. Anecdotally, many graduates of Khorugh State University are, at the very least, quadrilingual, with proficiency in one Pamiri language + Tajik + Russian + English. When considering the possibility of local-local bi-/multilingualism such as inter-Pamiri and/or Pamiri-Kyrgyz bilingualism, the number of languages in which some Badakhshanis have some proficiency is staggering to someone with a monolingual ethos.

Or take the example of someone raised in a Wakhi-speaking family in Murgab, learning oral Kyrgyz from neighbors and classmates, Tajik and Russian in school, and on arriving at Khorugh State University in the centre of the Shughni-speaking domain, adding Shughni informally and English formally to this long list of language repertoires for a grand total of six languages. Suggestions that Shughni actually functions as an L language lingua franca among all MBAP residents, possibly including Kyrgyz speakers, need substantiation. At the same time, if Shughni does indeed fulfill this role, how speakers of other Pamiri languages respond to the apparent centrality of Shughni in MBAP is in need of serious investigation, including the questions as to any concerns about the potential for hegemony of Shughni language and its speakers. On the question of language shift, language loss and language endangerment, the case studies in Clifton (2005) have made an excellent contribution, but there is a need for broader study of the phenomenon.

Among published studies, there is little sign of any rejection of the Tajik language among the different MBAP populations. Indeed, within certain registers and functional domains, such as the recitation of religious poetry, perhaps Tajik is the preferred language in MBAP. It seems therefore, that while individuals vary in number of languages in their repertoires, the MBAP population seems to highly value additive bilingualism, accepting the extrinsic utility and intrinsic worth of societal multilingualism and personal plurilingualism. Tajik/Russian/English seem to be sought by many and to coexist in a symbiotic additive fashion.

The next task for research on the language ecology of Pamir is to theorize the complexities of its multilingualism and pluralism, in particular to seek adequate understandings of how they exist, and of the persistence of Pamiri languages, where on the surface other languages in similar conditions have melted away rapidly. This not simply a question for MBAP, but also includes Xinjiang, where Chinese scholars Luo and Zhao (2004) have noted, not only the continued vitality of the Pamir languages in the remote home territory of Tashkurgan, but that educated Tajiks proficient in Uyghur and Chinese who live in the regional capital persist in using Pamiri languages in the home despite the lack of an external language environment to support its maintenance.

However, while it seems clear that Pamiri languages are in no way a threat to the learning of Tajik and other languages, the lack of use of these languages in early grades at least of primary school may limit the effectiveness of learning of some Pamiri children (Bahry 2005a, 2005b; Bahry et al. 2008; Jamshedov 1991; Niyozov 2001). The Pamiri language ecology is an extreme case for the testing of language ecology as an explanatory framework for understanding multilingualism, plurilingualism and language shift and maintenance. Much future insider research is needed that will take a more detailed, explicit language ecology approach, applying for example Hornberger's (2002) "Continua of Biliteracy" to the MBAP case. Such research should be fruitful not only for an understanding of multilingualism and language policy in MBAP, but would have much potential to generate many insights applicable to the entire region.

References

Abbess, Elisabeth, Katja Müller, Daniel Paul, Calvin Tiessen & Gabriela Tiessen. 2005. Literacy and the vernacular in Tajik Badakhshan: Research into Rushani, Khufi, Bartangi, and Roshorvi. In John M. Clifton (ed.), *Studies in languages of Tajikistan*, 187–221. Dushanbe, Tajikistan: National State University of Tajikistan: SIL International.

Backstrom, Peter C. 1992. Wakhi. In Peter C. Backstrom & Carla F. Radloff (eds.), *Sociolinguistic survey of Northern Pakistan. Volume 2. Languages of northern areas*, 57–76. High Wycombe, England: SIL International.

Bahry, Stephen A. 2005a. The potential of bilingual education in educational development of minority language children in Mountainous Badakhshan, Tajikistan. In Hywel Coleman, Jamilya Gulyamova & Andrew Thomas (eds.), *National development, education and language in Central Asia and beyond*, 46–63. Tashkent, Uzbekistan: British Council.

Bahry, Stephen A. 2005b. Language, literacy and education in Tajikistan. In Michael Gervers, Uradyn E. Bulag & Gillian Long, (eds.), *History and society in Central and Inner Asia* (Toronto Studies in Central & Inner Asia 7). Toronto, Canada: University of Toronto.

Bahry, Stephen A. 2013. Language in Afghanistan's education reform: Does it play a role in peace and reconciliation? In Carol Benson & Kimmo Kosonen (eds.), *Language issues in comparative education: Inclusive teaching and learning in non-dominant languages and cultures* [Comparative and International Education: A Diversity of Voices 24], 59–76. Rotterdam: Sense Publishers.

Bahry, Stephen A., Sarfaroz Niyozov & Duishon Shamatov. 2008. Bilingual education in Central Asia. In Jim Cummins & Nancy H. Hornberger (eds.), *Bilingual education* [Encyclopedia of Language and Education 5], 205–221. New York: Springer Science + Business Media LLC.

Baskakov, Aleksandr N. 1996a. Languages of interethnic communication in the area of Central Asia and Kazakhstan. In Stephen A. Wurm, Peter Mühlhäusler & Darrell T. Tryon (eds.), *Atlas of languages of intercultural communication in the Pacific, Asia, and the Americas*, Vol. 2.2, 913–918. Berlin: Walter de Gruyter.

Baskakov, Aleksandr N. 1996b. Languages of interethnic communication in Tajikistan. In Stephen A. Wurm, Peter Mühlhäusler & Darrell T. Tryon (eds.), *Atlas of languages of intercultural communication in the Pacific, Asia, and the Americas*, Vol. 2.2, 941–944. Berlin: Walter de Gruyter.

Beck, Simone. 2012. The effect of accessibility on language vitality: The Ishkashimi and the Sanglechi language varieties in Afghanistan. *Linguistic Discovery* 10(2). 157–233. http://journals.dartmouth.edu/cgi-bin/WebObjects/Journals.woa/1/xmlpage/1/archive (accessed 25 January 2014).

Beck, Simone. 2013. A sociolinguistic assessment of the Roshani speech variety in Afghanistan. *Language documentation and conservation* 7, 235–301. http://scholarspace.manoa.hawaii.edu/bitstream/handle/10125/4573/beck.pdf?sequence=1 (accessed 25 January 2014).

Clément, Matthieu. 2011. Remittances and household expenditure patterns in Tajikistan: A propensity score matching analysis. *Asian Development Review* 28(2). 58–87

Clifton, John M. (ed.). 2005. *Studies in languages of Tajikistan*. St. Petersburg: SIL International.

Clifton, J. M. 2010. Stable multilingualism in Tajikistan. In A. Baker, R. Baglini, T. Grinsell, J. Keane, & J. Thomas (eds.), *Chicago Linguistic Society* 46(2).

Cummins, Jim. 2000. *Language, power and pedagogy: Bilingual children in the crossfire*. Clevedon: Multilingual Matters.

Edelman, Dzhoi I. 1966. *Iazguliamskii iazyk* [The Yazgulami language]. Moscow: Nauka.

Edelman, Dzhoi I. & Leila R. Dodykhudoeva. 2009a. The Pamir languages. In Gernot Windfuhr (ed.), *The Iranian languages*, 773–786. New York: Routledge.

Edelman, Dzhoi I. & Leila R. Dodykhudoeva. 2009b. Shughni. In Gernot Windfuhr (ed.), *The Iranian languages*, 787–824. New York: Routledge.

Elnazarov, Akim. 2004. Endangered languages and education: A case of Badakhshan Province of Tajikistan. In Joan A. Argenter & R. McKenna Brown (eds.), *Endangered languages and linguistic rights: On the margins of nations. Proceedings of the 8th FEL Conference, Barcelona (Catalonia), Spain. 1–3 October*, 207–208. Bath, England: Foundation for Endangered Languages.

Elnazarov, Hakim. 2010. West and Central Asia. In Christopher Moseley (ed.), *Atlas of the worlds' languages in danger*, 43–46. Paris: UNESCO.

Ferguson, Charles A. 1959. Diglossia. *Word* 15. 325–40.

Fishman, Joshua A. 1967. Bilingualism with and without diglossia; Diglossia with and without bilingualism. *Journal of Social Issues* 23(2). 29–38.

Gao, Erqiang. 1985. *Tajike yu jianzhi* [A grammar of Tajik (i.e., Sarykoli and Wakhi)]. Beijing, China: Minzu Chubanshe.

Gryunberg, Aleksandr L. & Mikhail I. Steblin-Kamenskii. 1976. *Iazyki vostochnogo Gindukusha: Vakhanskii iazyk; teksty, slovar' grammaticheskii ocherk* [The languages of the eastern Hindukush: Wakhi language, texts, dictionary and grammatical outline]. Institute of Linguistics, Academy of Sciences. Moscow: Nauka.

Guboglo, Mikhail N. 1984. *Sovremennye etnoizykovye protsessy v SSSR: Osnovnye factory i tendentsii razvitiia natsional'no-russkogo dvuiazychiia* [Contemporary ethnolinguistic processes in the USSR: Basic factors and tendencies in the development of national-Russian bilingualism]. Moscow: Nauka.

Haugen, Einar. 1972. The ecology of language. In Anwar S. Dil (ed.), *The ecology of language. Essays by Einar Haugen*, 324–329. Stanford: Stanford University Press.

Hojibekov, Elbon. 2010. The use of Shughni language in Ghoron of Tajikistan and the causes of its demise. In Hakim Elnazarov & Nick Ostler (eds.), *Endangered languages and history: The Proceedings of the conference FEL XIII 2009, Khorugh, Tajikistan, 24–26 September 2009, Institute of Humanities, Academy of Sciences of Tajikistan, Khorugh Tajikistan*. Bath, England: Foundation for Endangered Languages.

Hornberger, Nancy H. 2002. Multilingual language policies and the continua of biliteracy: An ecological approach. *Language Policy* 1. 27–51.

Jamshedov, Parvona. 1991. Pamirskie iazyki i nekotorye voprosy prosveshcheniia [Pamiri languages and several questions of education]. *Russkii iazyk v SSSR* [The Russian language in the USSR], 1(9). 7–8.

Karabaev, Daniyar. 2011. *Minority education in Tajikistan: A case of Kyrgyz minority schools in Badakhshan Province*. Tsukuba, Japan: University of Tsukuba thesis.

Kieffer, Charles. 1983. Afghanistan. V. Languages. *Encyclopedia Iranica, Vol. I*, Fasc. 5, 501–516.

Landau, Jacob M. & Barbara Kellner-Heinkele. 2012. *Language politics in contemporary Central Asia*. London: I.B. Tauris

Luo, Jiayun & Jianguo Zhao. 2004. *Tajike zu: Xinjiang Tahsiku'ergan Xian Tizinafu Cun diaocha* [Tajik nationality: Xinjiang Tashkurgan County, Tizinafu village investigation]. Kunming, China: Yunnan University Press.

Marsden, Magnus. 2012. 'For Badakhshan-the country without borders!' Village cosmopolitans, urban-rural networks, and the post-cosmopolitan city in Tajikistan. In Caroline Humphrey

& Vera Skvirskaja (eds.), *Post-cosmopolitan cities: Explorations of urban coexistence*, 217–239. Oxford: Berghahn Books.

Moseley, Christopher (ed.). 2010. *Atlas of the world's languages in danger*, 3rd edn. Paris: UNESCO. http://www.unesco.org/culture/en/endangeredlanguages/atlas

Mostowlansky, Till. 2012. Making Kyrgyz spaces: Local history as spatial practice in Murghab (Tajikistan). *Central Asian Survey* 31(3). 251–264.

Müller, Katja, Elisabeth Abbess, Daniel Paul, Calvin Tiessen, & Gabriela Tiessen. 2005a. Language in community-oriented and contact-oriented domains: The case of the Shughni of Tajikistan. In John M. Clifton (ed.), *Studies in languages of Tajikistan*, 151–185. St. Petersburg: SIL International.

Müller, Katja, Elisabeth Abbess, Daniel Paul, Calvin Tiessen, & Gabriela Tiessen. 2005b. Ishkashimi: A father's language. How a very small language survives. In John M. Clifton (ed.), *Studies in languages of Tajikistan*, 223–250. St. Petersburg: SIL International.

Müller, Katja, Elisabeth Abbess, Calvin Tiessen, & Gabriela Tiessen. 2008. *Language vitality and development among the Wakhi people of Tajikistan*. SIL Electronic Survey Reports. http://www.sil.org/resources/publications/entry/9157U (accessed 8 November 2013).

Niyozov, Sarfaroz. 2001. *Understanding teaching in post-Soviet, rural mountainous Tajikistan: Case studies of teachers' life and work*. Toronto, Ontario: Ontario Institute for Studies in Education, University of Toronto doctoral dissertation.

Niyozov, Sarfaroz & Duishon Shamatov. 2006. Trading or teaching: Dilemmas of everyday life economy in Central Asia. *Inner Asia* 8(2), 229–62.

Olimnazarova, Tojiniso. 2012. *Using students' linguistic repertoires for teaching English as a Foreign Language in Tajikistan*. Birmingham, England: University of Birmingham M.A. thesis.

Olimova, S. & I. Bosc. 2003. *Labour migration from Tajikistan*. Dushanbe, Tajikistan: International Organization for Migration.

Owens, Jonathan. 2007. Endangered languages of the Middle East. In Matthias Brenzinger (ed.), *Language diversity endangered*, 263–277. Berlin, Germany: Walter de Gruyter.

Pakhalina, Tatiana N. 1975. *Vakhanskii iazyk* [Wakhi language]. Institute of Linguistics, Academy of Sciences. Moscow: Nauka.

Rahman, Tariq. 2006. Language policy, multilingualism and language vitality in Pakistan. In Anju Saxena & Lars Borin (Eds.), *Lesser known languages of South Asia: Status and policies, case studies and applications of information technology*, 73–104. Berlin: Walter de Gruyter.

Rastorogueva, Vera S. 1964. *Opyt sravnitel'nogo izucheniia Tadzhikskikh govorov*. Moscow: Nauka.

Republic of Tajikistan Statistics Agency 2012. *Population census of the Republic of Tajikistan, 2010. Volume III: Nationalities, languages and citizenship*. Dushanbe, Tajikistan: Republic of Tajikistan Statistics Agency. http://www.stat.tj/en/img/526b8592e834fcaaccec26a22965ea2b_1355502192.pdf (accessed 1 November 2014).

Rozenfel'd, Anna Z. 1964. *Vandzhskie govory Tadzhikskogo iazyka* [The Vanj dialects of the Tajik language]. Leningrad: Leningrad University Press.

Roy, Olivier. 2007. *The new Central Asia: Geopolitics and the birth of nations*. London: I.B. Tauris.

Silver, Brian D. 1975. Methods of deriving data on bilingualism from the 1970 Soviet census. *Soviet Studies* 27(October), 574–597.

Sokolova, Valentina S. 1959. *Rushanskie i Khufskie teksty* [Rushani and Khufi texts]. Leningrad: Academy of Sciences Press.

Sokolova, Valentina S. 1960. *Bartangskie teksty i slovar'* [Bartangi texts and dictionary]. Moscow: Academy of Sciences Press.

Šombezoda, Xosrov Dž. 1996. Languages of interethnic communication in the Gorno-Badakhshan province of Tajikistan. In Stephen A. Wurm, Peter Mühlhäusler & Darrell T. Tryon (eds.), *Atlas of languages of intercultural communication in the Pacific, Asia, and the Americas*, Vol. 2.2, 945–946. Berlin, Germany: Mouton de Gruyter.

Tiessen, Gabriela, Elisabeth Abbess, Katja Müller and Calvin Tiessen. 2005. Language access and Tajik language proficiency among the Yazghulami of Tajikistan. In John M. Clifton (ed.), *Studies in languages of Tajikistan*, 107–149. St. Petersburg, Russia: SIL International.

Voegelin, Charles F. & Florence M. Voegelin. 1964. Languages of the world: African fascicle one. *Anthropological Linguistics* 6(6). 1–149.

Wurm, Stephen. A. 1996. Shugni as a lingua franca in the Pamir area. In Stephen A. Wurm, Peter Mühlhäusler & Darrell T. Tryon (eds.), *Atlas of languages of intercultural communication in the Pacific, Asia, and the Americas*, Vol. 2.2, 947–948. Berlin: Walter de Gruyter.

Zarubin, Ivan I. 1960. *Shugnanskie teksty i slovar'* [Shughni texts and dictionary]. Leningrad, USSR: Academy of Sciences Press.

Zholdoshalieva, Rakhat. 2010. Inclusion and exclusion of indigenous knowledge, culture and language: The Kyrgyz minority in Central and Inner Asia. Paper presented at the annual conference of the Comparative International Education Society, University of Chicago, March 1–5, 2010.

Daniyar Karabaev and Elise S. Ahn

8 Language-in-Education: A Look at Kyrgyz Language Schools in the Badakhstan Province of Tajikistan

Abstract: Tajikistan is a multiethnic republic in Central Asia where ethnic Russian, Uzbek, Kyrgyz, Turkmen and other minorities live. The purpose of this research study was to examine the access that Kyrgyz students living in Tajikistan have to Tajik language Medium of Instruction (MOI) schools. Research findings show that the combination of lack of resources and exposure to the Tajik language and sustained Kyrgyz language education has restricted access to further schooling and career opportunities for participants. Through the interviews, educators at Kyrgyz language MOI schools shared that teaching Tajik language courses was difficult because of the general absence of appropriate textbooks, a shortage of necessary teaching materials and unqualified teachers. The experience of Kyrgyz language MOI schools provides an interesting case to examine the ways in which minority language-based education in Central Asia are changing.

Keywords: Kyrgyz schools; minority education; Murghab; Tajikistan

1 Introduction

Tajikistan became independent on September 9, 1991. The years following independence were tumultuous as a five-year civil war broke out (1992–1997), which subsequently created political and economic instability, widespread poverty, and seriously damaged the infrastructure of most sectors in the country. The civil war came to an end with the signing of the Peace Accord in 1997. But because of this period of socio-political unrest, Tajikistan's path to development post-independence has been different from the other Central Asian republics. As noted by Abdushukuorova (2008), Tajikistan (and specifically its education sector) is sometimes described as having "latecomer syndrome". This is because the education sector was particularly impacted by the civil war on a number of levels, including the brain drain of many professionals including many in the education sector (MoE 2005).

Today, the Tajikistani education system remains officially centralized. All schools are obliged to follow the state standards and curriculum set out by the

Tajikistani Ministry of Education (MoE). Subsequently, local schools report to the District Education Department (DED), which is in charge of overseeing all educational activities. The DED in turn, reports to the Regional Education Department, which is directly under the auspices of the MoE.

Murghab is one of the seven districts in the Mountainous Badakhshan Autonomous Province (MBAP) in Tajikistan. Murghab has one basic, two primary and 11 secondary schools, which totals to 14 schools. Among these schools, Tajik is the medium of instruction (MOI) in two schools, one is a mixed Kyrgyz-Tajik school, and the other 11 are Kyrgyz MOI. It should be noted that Kyrgyz is a Turkic language like Kazakh and Uzbek, whereas Tajik is an Indo-Iranian language along with languages like Farsi/Persian, Pashto, and Dari.

Similar to research conducted about other parts of Central Asia, language and education-related research in Tajikistan has often focused on macro-level policy and infrastructure issues or specifically at different stakeholders (i.e., teachers' perspectives and lived experiences) (Abdushukurova 2008; Bignell 2007; DeYoung 2004; Niyazov 2001, 2011; Olimov and Olimova 2002; Silova 2009). However, this chapter focuses on the experiences of different stakeholders' experiences with the education system in Murghab with a specific focus on stakeholders' perspectives on the MOI of their schools (Kyrgyz) and its relationship to the official state language (Tajik). Examining the MOI provide an interesting and challenging look into the complex process of nation-state building and civic identity building. As Bakhtin (1981: 291) noted "At any given moment of its historical existence, language is heteroglot from top to bottom; it represents the co-existence of socio-ideological contradictions between the present and the past, between differing socio-ideological groups in the present." By using this perspective as a lens through which to understand people's lived experiences, this chapter aims to examine the complex ways in which people identify with different languages in post-Soviet contexts.

2 Background

According to the 2012 data released by the Tajikistani government, there are 93 different nationalities represented in the country. Of the 93 different nationalities recorded, Tajiks make up 84.3% of the total population (Tables 8.1 and Figure 8.1).

Table 8.1: Population Overview

	1989	1989 (%)	2000	2000 (%)	2010	2010 (%)
Total	5,092,603	100.0	612,7493	100.0	756,4502	100.0
Tajiks	3,172,420	62.3	4,898,382	79.9	6,373,834	84.3
Minorities	1,920,183	37.7	1,229,111	20.1	1,190,668	15.7

Source: *Population and Society [Демоскоп Weekly]* Number 191–192. 2005, February 21–March 6. http://demoscope.ru/weekly/2005/0191/analit05.php; Results of the census of Tajikistan in 2000: National, age, gender, family and educational compositions. (2010). Retrieved from http://www.stat.tj/en/img/526b8592e834fcaaccec26a22965ea2b_1355502192.pdf

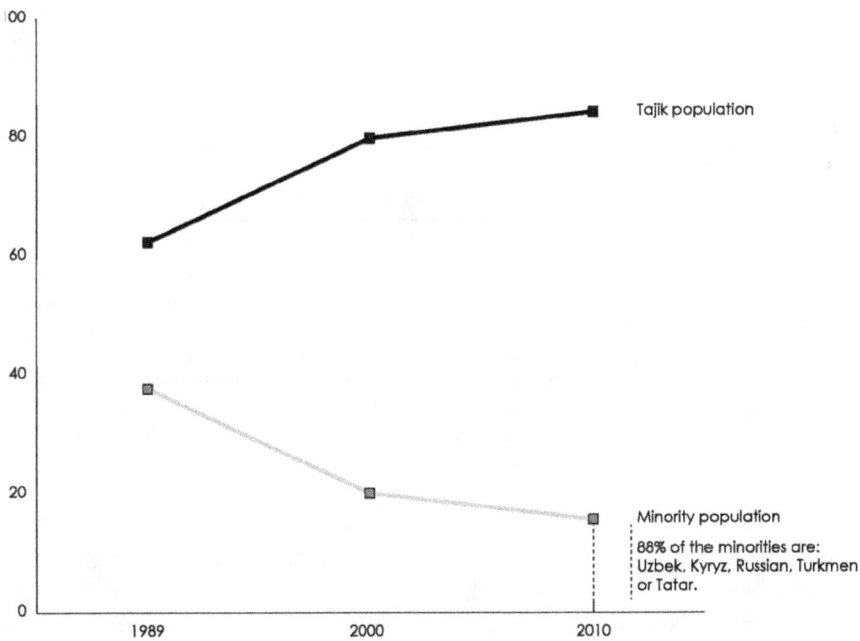

Figure 8.1: Population shift between 1989 and 2010
Sources: *Population and Society [Демоскоп Weekly]*, Number 191–192. 2005, February 21–March 6. http://demoscope.ru/weekly/2005/0191/analit05.php; Statistical Agency under the President of the Republic of Tajikistan (2012). Retrieved from http://www.stat.tj/en/img/526b8592e834fcaaccec26a22965ea2b_1355502192.pdf

The largest minority nationalities include: Uzbeks, Kyrgyz, Russians, Turkmens, and Tatars (Table 8.2).

Table 8.2: Largest Minority Nationalities

	1989	1989 (%)	2000	2000 (%)	2010	2010 (%)
Uzbeks	1,197,841	23.5	936,703	15.3	926,344	12.2
Kyrgyz	63,832	1.3	65,515	1.1	60,715	0.8
Russian	388,481	7.6	68,171	1.1	34,838	0.5
Turkmen	20,487	0.4	20,270	0.3	15,171	0.2
Tatar	72,228	1.4	18,939	0.3	6,495	0.1

Source: Statistical Agency under the President of the Republic of Tajikistan (2012). Retrieved from http://www.stat.tj/en/img/526b8592e834fcaaccec26a22965ea2b_1355502192.pdf

Table 8.3 provides an overview of the language affiliations of the largest minority populations.

Table 8.3: Largest Minority Nationalities (%)

	Population	Language of nationality	Tajik	Russian	Other
Uzbeks	926,344	97.5	2.4	0.08	0.02
Kyrgyz	60,715	97.9	1.5	0.1	0.5
Russian	34,838	94.0	2.4	–	3.6
Turkmen	15,171	90.0	1.1	0.3	8.6
Tatar	6,495	61.5	7.3	26.2	5.0

Source: Statistical Agency under the President of the Republic of Tajikistan (2012). Retrieved from http://www.stat.tj/en/img/526b8592e834fcaaccec26a22965ea2b_1355502192.pdf

Further disaggregating this data provides a glimpse into how these numbers are distributed between urban and rural populations (Table 8.4). For example, in light of discussions regarding global urbanization, in 2012, out of the total population of 7,564,502 people, only (26.5%) were identified as being urban residents. Table 8.4 provides an overview of the different nationalities and their languages based on place of residence (urban/rural).

As seen in Table 8.4, about 74% of the Tajikistani population is identified as living in rural locales. This is notable because while Russian and Tatar minorities are small, they are predominantly located in urban contexts, whereas the titular nationality, i.e., Tajiks, as well as Uzbek, Kyrgyz and Turkmen communities primarily reside in rural areas.

Table 8.4: Distribution of Nationalities by Location (Urban/Rural) and Language (%)

Nationality	Total population	Distribution	%	Language identifier (urban/rural)			
				Nationality	Tajik	Russian	Other
Tajik	6,373,834	Urban	27.9	99.5	–	0.2	0.3
		Rural	72.1	99.8	–	0.0	0.2
Uzbek	926,344	Urban	19.1	94.3	5.2	0.4	0.1
		Rural	80.9	98.3	1.7	0.0	0.0
Kyrgyz	60,715	Urban	12.0	94.7	3.2	0.6	1.5
		Rural	88.0	98.3	1.2	0.0	0.5
Russian	34,838	Urban	93.5	94.4	2.1	–	3.5
		Rural	6.5	88.0	6.2	–	5.8
Turkmen	15,171	Urban	7.7	68.4	8.3	3.3	20.0
		Rural	92.3	91.8	0.4	0.0	7.8
Tatar	6,495	Urban	85.3	60.7	6.4	29.5	3.4
		Rural	14.7	66.1	12.1	7.4	14.4

Note: If zero percent is present this means that there were language speakers recorded but that the number was too small to be represented after rounding. Source: Statistical Agency under the President of the Republic of Tajikistan (2012). Retrieved from http://www.stat.tj/en/img/526b8592e834fcaaccec26a22965ea2b_1355502192.pdf

2.1 The Kyrgyz community in Murghab

In eastern Tajikistan, there is a Kyrgyz population, which resides in the Murghab district of Mountainous Badakhshan Autonomous Province (MBAP) (Figure 8.2). In comparison with other Kyrgyz living in Tajikistan, the Kyrgyz of the Murghab district have been able to preserve their traditions, culture and the Kyrgyz language. Relatedly, the Kyrygyz people in this region are oftentimes unable to speak Tajik, the official language of the country.

During the Soviet era, Kyrgyz school children in this region did not study Tajik language or literature in schools. Rather, Kyrgyz schools in Tajikistan which was taught curriculum provided by the Kyrgyz Soviet Socialist Republic's (SSR) in the Kyrgyz language. After 2000, however, Tajik language and literature courses were introduced to Kyrgyz schools in the Murghab district. Prior to 2010, in addition to the Kyrgyz language, Kyrgyz students studied Russian, English and German as foreign languages.

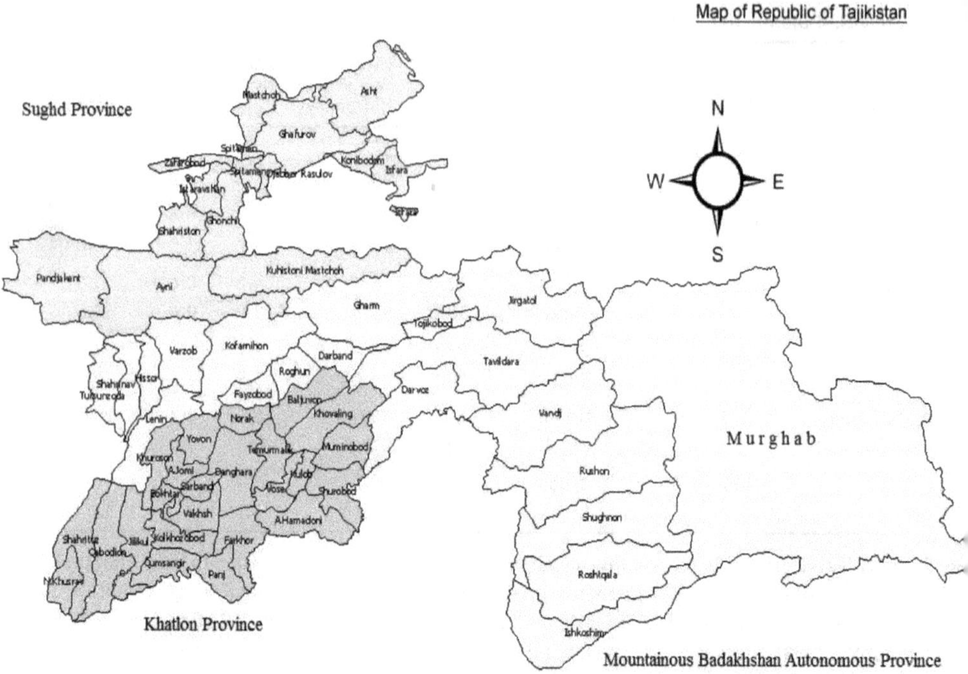

Figure 8.2: Administrative map of Tajikistan
Retrieved from http://tva.tj/ru/index/index/pageId/66/

2.2 Changing language and education laws

Like the other Central Asian republics, Tajikistan initially passed a language law
in July of 1989 establishing Tajik as the official language. On November 6, 1994,
the new Constitution allowed everyone the right to use their titular language in
private and in education settings (i.e., formal schooling); however, the Constitution did specify that Tajik was the state language and Russian the language
of interethnic communication. In 1997, a resolution providing a more specific
overview of the government's language policy and planning activities was
passed. On July 26, 2007, President Rahmon passed a decree declaring 2008 as
the "Year of the Tajik Language", which led to the eventual formation of a working group on revisiting and revising the language law. Later in 2009, the president referenced language issues in public and political speeches, concluding
that the language law should be changed so that only Tajik would be used in
state documents and official correspondence, thereby continuing to increase

both its utility and its official symbolic value. This law was passed on October 5, 2009 and "confirmed Tajik as the state language and the only language to be used officially in the course of law, in administration, and in the economy" (Landau and Kellner-Heinkele 2011: 179).

Regarding education, the Constitution guaranteed all citizens free compulsory education (Article 41; Law about Education in Tajikistan 2004). Table 8.5 provides an overview of the Tajikistani education infrastructure.

Table 8.5: Overview of the Tajikistani Education System

Levels of education	Length of study (years)	Age	Educational institution
Preschool	1–6	1–6 (7)	Kindergarten, nursery
General	11	7–18	General secondary schools, gymnasiums,
Primary	4	7–11	lyceums
General basic	5	11–16	
General secondary	2	16–18	
Professional	Varies	16+	Vocational schools, centers, technical
Primary	1–4		colleges, colleges, special secondary
Secondary	2–4		schools, universities, academies, institutes
Higher education	4–6		
Post-diploma			Master, doctoral, other post-graduate work

Source: MoE (2005: 7)

The Law on Education was adopted on December 27, 1993 and has been amended five times between 1994 and 2003, with the current form having being adopted in 2004 (MoE 2005). Similar to the experiences of the Central Asian republics in the 1990s, Tajikistan also partnered with a number of non-governmental organizations (NGOs) and inter-governmental organizations, e.g., UNICEF, USAID, the Aga Khan Foundation, Open Society, Asian Development Bank and World Bank, to rebuild various sectors including education (Abdushukurova 2008; Silova and Steiner-Khamsi 2008). These partnerships helped the Tajikistani MoE produce its strategic plan (2005) which was influenced by the various donor agencies which helped shape the government's education agenda as seen in the discourse used throughout the document. Discourse from the World Bank's Poverty Reduction Strategy Paper, the United Nations' Millenium Development Goals, and UNESCO's Education for All initiatives was referenced and used throughout the strategic plan.

2.3 Changes for minorities

As aforementioned, during the Soviet times, all of the schools and educational institutions of the Tajik Soviet Socialist Republic (SSR) followed the same educational standard and instructions, which were produced and provided by different SSRs (e.g., all Kyrgyz schools received textbooks and curriculum from the Kyrgyz SSR). The MOI for ethnic Russian, Uzbek, Kyrgyz and Turkmen minorities were their native languages respectively, with an emphasis placed on the learning and mastering of the Russian language and literature. After the collapse of the Soviet Union, Kyrgyz schools in Murghab continued to follow the curriculum and educational programs developed by the MoE of the Kyrgyz Republic (Niyozov 2001). In 2000, however, this changed when the Tajikistani MoE required all schools (regardless of nationality) to follow the curriculum and standards which it set. This included becoming familiar with emergent Tajik national history, literature, and being able to demonstrate Tajik language proficiency (Kazimzade 2011; Khan 2003).

Although the state language is Tajik, the Constitution maintains that schooling can be conducted in other languages and that populations have the freedom to choose the MOI where numbers warrant (Article 8). Currently, general secondary education in Tajikistan is offered in Tajik, Russian, Uzbek, Kyrgyz, and Turkmen (the minorities with the largest officially recorded numbers of other language speakers as seen in Tables 8.2 and 8.3). However, regardless of the school's MOI, as the state language, Tajik must be taught in schools, along with Russian and a foreign language, which are also compulsory subjects in all ethnic minority schools.

2.4 General education curriculum and standards for minorities

According to the curriculum set out by Tajikistan's MoE for the 2009–2010 academic year, separate curricula for the ethnic Uzbek, Kyrgyz and Turkmen schools were delineated (MoE 2009) (Table 8.6). The curricula prescribed the school subjects and hours to spend in each subject for all grades. Consequently, all school textbooks have to correspond to the course learning outcomes and topics that are prescribed by the MoE.

Table 8.6: The MoE Curriculum for Primary Education in Uzbek, Turkmen and Kyrgyz Schools (AY2008–09)

Subject category	Subject titles	Grades				Total hours
		1	2	3	4	
Philology	1. Uzbek, Turkmen and Kyrgyz Languages	10	10	8	8	36
	2. State Language (Tajik)	–	2	2	2	6
	3. Russian Language	–	2	2	2	6
	4. Foreign Language	–	–	2	2	4
Mathematics	5. Mathematics	5	4	4	4	17
Science	6. Science	–	–	–	2	2
Technology	7. Manual Training	2	2	2	2	8
Art	8. Music	1	1	1	1	4
Physical training	9. Physical Training	2	2	2	2	8
		20	23	23	25	91

Source: MoE (2009)

As seen in Table 8.6, the greatest proportion of class hours is spent in language classrooms (e.g., Kyrgyz) and mathematics. Note that students start their Tajik language courses in second grade, hours per week.

Table 8.7 provides an overview of the curriculum and contact hours in basic education.

Table 8.7: Curriculum of Basic Education in Uzbek, Turkmen and Kyrgyz Schools (AY2008–09)

Subject category	Subject title	Grades					Total hours
		5	6	7	8	9	
Philology	1. Uzbek, Turkmen and Kyrgyz Languages	3	3	3	2	2	13
	2. Uzbek, Turkmen and Kyrgyz Literature	2	2	2	2	2	10
	3. State Language (Tajik)	2	2	2	2	2	10
	4. Russian Language	2	2	2	2	2	10
	5. Foreign Language	2	2	2	2	2	10
Social science	6. History of Tajik Nation	1	2	2	2	1	8
	7. Common History	1	1	1	1	1	5
	8. Basic of Law	–	–	–	1	1	2
Mathematics	9. Mathematics	4	4	–	–	–	8
	10. Algebra	–	–	2	2	3	7
	11. Geometry	–	–	2	1	1	4
Technology	12. Technological Information (Computer)	–	–	1	1	1	3
Science	13. Chemistry	–	–	–	2	2	4
	14. Physics	–	–	2	2	2	6
	15. Biology	2	2	2	2	2	10
	16. Ecology	–	–	–	–	1	1
	17. Geography	–	1	2	2	2	7
Art	18. Drawing	1	1	1	1	1	5
	19. Music	1	1	–	–	–	2
Physical training	20. Physical Training	2	2	2	2	2	10
Technology	21. Manual Training	1	1	1	1	1	5
		24	26	29	30	31	141

Source: MoE (2009)

According to the state curriculum, Russian language classes were supposed to start in grade two and foreign language in third grade. In basic school (or lower secondary school), Kyrgyz students were required to take 21 subjects, which included two hours of class for Tajik language per week as prescribed for Russian and foreign language. It is worth noting that children attending non-Tajik MOI schools are supposed to acquire a total of four languages (i.e., the language of their nationality, Tajik, Russian, and a foreign language).

At the general secondary school level (upper secondary), the curriculum prescribed two hours of class for Tajik language per week in Kyrgyz schools. Table 8.8 provides an overview of the requirements for secondary education.

Table 8.8: Curriculum of Secondary Education in Uzbek, Turkmen and Kyrgyz Schools (AY2008–09)

Subject category	Subject titles	Grades 10	11	Total hours
Philology	1. Uzbek, Turkmen and Kyrgyz Languages	2	2	4
	2. Uzbek, Turkmen and Kyrgyz Literature	3	3	6
	3. State Language (Tajik)	2	2	4
	4. Russian Language	3	3	6
	5. Foreign Language	2	2	4
Social science	6. History of Tajik Nation	1	1	2
	7. Common History	1	1	2
	8. Human Rights	1	1	2
Mathematics	9. Algebra	3	3	6
	10. Geometry	2	2	4
Technology	11. Technological Information (Computer)	2	2	4
Science	12. Chemistry	2	2	4
	13. Physics	3	3	6
	14. Biology	2	2	4
Physical training	15. Physical Training	2	2	4
	16. Military Training	1	1	2
		32	32	68

Source: MoE (2009)

Kyrgyz schools in the Murghab district must follow this prescribed curriculum and subjects. Teachers are required to teach these topics and subjects and schoolchildren have to acquire knowledge on the prescribed subjects in the curriculum.

In one perspective, the continued allowance of minority language schools can be seen as promoting inclusion and being promotive. However, sometimes, this can have other effects by limiting the long-term choices that are available to students. For example, students who want to go to university in Tajikistan must take a university entrance and school exit exam. This exam is conducted in Tajik. Applicants to any civil service jobs need to be proficient in Tajik. And increasingly, Tajik is being utilized in other areas, e.g., legal courts (Landau and Kellner-Heinkele 2011). In this way, the allowance of Kyrgyz MOI without providing adequate Tajik language support can produce a gatekeeping effect for non-Tajik minorities by limiting the different career and education options that are available to them in certain sectors.

What was interesting about the MoE's (2005) strategic plan is that it made very little reference to language, culture, and nationality. The report attributes low educational participation to poverty (MoE 2005: 10). Relatedly, targeted objectives are related to infrastructure development, e.g., developing and reno-vating the school infrastructures to include access to clean drinking water, central heating and gender-separate washrooms, providing support for poor students, providing textbooks for students, and increasing teacher salaries (MoE 2005; UNICEF n.d.). Later, the report describes schools at their respective levels. For secondary schools, the report states that in particular, rural schools are more impacted by their local governments and their budgets and notes that needs and resources range across districts (MoE 2005).

The report also candidly noted that poverty (as reflected in families being unable to pay for books, clothes, shoes) and poor physical school infrastructure (seen in lack of heat and clean water) have worked as disincentives for students to attend school, particularly in rural areas and especially in the winter (MoE 2005: 14). In general, it was reported that all schools suffered from lack of access to (1) any resources and (2) in particular, quality resources (MoE 2005). Amidst discussions about poverty alleviation and economic improvement, it is worth noting that the language used in the report was careful not to mention particular ethnolinguistic groups or nationalities.

According to the MoE (2005: 18-19), education reforms were "aimed at up-dating the education system, ensure equal access to education, address gender issues in education, improve the quality of education, and address the issue of poverty reduction through increased levels of literacy of the population." The MoE (2005: 23) mission statement for this strategic plan was "to ensure the effective and efficient delivery of education services and access to relevant and quality education for all."

In a more specific outline of the different objectives, under the third strategic goal ("To ensure quality of the educational services delivered at all levels in accordance with Education for All goals and Millenium Development Goals"), there was a note which stated that there was a need to "work out plan of publishing textbooks, teaching methodological manuals, according to the needs, including languages of instructions" (MoE 2005: 33). This was the first mention of language or languages at all in the entire document. Under the strategies for objective 3.2, there was an item that stated "Develop a plan and agreements for the implementation of annual training of teachers at pedagogical higher schools in countries which are ethnical [sic] Motherland for national minorities living in Tajikistan (Kyrgyzstan, Uzbekistan, and Russia)" (MoE 2005: 34) (Table 8.9).

Table 8.9: Language or Culture-Related Action Items

Strategic goal	Objective	Action item(s)
3. "To ensure quality of the educational services delivered at all levels in accordance with 'Education for All' goals and Millenium Development Goals" (p. 33)	3.1. Upgrade the content of state standards, curricula, textbooks and teaching manuals (p. 33).	"Work out plan of publishing textbooks, teaching methodological manuals, according to the needs, including languages of instructions" (p. 33).
	3.2. Ensure pre-service and in-service training for pedagogic staff and training of personnel in the education system in accordance with the new requirements (p. 34).	Develop a plan and agreements for the implementation of annual training of teachers at pedagogical higher schools in countries which are ethnical Motherland [ethnic Motherland] for national minorities living in Tajikistan (Kyrgyzstan, Uzbekistan, and Russia)" (p. 34).
4. To ensure the equitable access to basic education and merit-based access to other levels of education (p. 35).	4.1. Support children who have limited access to education in accordance with PRSP, RT (p. 35).	Develop regional programs for the development of the system of pre-school upbringing and learning by 2010 with regard to national, social, cultural, and demographic characteristics (p. 35).

3 Methodology

In order to look at how macro-level language and education policies and planning efforts have impacted the Kyrgyz community in Murghab, data was collected through 43 interviews (structured, semi-structured, and informal). These interviews were conducted between September 2010 and July 2011. While most of the interviews were conducted in Kyrgyz, seven was in Russian and one in English. The interviews were recorded with the participants' consent. These interviews helped to provide insight into the participants' thinking, attitudes, opinions, and perceptions regarding this topic. The participants were stake-holders in the education system including: various district and regional education authorities, policy-makers, Kyrgyz school administrations, teachers, students and their parents. Translated excerpts from the interviews highlight and/or illustrate the themes and topics which emerged from the transcripts.

4 Teaching and learning Tajik in Kyrgyz-medium schools

4.1 Access to textbooks and teachers

Although two hours of Tajik language class is prescribed for each grade in the national curriculum for students attending minority language MOI schools, Kyrgyz schools in Murghab usually spend three hours for Tajik language class per week so that students become more proficient at the Tajik language. One education specialist in the Murghab DED commented that

> To learn a language is a difficult process, specially, when only two hours are spent per week. To be a successful language learner, it takes more time and frequent practice. There-fore, we permitted to have one more additional hour for teaching of the State language (Tajik) in Kyrgyz schools. (MR1, personal communication, 15 September 2010)

However, the Tajik language textbooks for non-Tajik schools that are available contain vocabulary translations, which are in the Russian and Uzbek languages. Russian and Uzbek vocabulary translations create problems for Kyrgyz language teachers and children to successfully learn the Tajik language. The following interview with a Tajik language teacher from an urban school describes these types of problems. Interestingly, the teacher was ethnically Tajik but taught in a Kyrgyz MOI school.

> It is really difficult to teach Tajik language for Kyrgyz children for following reasons: (1) the textbook content is very difficult which is designed for children who already speak Tajik language. For example, for grade two, textbook starts with expressive reading of texts and songs while Kyrgyz children even do not know yet Tajik alphabet by heart; and (2) vocabulary translations are given in Russian and Uzbek languages that make more problematic teaching process. Especially, primary class children do not understand both Russian and Uzbek translations. Therefore, I have to explain in Kyrgyz language topic names and main points. (FT1, personal communication, 20 September 2010)

In a different instance, due to the difficult content of Tajik language text-books for Kyrgyz students, Tajik language teachers decided to use textbooks in the following way: Textbooks for the second grade would be used for fourth grade, the grade three textbooks for grade five, the grade four textbook for six and so on, ending with grade nine textbooks being used for grade 11. This meant that grades two and three did not have any grade-appropriate Tajik language textbooks. This not only illustrates the difficulty of the content but it also reflects the difference in access to textbooks between urban and rural schools. One rural teacher noted

> We have no textbooks for grades two and three, since it is decided to use the textbooks for these grades for upper grades. For grade two, mainly we work with pictures and posters. Based on curriculum requirements for Tajik language, I do all my best to teach Tajik language, but it is really difficult. (FT2, personal communication, 5 October 2010)

Another teacher from an urban school shared that s/he just continued using an old textbook for grades two and three, which was basically a Tajik language textbook for Russian schools published during the Soviet period. But since only this teacher owned this book, this resource was only used in this one classroom.

The third challenge for Tajik MOI language education is the general shortage of teachers. In most cases, Tajik language is taught by teachers whose area of expertise is not the Tajik language. If Kyrgyz schools have no specialized Tajik language teachers, they will try to find Tajik or Kyrgyz teachers who speak Tajik. For instance, three of the research interview respondents were non-specialized teachers. One teacher was specialized in Russian language, the second in chemistry-biology and the third in history. They graduated from Tajikistani universities where they became proficient in the Tajik language.

4.2 Access to other activities and resources

Children from urban schools had more opportunity to attend additional Tajik language classes outside of school. For example, among project participants, some urban schools had organized Tajik language circles in response to parents and schoolchildren who wanted to learn the language better. Usually, they were run by Tajik language teachers and held three classes per week. Every month parents would pay anywhere from five to 10 Tajik somoni per student (about $1.05–2.10 USD at the time of publication). One Tajik language teacher who also taught in one of these language circles described it like this.

> Our Tajik language circle was organized upon the request of schoolchildren and their parents. I have additional classes for them on Monday, Friday, and Saturday. Our program is very flexible and again based on children's request and interest I designed a program myself. I started to teach from Tajik alphabet, basic of grammar explanation, and have many practical dialogues with them. (FT3, personal communication, 16 March 2011)

On the other hand, school children from rural schools had limited or no opportunity to participate in these types of additional Tajik language circles. During a field visit to one rural school, it was found that in the 2009–2010 academic year they organized some additional classes for Tajik language. This meant that students would have four (every Saturday) additional classes per month. In the end, however, this particular rural school did not organize a Tajik language circle in 2010.

Because of the lack of exposure to Tajik speakers, Tajik language classrooms and teaching/learning materials, despite wanting to learn the language, Kyrgyz students are disadvantaged if they want to pursue higher education, where Tajik is essential to being able to pass the entrance exams. One urban school Tajik language teacher mentioned that

> There is a big interest of students to learn Tajik language in our school. Many students want to speak and write in Tajik language. They want to continue their higher education in Tajikistan universities, therefore, they have to speak Tajik language [to enter to Tajikistan universities]. (FT4, personal communication, 22 November 2010)

Some Kyrgyz schoolchildren were able to successfully learn the Tajik language. These schoolchildren generally worked hard and took additional classes. According to an education specialist from Murghab DED, these schoolchildren had good results in district-level education competitions among all of the Kyrgyz and Tajik schools in 2009.

> Last year (in 2009) we had annual competition among all schools and schoolchildren in Murghab district. They competed with each other in all school subjects. Some Kyrgyz students had good results in Tajik language too. They had very good dictation and essay results in Tajik language, equally with Tajik students. (MR2, personal communication, 25 September 2010)

However, what should be noted is that their academic success was attributed to the extra resources these students (and their families) had access to and not the provisions available to them through the public education system.

The absence of a language immersive environment conducive to communicating to native speakers can be challenging for any language learner. Another particularity about Murghab is that the local Tajik populations speak a variety of dialects, e.g., Shugni, Wakhi and Bartangi. There are very few standard Tajik language speakers that reside there. The Kyrgyz language is spoken everywhere since the majority of the Murghab district population are ethnic Kyrgyz. One Tajik language teacher in a Kyrgyz MOI school commented,

> Our government and education authorities should not compare us [Kyrgyz schools] with other ethnic minority schools. Other ethnic minorities in Tajikistan have no problem with Tajik language. For example, all Uzbek and Kyrgyz students from Jergetal district freely speak Tajik language, because they live among the native Tajik speakers. From the childhood they [other ethnic minorities] mastered in Tajik language. Here, [in Murghab district] we have not native speakers to communicate in Tajik language. (MR3, personal communication, 9 April 2011)

Another Tajik language teacher from urban Kyrgyz MOI school added an interesting point about the successful learning of Tajik language. She said

> My students work really hard. They have many Tajik language vocabularies and expressions; they can recite Tajik songs and poems. Even if they cannot understand everything, they can read texts from the books. I think and I am sure that if my students spend at least one month among native speakers, they quickly become fluent in Tajik language. (FT5, personal communication, 23 November 2010)

As seen earlier in this chapter, students have three hours of Tajik language class in schools, and additional courses are more easily accessible primarily by those living in urban areas. But successful language learning requires more hours and more practice. As one Russian language teacher from a Kyrgyz MOI school observed, during the Soviet times, Kyrgyz MOI schools had five hours of Russian language and two hours of Russian literature class per week. In contrast, Kyrgyz schools now have only three hours of integrated Tajik language and literature class per week. Tajik language teachers argue that having three hours of Tajik language class, which last for 45 minutes, is not enough to teach and learn the Tajik language.

> My students already learned the words and expressions used in everyday class. They know a lot of Tajik words and expressions. They can learn by heart the given tasks, but unfortunately, cannot freely retell and express their opinion. If you ask additional questions, they cannot answer. I think they need more classes and more practice. Out of all possible efforts and possibilities we try to teach and help them to learn Tajik language enough good. (FT6, personal communication, March 10, 2011)

While talking to different teachers, administrators and students during the field work phase in Kyrgyz MOI schools, it became clear that there was great interest in learning the Tajik language. Teachers, students and parents alike acknowledged that it is really important to learn the Tajik language. They understand that the learning of the Tajik language from schools enables Kyrgyz students to successfully pursue their higher education from Tajikistani universities, and in the future to have an opportunity for career development in their home country. One education specialist who had extensive work experience in Kyrgyz MOI schools said,

> We [Kyrgyz schools] must to obey laws, political decisions and other educational require-
> ments of Tajikistan. It is our duty. Today, even if we have problems with school textbooks,
> teaching materials and shortage of teachers, we must make all our efforts to provide good
> knowledge and learn Tajik language. (MR4, 25 September 2010)

Among the project participants, there were some Kyrgyz families who were able
to send their children to a Tajik MOI school. As one Kyrgyz father who sent his
two sons to Tajik school shared,

> I decided to send two of our junior sons to Tajik school. We wanted that our sons to learn
> good Tajik language. It is good for their future career. During the Soviet times who spoke
> good Russian language was hired easily for good jobs, but now our children need to know
> Tajik language. (KF, personal communication, 10 November 2010)

4.3 Discussion

Before discussing the particularities of the Kyrgyz experience in Murghab,
it should be noted that the challenges discussed are primarily resource and
infrastructure-related (i.e., lack of textbooks, resources, and teachers) and are
not unique to MBAP but is true throughout the Tajikistani education system.
For example, data from the MoE (2005) shows that after the civil war, Tajikistan
experienced brain drain particularly in the education sector (Figure 8.3).

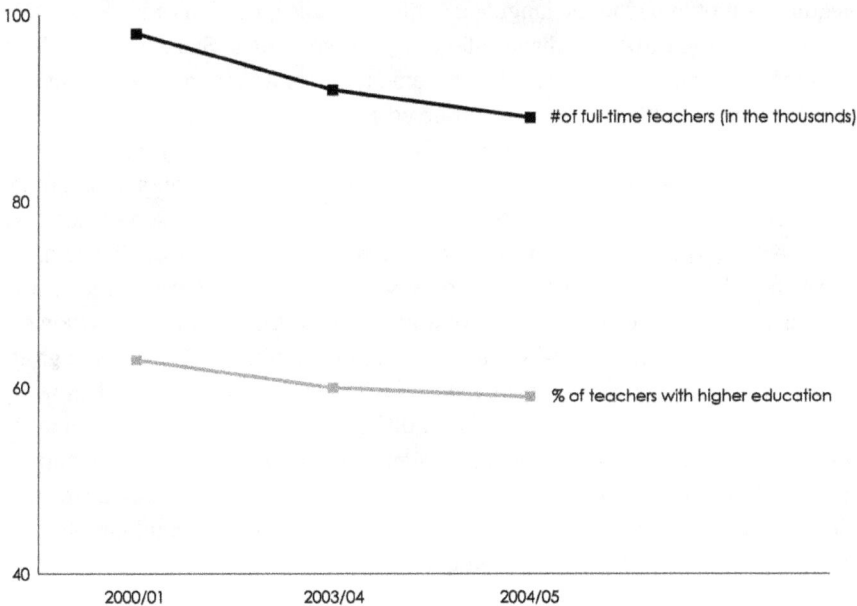

Figure 8.3: The total number and the percentage of teachers with degrees in higher education
Source: MoE (2005)

This massive migration of educators from the country can be attributed to a number of factors, including the fact that the "average salary of a primary school teacher today is lower than the per capita income of the country, which at the time the report was written 724 *somoni* (approximately $124 USD) (MoE 2005). Consequently, this was reflected in a 2003–04 statistic, where 35.7% of teachers had a secondary education degree (general or specialization) or had not completed a higher education degree (MoE 2005).

While looking at systemic challenges situates local experiences, examining other features, e.g., socio-economic, cultural, and linguistic attributes, allows researchers to consider what other attributes should be seen as salient in understanding how public policies are implemented and how social change is being shaped. Schermerhorn (1979: 81) observed "Centripetal tendencies refer both to cultural trends as acceptance of common values, styles of life, etc... Conversely, centrifugal tendencies among subordinate groups are those that foster separation from the dominant group or from societal bonds in one way or another. Culturally this most frequently means retention and presentation of the group's distinctive tradition in spheres like language, religion, recreation, etc." (as cited in May 2008). In the case of the Tajikistani government, while its language policy can be seen as centripetal, it has taken a more centrifugal approach in its education policies. Khan (2003: 77) noted that across the Central Asian republics "the requirement of knowing the language of titular ethnic groups in order to get state positions has led to the indigenization of state structures. State language laws and their implementation have thus become tools for an ethnocentric policy."

Moreover, as Khan (2003: 74) observed in the Central Asian, post-independence, nation-state building process, "The paradox is that in trying to preserve their own national cultures under the conditions of globalization and standardization, the governments of these countries do not notice that sometimes they themselves assume a standardizing role... refusing the right of diasporas to have their own ethnic identity and to be what they are." However, the Kyrgyz case is also an interesting example of a government that is not actively homogenizing or assimilating a particular ethno-linguistic minority but is, through its minimal support, can be considered complicit in the production of growing inequality in those communities. This is different from cases in post-colonial or developed countries that take a more assimilationist approach toward minorities (May and Hornberger 2008). Thus, amidst the broader, systemic challenges that students going through the education system face, minority students face an ever-increasing burden to avoid being left behind.

5 Conclusion

This chapter explored the educational experiences of Kyrgyz students attending Kyrgyz MOI schools in Murghab (MBAP). The study found that there is a shortage of necessary teaching materials, an insufficient number of qualified teachers, and an insufficient amount of time allocated for Tajik language classes. Despite this, Kyrgyz MOI schools and teachers are doing their best in order to implement national curriculum requirements and provide students with accurate knowledge.

Moreover, the Kyrgyz experiences provided in this section challenge frequently made assertions is regarding assimilation in post-Soviet, Central Asian contexts. As Landau and Kellner-Heinkele (2011) asserted that the government is implementing a process of "nation-state building focusing on state language" and concluded that this is at the expense of the minority languages, which are consequently neglected. However, the examples provided in this chapter demonstrate that Kyrgyz stakeholders in Murghab are not discontent with their Kyrgyz language capacity; rather, they are dissatisfied with their limited access to the dominant language, Tajik. The Kyrgyz case shows that processes of creating new national identities in Central Asian (and post-Soviet) contexts is more nuanced than often appears when simply looking at macro level policy discourse. This is all the more complicated by the fact that it is unclear what is being revived or created and for what purpose, since "national revival for a titular ethnos is considered by Central Asian authorities as the revival of past power and past roles" where the "past becomes even more real than the present" (Khan 2003: 70). These types of tensions that run throughout macro-level policies and how they are implemented (or not) in local communities provide interesting insight into how multi-scaler socio-political policy changes are experienced. Moreover, the post-Soviet context provides different cases to examine ideas regarding the dynamic between dominant and minority populations that have typically been written about in post-colonial or in developed, Western contexts.

References

Abdushukurova, Tatiana. 2008. The latecomer syndrome. Beyond project implementation toward an education policy think tank in Tajikistan. In Iveta Silova & Gita Steiner-Khamsi (eds.), *How NGOs react. Globalization and education reform in the Caucasus, Central Asia, and Mongolia*, 191–210. Bloomfield, CT: Kumarian Press.

Kazimzade, Elmina. 2011. In the margins: Minority education in Central Asia. *Khazar Journal of Humanities and Social Sciences* 14. 5–20.

Khan, Valeriy S. 2003. On the problem of revival and survival of ethnic minorities in post-Soviet Central Asia. In Birgit Schlyter (ed.), *Prospects for democracy in Central Asia*, 69–80. Istanbul: Swedish Research Institute in Istanbul.

Landau, Jacob M. & Barbara Kellner-Heinkele. 2011. *Language politics in contemporary Central Asia. National and ethnic identity and the Soviet legacy.* New York: I.B. Tauris.

May, S. 2008. Language education, pluralism, and citizenship. In Stephen May & Nancy H. Hornberger (eds.), *Language policy and political issues in education* [Encyclopedia of Language and Education, Vol. 1], 15–29. New York: Springer.

Ministry of Education of the Republic of Tajikistan, The [MoE]. 2005. The national strategy for education development of the Republic of Tajikistan. Dushanbe, Tajikistan. http://planipolis. iiep.unesco.org/upload/Tajikistan/Tajikistan%20Education%20Plan%202006-2015.pdf (accessed January 2014).

Niyazov, Sarfaroz. 2001. *Understanding teaching in post-Soviet, rural, mountainous Tajikistan: Case studies of teachers' lives and work.* Toronto, Canada: University of Toronto dissertation.

Niyazov, Sarfaroz. 2011. Revisiting teacher professionalism discourse through teachers' professional lives in post-Soviet Tajikistan. In Iveta Silova (ed.), *Globalization on the margins. Education and postsocialist transformations in Central Asia*, 287–312. Charlotte, NC: Information Age Publishing.

Olimov, M.A., & Saodat Olimova. 2002. Ethnic factors and local self-government in Tajikistan. In Valery Tishkov & Elena Filippova (eds.), *Local governance and minority empowerment in the CIS*, 235–262. Budapest: Open Society Institute.

Schermerhorn, Richard A. 1979. *Comparative ethnic relations: A framework for theory and research.* Chicago: University of Chicago Press.

Silova, Iveta. 2009. *Private supplementary tutoring in Central Asia: New opportunities and burdens.* Paris: UNESCO.

Silova, Iveta & Gita Steiner-Khamsi. (eds.). 2008. *How NGOs react. Globalization and education reform in the Caucasus, Central Asia, and Mongolia.* Bloomfield, CT: Kumarian Press.

UNICEF. (n.d.). Country profile. Education in Tajikistan. Retrieved from http://www.unicef.org/ ceecis/Tajikistan.pdf (accessed January 2014).

Ruth Bartholomä

9 The Construction of the Tatar Nation in the Debate About the Introduction of Latin Script in the Republic of Tatarstan

Abstract: This chapter examines the construction of nation-building in language policy discourse by focusing on the role of script change in the introduction of a Latin script in the Republic of Tatarstan (Russian Federation). The choice of a certain alphabet can create emotions like a feeling of the unity of a nation or the necessity of distancing the own group from another; language policy thus serves as a mean for nation-building. Scripts are, as Sebba (2007: 39) stressed, "particularly powerful identity markers, as they often have associations with particular secular and – especially – religious cultures, and this may evoke strong positive or negative reactions." This was the case with the planned script change for Tatar. This change was intended approximately 15 years ago, but was forbidden at the federal level of the Russian Federation. In the discourse about these events, different connotations and ideas of a Tatar nation were expressed. In contrast to similar processes among other speech communities, the situation was and is complicated by the fact that Tatarstan is part of the Russian Federation and has only limited possibilities to pursue its own policies as the script change example shows. The aim of this chapter is to show that the shift from Cyrillic to Latin evoked strong reactions at different levels. By examining the discourse, it becomes clear that the idea of one Tatar nation united by – amongst other factors – a common language and script was and still is existent; nevertheless, it often remains unclear who is included in the idea of a "Tatar nation".

Keywords: Tatar script reform; language policy; nation-state building

1 Introduction

In the 1990s, the Republic of Tatarstan (Russian Federation) planned to change its script system from a Cyrillic alphabet that had been used for the Tatar language since 1939 to a Latin script. The introduction of a Latin-based alphabet had been the object of long-lasting discussions which resulted in the adoption of a law at the republican level in 1999 (Minnullin et al. 2006). The law stated that the new script was to be introduced over the course of the next years. This step caused serious resistance at the federal level and resulted in a change of the Russian Federation's Language Law (Minnullin et al. 2006: 74–75). In the broader debates about these events, it soon became clear that many people did not see the introduction of a Latin script as a decision based on linguistic reasons as Tatar politicians and intellectuals argued. Rather, opponents viewed the decision as political, arguing that a script change would be a potential danger to the unity of the Tatar nation as well as a threat to the unity of the Russian Federation.

This chapter analyzes some of the conflicting discourses about script change with a focus on arguments that refer to different aspects of nation-building. It first provides an account of the script choice developments in the Republic of Tatarstan, followed by a brief overview of the theoretical and methodological background. The article then continues to analyze the discourses that can be seen in statements from different sources and positions of the debate. The following issues of dispute are discussed in detail: How did the discussants view the attempt to introduce a Latin script? Was it a step of dissociation from the Russian element, i.e., an attempt to strengthen the perception of the own group as different from another? And has the awareness of the importance of this issue changed over the years? How was the Tatar nation constructed, and which arguments were used in the debate around how the introduction of a Latin script would contribute to – or disrupt – the idea of Tatar nation-building, especially with the consideration that two-thirds of Tatars of the Russian Federation do not live in the Republic of Tatarstan? This chapter argues that changes in the relation between the federal and the local levels have caused a shift in the discourse of distancing, while the issue of Tatars living outside Tatarstan remains important.

2 Background information

After the dissolution of the Soviet Union, and the subsequent independence of the former Union Republics (FSU) in the beginning of the 1990s, several of the newly emerged states that had a Turkic language as their titular language switched from a Cyrillic to a Latin alphabet.[1] And in other states, script changes

---

1 Azerbaijan "adopted a modified version of the Latin script for the official Azerbaijani alphabet" in 1991 (Garibova 2009: 17). Uzbekistan adopted the "Law on the Introduction of the Uzbek Alphabet Based on Latin Graphics" in September of 1993 (Azimova 2008: 194). And Turkmenistan "began crafting the 'New National Turkmen Alphabet' in the early 1990s"

were discussed. Choosing a Latin script was considered a highly symbolic step. Clement (2008: 171) called the newly adopted Latin alphabet for Turkmen an "emblem of independence," and Wright (2004: 51) highlights that "[c]hanging alphabet can also be a way of reaffirming identity or signaling new orientations." Thus, an alphabet change is not only a purely linguistically based decision, but a step which is both influenced by and influences political and social debates and discourses. However, script choice had an additional role in the nation-building processes of the newly established republics. Selecting the titular language as the state language and choosing a different script system created a new awareness for the often long neglected language. At the same time, this also created a group mentality within the titular nation centered on the language of the ethnic group.

A script change was also planned for the Tatar language in the Republic of Tatarstan at the end of the 1990s. There was a fundamental difference between Tatarstan and the other primarily Central Asian republics: Tatarstan was (and is) not an independent state. However, as a *субъект* or, more precisely, an autonomous republic of the Russian Federation, it had attained a degree of autonomy in the course of the 1980s and 1990s. The Tatars, the titular nationality of this republic (also called "Volga Tatars" or "Kazan Tatars"), are the largest minority group within the Russian Federation. Even though about 62% of the Tatars who live in the Russian Federation reside outside the borders of the Republic of Tatarstan, they still constitute the majority of the republic's population.[2] According to the 2010 Russian Census, Tatarstan's population is about 53.2% Tatar, 39.7% Russian, and the rest is composed of other ethnicities, e.g., Chuvashs, Udmurts and others (Federal'naia Sluzhba Gosudarstvennoi Statistiki 2010).

After presenting its Declaration of Independence in 1990 (Verkhovnyi Sovet Respubliki Tatarstan 1990), Tatarstan's leaders pursued emancipation from the Russian Federation. They did not sign the Federation Treaty in 1992, as did President Yeltsin and almost all other federal unit leaders. However, in 1994, Tatarstan and Russia signed a power-sharing agreement (Cashaback 2008: 251),

---

(Clement 2008: 175). Interestingly, despite the fact that two different conferences took place in order to create a common alphabet, each state introduced its own version of the Latin script, unlike the situation in the 1920s, when a "unified alphabet" was established for all Turkic languages of the Soviet Union (Garipov and Faller 2003: 180; Sebba 2006: 105).

2 The exact data from the 2010 Russian Census are: 5, 310, 649 Tatars in the Russian Federation (Federal'naia Sluzhba Gosudarstvennoi Statistiki 2010); 2, 012, 571 Tatars in Tatarstan (Federal'naia Sluzhba Gosudarstvennoi Statistiki 2010). According to these figures, 37.9% of the Tatars living in the Russian Federation resided in the Republic of Tatarstan; the others mostly lived either in those units of the Russian Federation adjacent to Tatarstan, in Siberia, or in large cities like Moscow and St. Petersburg.

which made comparatively far-reaching concessions.[3] But as the Tatar historian Iskander Giljasov (1994: 199) emphasizes, the often-used keyword "sovereignty" did not mean complete and unlimited autonomy from the Russian Federation; rather, this reflected Tatarstan's ambitions to increase its political status. This was also stressed by Mintimer Shaimiev, the president of Tatarstan, who explained that the referendum which was held in 1992 "was not about secession from Russia and was not intended to change the territorial integrity of the Russian Soviet Federative Socialist Republic" (Suleymanova 2010: 46). Nevertheless, in the referendum on Tatarstan's status, 61.4% of its population supported the demand that Tatarstan should be a "sovereign state, subject to international law" (Suleymanova 2010: 46).

Regarding its language policies, the first decisions taken in the 1990s focused on equalizing the official status of the Tatar and Russian languages. With the Tatarstan's Declaration of Independence, passed in 1990, and its Constitution, which was passed in 1992, both Tatar and Russian were declared official languages equal before the law and were to be used in public authorities, local authorities and public institutions (Minnullin et al. 2006: 205).[4] Different programs and measures, e.g., a Language Program from 2004–2013 (Respublika Tatarstan 2005), were aimed at reaching symmetric Russian-Tatar bilingualism within all parts of the population. The law decreed the teaching of Russian and Tatar in general education schools in equal measure (Respublika Tatarstan 2005: 7–8), as well as the provision of financial means for the realization of the program (Respublika Tatarstan 2005: 18–35).

Discussions about the introduction of a Latin alphabet for Tatar re-arose in the years around the dissolution of the Soviet Union. However, this debate about script systems was nothing new. By the end of the 19th century, script issues were already being debated among Tatar intellectuals as well as among other Turkic-speaking peoples (Baldauf 1993). In the early 1920s, the Tatar Autonomous Soviet Socialist Republic reformed the Arabic alphabet and established a Latin-based alphabet which was called *Yaŋalif* [new alphabet].[5] The *Yaŋalif*

---

3 For further consideration of the Tatar efforts to gain autonomy, see Graney (2001) and Derrick (2008, 2010). Additionally, Bowring (2010) describes the Russian constitutional system with regard to the "asymmetrical" relation between the republican and the federal levels and Cashaback (2008) analyzes the language policy of the Republic of Tatarstan referring to this aspect.

4 The Russian term used in the Constitution (государственный язык), as well as the Tatar expression (дәүләт теле) include the connotation of state (государство in Russian and дәүләт in Tatar) (Respublika Tatarstan 1992). To avoid the term "state language" since Tatarstan is not an independent nation-state, the expression "official language" was chosen here.

5 The Tatar ASSR was officially created in May 1920 and its borders are identical to that of the Republic of Tatarstan today.

contained 33 letters and a sign and was used from 1927 to 1939. (Alparov et al. 1934: 4)

That script change to a Latin-based alphabet was not unique to Tatarstan, but occurred in most of the non-Russian minority languages and was part of the Soviet policy of коренизация [indigenization] of the different ethnic minorities in the Soviet Union. Even then however, a heated discussion arose. There were arguments in favor of the introduction of a Latin script focusing primarily on the internationality and the broad dissemination of this script for numerous languages of the world (Frings 2007: 78–79; Fierman and Garibova 2010: 432). The Latin script was considered a "symbol of modernity, of European-isation" (Haarmann 1995: 11), as well as the "alphabet of revolution" (Kreindler 1995: 192), the "alphabet of the Great October" (Fierman and Garibova 2010: 432), and a script change for Russian from the Cyrillic to a Latin alphabet was expected to happen shortly after (Glück 1984: 539; Kreindler 1995: 192).

Another aim of the 1920s alphabet reform was to replace the Arabic script, which was associated with Islam and especially religious texts. Arabic script had been used for the Tatar language for centuries before (Faller 2011: 118–124). Thus, conservative forces among the Tatars, i.e., Qadimists (from the Arabic *qadīm* [old]), "vigorously objected to any attempts at alphabetic reform and the use of Cyrillic or Latin scripts in relation to the Qur'an, Sunnah, or other sacred Islamic texts" (Yemelianova 1997: 560). Qadimists shared this view with a group of modernizers called the Djadidists (from the Arabic *ğadīd* [new]), who "favored a modernized form of Islam" and suggested several changes for the Arabic script, including additional diacritic marks, the introduction of a so-called "one-form script" with only one sign for each letter (in spite of the different forms in initial, medial and final position) and the "elimination of letters to write borrowed Arabic words which lacked phonemic significance in local languages" (Fierman and Garibova 2010: 431). But despite these objections, the script change took place quickly.

At the All-Union Turkological Congress in Baku in 1926, most of the delegates argued for a change to a Latin-based alphabet. Of the 117 delegates, 101 delegates voted for a corresponding resolution, seven against, and nine abstained (Crisp 1989: 26–27).[6] While the Tatar administration initially tried to delay the introduction of the Latin alphabet, mainly because they feared to be

---

6 According to Theodor Menzel (1927: 21), a German orientalist and participant of the Congress, the Tatar delegation consisted of 15 persons from Kazan, so at least one person of another delegation must have voted against the resolution or have abstained from voting, respectively. For a detailed account of the discussions about the script issue, as well as a German translation of the adopted resolution in favor of an introduction of a Latin script see Menzel (1927: 173–203).

cut off of what they perceived as a century-old tradition, reactions from Moscow signaled that this was understood as pan-Turkism and therefore as bourgeois nationalism, a dangerous accusation at that time (Frings 2007: 182–187; Garibova 2011: 275). As a consequence of this, the script change was decreed in August 1927 and implemented within a few months.

However, on May 5, 1939, the Supreme Soviet of the Tatar ASSR passed a decree replacing the *Yaŋalif* with a Cyrillic script based alphabet (TASSR Verxovnьj Sovetь Prezidiumь 1939). This new alphabet consisted of 38 letters, including six which were not part of the Cyrillic script that was used for the Russian language. These six characters – representing three vowels and three consonants – were grouped at the end of the alphabet and expressed sounds specific for Tatar (Wertheim 2012: 71–73). In contrast to the 1920s, the issue at the late 1930s was rarely publicly discussed (Frings 2007: 353) and no official campaign in support of the Cyrillic script was launched as it was 10 years before with the Latin script (Crisp 1989: 28). Therefore, it is more difficult to speculate about the motives for this change and arguments in favor or against it. In general, most researchers assume that one of the main aims was "russifying the non-Russian languages" (Bruchis 1984: 135–136) or "to distance the writing of 'Soviet' Turkic languages from Turkish and bring them closer to Russian" (Fierman and Garibova 2010: 432). This is also thought to be the cause for other measures of that time, such as the introduction of compulsory teaching of the Russian language in schools in 1938.

An argument in favor of the script change often expressed by Soviet scholars in later years was that the non-Russian peoples had disadvantages in acquiring the Russian language because they had to learn two different alphabets, i.e., a Latin-based alphabet for their mother tongue as well as the Cyrillic script for Russian. In their opinion, this problem had been solved by the introduction of Cyrillic-based scripts for the non-Russian peoples (Tenishev et al. 1968: 268). Frings (2007: 378–380) criticized these views and spoke of a "self-fulfilling prophecy." Thus, in an atmosphere of fear and insecurity during and shortly after the Stalinist purges, the Tatar ASSR's administration decided to change the alphabet for fear of consequences in case that change came too late. Moscow saw no reason for forbidding this step, which was, in turn, an affirmation for the republic's administration (Frings 2007: 396).

During the rest of the Soviet era, the use of a Cyrillic alphabet for the Tatar language remained unchanged. It was only in 1997 that a law concerning the rearrangement of the Cyrillic letters used for Tatar was adopted. With this law, those six specific signs which were used for Tatar sounds were rearranged to stand next to those signs from which they were derived or to which they were most similar (Minnullin et al. 2006: 216–218). However, in that same year, at the second World Congress of Tatars in Kazan, the deputies passed a resolution demanding the transition to a Latin script. This resolution was quickly moved to the political arena and on September 15, 1999, the parliament of the Republic of Tatarstan adopted the law "On the restoration of the Tatar language based on the Latin alphabet" (Minnullin et al. 2006). This *восстановление* [restoration] was "meant to link Tatarstan's 1999 law with the period from 1927 to 1939 when Tatar was based on a Latin script" (Cashaback 2008: 265).

However, it was not the original *Yaŋalif* which was reinstated but rather an alphabet with partly new elements which consisted of 34 letters, some of which were provided for Tatar-specific sounds. While a couple of the special characters were already in use in the *Yaŋalif*, a few were borrowed from other Latin-based Turkic language scripts, e.g., the Turkish language alphabet. To reference the historical link, this alphabet was called *Yaŋalif–2* at times (Khisamova 2004; Sokolovskii 2007: 14).

In contrast to the previous script changes which took place with almost no preparation and were implemented within a very short period of time, this transition was to happen during the course of 10 years. The law would go into force on September 1, 2001 but until September 1, 2011 both the Cyrillic and the Latin alphabets would be used in parallel. A special program for the introduction of the Latin script was to be prepared by Tatarstan's administration by March 1, 2001 (Minnullin et al. 2006: 218–220). The law was adopted by the parliament of the Republic of Tatarstan and was valid for the Tatar language within the borders of the Republic of Tatarstan.

The enthusiasm for the new script was reflected in the appearance of Tatar words written in the Latin alphabet in public places during those years. One can still find several street signs or name plates on different types of institutional buildings in Kazan today. Examples of this type of sign can be found at the National Library (Figure 9.1) and another at the Kazan Kremlin (Figure 9.2).

As seen in Figures 9.1 and 9.2, besides the English and the Russian texts, one can see the Tatar expression, *bøtenønya mirasi* [World Heritage] in Latin script at the top of the sign.

In contrast to the enthusiasm in large parts of the Tatar community in Tatarstan, the adoption of the law provoked strong resistance in Moscow as well as within other parts of the Russian Federation. Soon afterwards, a broader debate began in which both journalists and politicians accused Tatarstan of "a kind of treachery" (Cashaback 2008: 267; Garipov and Faller 2003: 180; Sebba 2006: 107). The measure was seen as an attempt to separate Tatarstan from the rest of the Russian Federation, as well as a potential threat to the unity of the Tatar nation. In 2002, the Russian Duma adopted an amendment to Article 3 §5

Figure 9.1: Sign at the National Library of the Republic of Tatarstan, Kazan

of the Federation's Language Law, which stated that the Federation's state language, i.e., Russian, as well as the republics' official languages had to be written in an alphabet based on the Cyrillic script (Minnullin et al. 2006: 74–75). A group of State Duma deputies under the leadership of Kaadyr-ool Bicheldei from Tuva, the Deputy Head of the Committee on Nationalities Affairs, supported the bill, arguing that "script reform posed a threat to Russia's integrity and consequently the federal government needed to act to prevent republics from falling into the sphere of influence of foreign states" (Cashaback 2008: 266–267). The amendment was accepted by both houses of the parliament in November 2002 (Sebba 2006: 108) and signed into law by President Putin a month later (Cashaback 2008: 267).

Figure 9.2: Sign at the Kazan Kremlin

In response, in 2003, the Constitutional Court of the Republic of Tatarstan published a ruling in which it declared that "competence over script reform belongs to the republic" and "that the power granted by the federal constitution to establish a state language 'necessarily assumes a right to determine its alphabet'" (Cashaback 2008: 268). The Constitutional Court of the Russian Federation came back with a ruling handed down in November 2004, where it decided that "since the status of state languages of republics affects [...] the rights and freedoms of the citizens of the Russian Federation in the spheres of education and culture, it cannot be an area of exclusive republican competence" (Cashaback 2008: 269). Therefore, the Constitutional Court's conclusion was that the decision about which alphabet should be used for Tatar (and other official languages within the Russian Federation) was a federal issue.

Approximately 10 years have passed since the ruling and the decision appears to be final and accepted by the government of the Republic of Tatarstan. In the law "On the use of the Tatar language as official language of the Republic of Tatarstan," which was adopted in January 2013, the use of the Cyrillic script for Tatar on the basis of the federal law is specified in Article 3 (Respublika Tatarstan 2013). Nevertheless, the issue remains an emotional and controversial one as seen later in this chapter.

3 Theoretical framework: Language and nation, language policy and nation-building

Language and language planning often plays an important role in nation-building processes. In the Soviet Union, language planning was an integral part of Soviet nationality policies and was extended to the languages of all peoples living in the state. For Soviet language planners, language was "the most prominent factor for the definition of nationality" (Haarmann 2006: 2414). *Natsional'nost'* [nationality] referred more broadly to individual ethnic groups. As Haarmann (2006: 2414) stresses, the Soviet view of language as a key element "not only reflected the typical European tradition of the nineteenth century, it was also in accordance with the reality of self-awareness among most of the speech communities in the Soviet Union". This view remains prevalent, even though the members of different speech communities may no longer be fluent in the language which they and others regard as their mother tongue (i.e., the titular language of their ethnic group).

Nevertheless, it is necessary to differentiate between two types of "nation," both of which should be considered an "imagined" group, as Anderson (1998: 6–7) put it. On one hand, a "nation" can be a group based on the idea of an "ethnos", i.e., a number of people with certain common characteristics. Ethnic identity here means the identification (or self-identification) of a person as a member of a certain ethnic group, or, as in the case which is considered in this chapter, mainly as "Tatar" or "Russian". Edwards (2009: 162) defines ethnic identity as an

... allegiance to a group – large or small, socially dominant or subordinate – with which one has ancestral links. There is no necessity for a continuation, over generations, of the same socialisation or cultural patterns, but some sense of a group boundary must persist. This can be sustained by shared objective characteristics (language, religion, etc.), or by more subjective contributions to a sense of "groupness", or by some combination of both. Symbolic or subjective attachments must relate, at however distant a remove, to an observably real past.

On the other hand, a nation can be seen as a group of people belonging to a certain state, i.e., a civic nation. The civic model of the nation is, according to Smith (1991: 9), "in the first place, a predominantly spatial or territorial conception." Smith (1991: 14) continues, stating that "A nation can therefore be defined as *a named human population sharing an historic territory, common myths and historical memories, a mass, public culture, a common economy and common legal rights and duties for all members*" [italics in original]. In the case of Tatarstan, this can be the identification with the Russian Federation (i.e., Russian in the sense of the Russian word *российский*), or, respectively, with the Republic of Tatarstan, i.e., a Tatarstani identity (Bartholomä 2010: 171–172).

In this broader framework, language can be, but is not necessarily an important element in the (self-) definition of a nation, as Fishman (2007: 330) argues, writing

However, just as ethnicity itself is perspectival and situational, and therefore variable in saliency, so the link between language and ethnicity is also variable. For some (and in some historical and situational contexts) language is the primary indicator and expression of their own and another's ethnicity; for others, language is both merely marginal and optional (i.e., detachable) vis-à-vis their ethnicity (and that of "others" as well).

Thus, language can be (but is not necessarily) used not only as a marker for the own group, but, as Fishman points out, for defining the ethnicity of others. Therefore, here it is crucial to show "both that *they* are different from *us* and that *we* are different from *them*" (Tabouret-Keller 2007: 316; italics in original). In this way, language plays a key role as element of distancing from "others" as well as a factor for defining and limiting the own group.

For Tatarstan, language has been seen as an important marker for the titular nation in the definition of the own group, especially in contrast to the dominant Russian element. In an ethnosociological research study, of those Tatars who answered the question, "What binds you to people of your nationality?" the majority (over 70%) "consider[ed] language the principal feature of an ethnic group" (Musina 2004: 82). Even though sociolinguistic studies showed a decreasing proficiency in Tatar as well as diminishing areas in which the language is functional among Tatars (Musina 2004: 83–84), it is still seen by an overwhelming majority to be the mother tongue, irrespective of the actual knowledge or use of the language. In the 2010 Russian census, 92.4% of the Tatars in the Republic of Tatarstan stated that Tatar was their mother tongue, while only 5.7% named Russian (Federal'naia sluzhba gosudarstvennoi statistiki 2010).[7] By claiming Tatar to be one's mother tongue, this person differentiates himself from the "other" group. Another attempt to create a distance from the Russian element was often seen in the efforts to introduce the Latin script for Tatar in the late 1990s, as the Cyrillic script was frequently equalized with "Russian".

4 Methodology

After situating the language debate in its historical context, the rest of this chapter focuses on analyzing the script change debate vis-à-vis qualitative discourse analysis of statements from various sources. This chapter is the result of a research project that was more broadly aimed at analyzing constructions of identity in debates about language policy by comparing developments in the Republic of Tatarstan (Russian Federation) and the Republic of Kazakhstan.[8] Although the Russian Federation's Constitutional Court ruling in 2004 seemed to be the end of the matter and the issue did not attract special attention over the past years, we addressed the issue in interviews which were conducted for the project. We did so in order to see how the former events and reactions are being perceived after several years, and the respondents commented on it in an interesting and clear way.

Statements were extracted from different texts as well as comments which were expressed in sociolinguistic interviews. For this chapter, excerpts from

---

7 This result may have been affected by the fact that only one language can be named as mother tongue. Already in 1991, a sociolinguistic investigation showed differing results: In this investigation, it was explained that mother tongue and ethnic belonging did not necessarily have to coincide. When given the possibility to name both Tatar and Russian as mother tongue, 6.8% of the Tatars named Russian as their mother tongue, 66.5% Tatar and 26.1% Tatar and Russian equally (as cited in Rom-Sourkova 2004: 206–207).

8 The findings in this chapter were part of an interdisciplinary project that was conducted at the Institute of Slavic Studies (project leader: Prof. Dr. Monika Wingender; assistant: Dipl.-Phil. Aksana Braun) and the Professorship of Turkology (project leader: Prof. Dr. Mark Kirchner; assistant: Dr. Ruth Bartholomä). Within the project, the regions of Kazakhstan and Tatarstan were taken into account from a Slavistic as well as from a Turkological point of view. For more information in German, see https://www.uni-giessen.de/cms/fbz/fb04/institute/turkologie/abgeschlossene%20projekte_n/russ-turk-sprachgem.

official documents, statements from newspaper and magazine articles and open letters, which revolved around script choice in Tatarstan and were published in the late 1990s and early 2000s, were considered. The individuals who engaged in public debate about the script change were either public figures or journalists.

Out of the sociolinguistic interviews which were taken during two fieldtrips to Kazan in September 2010 and in April/May 2011, statements from three interviews with four respondents were considered for this chapter.[9] The interviewees were persons working in the Republic of Tatarstan's Ministry of Education, in the Kazan municipal education department, and a journalist. They were chosen because they all were not only affected by the official language policy as individuals, but had to take certain decisions in their work regarding language which have the potential to influence other people and/or the discourse on language as well (i.e., are disseminators). To maintain participant anonymity, they are identified simply by their nationality, birth year, and gender. By analyzing these different sources, different perspectives were taken into consideration. The politicians and journalists who contributed to the debate and, respectively, the interviewees articulated statements which reflected their perceptions of their own group, as well as their idea of how language (and script as a part of it) could contribute to, or detract from, the building of a Tatar nation. Thus, this provided insight into how the language-nation-state relationship was publicly being constructed and conceptualized by these different actors.

Discourse in this chapter is generally situated with a Foucaultian perspective. Jung (1996: 463) defined "discourse" as "*Gesamtheit der Beziehungen zwischen thematisch verknüpften Aussagekomplexen* [the entity of relations between thematically associated statements]." Furthermore, according to Jung (1996: 461), a "statement" is "*eine bestimmte thematisch definierte Behauptung* [a certain, thematically defined proposition]." A "text" contains statements that relate to different discourses (Jung 2000: 25). In this chapter, texts include not only written but also verbal statements.[10]

---

9 In total, 43 semi-structured interviews with 56 interviewees were conducted in Kazan during these two fieldtrips. Not all participants gave their opinion about the introduction of a Latin script for Tatar, and some confined themselves to short statements with a mere reproduction of facts. The project interviews for Kazakhstan (Almaty and Astana) took place in March 2011. These interviews, not considered for this chapter, were semi-structured as well and based on a similar questionnaire, with only some questions slightly modified to be in line with some specific conditions in Kazakhstan, different from Tatarstan (laws, certain formulations in language programs, etc.).

10 In this project, text was defined broadly, i.e., "[b]asically, we thus subsume all communicates (notwithstanding the modality or mediality) as *texts*, if they are perceived as being concluded and autonomous to a significant degree" (Spitzmüller and Warnke 2011b: 91; italics in original).

An analytical framework based on the DIMEAN-model by Jürgen Spitzmüller and Ingo Warnke (Spitzmüller and Warnke 2011a, 2011b) is used in this chapter for analysis. DIMEAN is an acronym for *Diskurslinguistische Mehrebenen-Analyse* [Discourse-Linguistic Multilayered Analysis]. Within the DIMEAN-model, a distinction is drawn between three different basic layers (Spitzmüller and Warnke 2011b: 81–82). Besides the "intratextual layer"[11] and the "agent layer",[12] the "transtextual layer (knowledge)" represents the "actual goal of discourse analysis" (Spitzmüller and Warnke 2011b: 86) and is the result of "a research for *patterns* that emerge from multiple texts" (i.e., "*recurrent* phenomena) (Spitzmüller and Warnke 2011b: 86–87; italics in original). In this chapter, the main focus of analysis is the transtextual layer; thus the discussion focuses on specific discourse patterns, e.g., the use or avoidance of personal pronouns and certain keywords in order to reach certain goals, as well as repeating argumentations within the discourse.

5 The script change debate: Nation-building within arguments for and against a Latin alphabet

As aforementioned, earlier discussions about the introduction of a Latin script for Tatar was a controversial issue and led to heated debates. Several types of arguments reoccurred during the conflict, both in favor of and against a change of the script system for Tatar. Although they cannot be treated in detail here, due to space limitations, the most important will be examined briefly.

Some of the reasons that were articulated in favor of the script change included:

---

11 The intratextual layer (texts) is the starting point and aims at investigating "concrete manifestations... discursively contextualised linguistic practices" (Spitzmüller and Warnke 2011b: 82). In this project, this is done by an investigation on the word, proposition and text level.
12 The agent layer (actors) is "deliberately positioned between text and discourse" in the scheme provided by the authors, as the actors "can be regarded as 'mediators' between intra- and the transtextual strata" (Spitzmüller and Warnke 2011b: 85). Or, as the authors put it, "the discursive practices (and hence the texts) are on the one hand shaped by the discursive dispositions, but on the other hand, the discourse itself is also influenced by the practices of the actors" (Spitzmüller and Warnke 2011b: 85).

- History, i.e., the fact that Tatar was written in a Latin script in the late 1920s and 1930s.
- Philology, i.e., the belief that a Latin script was more suitable to express specific Tatar sounds than the Cyrillic alphabet that was currently in use.
- Associations of "modernity", i.e., the perception of Latin alphabets as progressive scripts, amongst other reasons due to the association with computers and the internet and terms like "globalization".

In contrast, the opponents of a script change often referred to the following arguments:
- Cultural, i.e., the fear of losing large parts of the cultural heritage.
- Economic, i.e., the financial costs and the expenditure of time which would incur in the event of a script change.
- Habitual, i.e., the fact that, after decades of using the Cyrillic script, a readjustment would be difficult.[13]

Hereon after, the focus in the following sections is the question of how various discussants constructed their idea of a "Tatar nation" (i.e., how they debated issues connected with questions of nation-building). Did they see the process of drawing a border to the Russian element as a necessary prerequisite of building a Tatar nation? Should the Tatar nation be built by distancing itself from "the other" or was this something considered unimportant in the debate? And whom did those who took part in the discussion include in their concept of a Tatar nation, and how did they discuss the fact that bigger parts of the Tatar community do not live within the borders of the Republic of Tatarstan but in other parts of the Russian Federation? How did this group take part in the debate?

5.1 Dissociation from "the other"

As mentioned earlier, in the process of creating an increased awareness for the own group, distancing from "the other" is an important element. This can also be observed in the discourse about the introduction of a Latin script in Tatarstan which is seen as a step of distancing from "the Russian." However, it was interesting to see that this distancing approach was used more frequently by the Russian side to prevent alphabet change rather than on the Tatar side.

---

13 As mentioned before, these arguments cannot be considered here (Khasanova 1997; Sebba 2006: 109–116).

Opponents of a script change claim that the change was intended as a sign of separatism, while supporters of the Latin script sometimes mention the necessity of drawing a boundary towards the dominating Russian element.

At the end of the 1980s and the beginning of the 1990s, there was a growing awareness among the Tatars about their own culture and traditions. This resulted in the desire to distance themselves from the Soviet legacy and the idea of a homogenous Soviet people that had developed in the 1930s. Through a convergence (*сближение*) of all the Soviet peoples and their cultures, a fusion (*слияние*) would be reached so that nationality, language, etc. would not continue to play a major role (Grenoble 2003: 42). This international proletarian class identity "would transcend national, ethnic, linguistic, and other boundaries" and seems at first sight a paradox to the politics of *коренизация* ("indigenization", i.e., the building of nations and languages in the 1920s). However, "according to the Bolshevik version of Marxist ideology, history was to progress in stages, and nations had to be created before proceeding to the stage of history where an 'international proletarian' identity would unite the entire world" (Fierman and Garibova 2010: 427). A shift came in the mid-1930s, when "the Soviet international identity promoted by the USSR's leaders became filled with a Russian component" (Fierman and Garibova 2010: 428).

Despite the fact that a dominant position for the Russian language was not planned in the Soviet Union, as was mentioned explicitly at times, Russian played a key role in practice, especially after Khrushchev's educational-reform laws of 1958/1959 (Kreindler 1982: 13). Therefore, as Faller (2011: 110) observes "for Tatars and other non-Russians, attitudes about orthography [in the 20th century] have served as significant indicators of integration into and disaggregation from the Russian-run state, while Russians' attitudes towards different alphabets indicate fluctuations in the strength of collective xenophobia." This tendency of drawing up frontiers was an important motive for the introduction of a Latin script in post-Soviet times, not only in Tatarstan but in several successor states as well. Fierman and Garibova (2010: 447) posited that it as an anti-Russian sentiment that informed or was "undoubtedly part of the reason for the eagerness to adopt Latin letters." The motive could be found in several statements in the debate that took place in Tatarstan in the end of the 1990s and the early 2000s. Nevertheless, it seems that it is more often perceived by the opponents of a script change outside the borders of the Republic of Tatarstan than it was explicitly mentioned by the supporters of such a step within the republic.

One example for this tendency to see the introduction of a Latin script as a step towards creating a distance to the Russian element is found in an article quoting Vladimir Alpatov, the Director of the Institute of Linguistics of the

Russian Academy of Sciences. Alpatov stated that "[...] the question of a script change is advantageous for those who wish 'to alienate Tatarstan from Russia'" (*"Перевод письменности"* 2001). Sycheva (2001), a well-known writer and journalist living in Moscow, also criticized the intended script change in Tatarstan. Sycheva cited two letters to the editor of the newspaper *Вечерняя Казань* [Evening Kazan] in which such this attitude becomes clear,

> The readers of the newspaper *Вечерняя Казань*, the only sharp-tongued mass media, were at a loss: Why, if the authorities are on fire for the national rebirth in such a way, should one not return to the Arabic alphabet, after all, the Tatars used it for a whole millennium, and the Koran, as is known, is created in Arabic. Gul'nara Kalganova writes: "The motives of a change to the Latin script today do not only lie in the correctness of pronunciation, but it is more a political step, the wish to separate from Russia".[14] Another reader, L. Urasin, adds: "It is not necessary to change the Cyrillic script for a Latin one because Latin is more suitable. The whole trouble is that the Russians use the Cyrillic script. It's their language. If the Turks used the Cyrillic script and Russia was Latinized, no problems would emerge. We would thank Allah that he gave us the Cyrillic script."[15]

In contrast, supporters of a change to the Latin script saw this step as an instrument to impede assimilation to the Russian culture among Tatars. Sokolovskii (2007: 34) cited an interview with Damir Iskhakov, a thought-leader regarding Tatar cultural revitalization. The correspondent of the Tatar newspaper *Восточный экспресс* [Orient Express] asked Iskhakov, "Is not the Latin script to which we are switching also surely a powerful factor impeding assimilation?" Iskhakov answered, "I think that Latin script raises the status of the Tatars as a national group. It 'marks' them as a part of the developed Western world. And this too may slow down assimilatory processes" (cited in Sokolovskii 2007: 22). By mentioning the "developed Western world", Iskhakov puts the Latin script in a broader context and implicitly mentions the distance which a script change could create, i.e., more Western and less Russian.

Though clearly prominent in the discourse in the beginning of the 2000s, in our interviews which were conducted between 2010 and 2011, discursal distancing from the Russian element was rarely mentioned by both sides of the debate. Only one interviewee mentioned this and this example is more the reproduction of an (maybe even unjustified) accusation of those who were opposing a script change for Tatar, but not the expressed of the wish of the interviewee herself, a

---

14 Kalganova is a lecturer at Kazan Federal University who wrote her dissertation about the functioning of the Tatar language in the sphere of business (http://kpfu.ru/Gulnara.Kalganova) (accessed 05/11/2014).

15 Quotes from newspaper articles and official documents as well as statements from the interviews have been translated from the original Russian.

young journalist. She purported that "... there was, of course, I think, some political attempt, nevertheless, to get rid of the Russian language, to get rid of the Russian culture, well, that is why they stopped, I think, they saw in it a political underlying reason" (personal communication, Tatar, *1976, female). While she speculates that there was some political motivation, from her comment it is unclear whether there really was a reason for being suspicious of the Russian element.

In other interviews this motive was not expressed at all. The reason for not mentioning the wish to create a distance to the Russian element might be in a changed reality today, i.e., the altered relation between Kazan and Moscow. Tatarstan is closer connected with the Russian Federation than was the case in the 1990s. Soon after the breakup of the Soviet Union, as Derrick (2010: 356–357) pointed out, "Tatarstan operated largely independently of Moscow... redeveloping a Tatar culture influenced by centuries of Russification", while "large anti-Muscovite demonstrations were common." However, in the years following Vladimir Putin's rise to power as president of the Russian Federation in 2000 (and despite his politics of recentralization of the Russian Federation) "no significant protests have taken place in the republic since Putin assumed power; and Kazan's political elite, including a president who once brazenly defied Moscow, has not attempted to mobilize its citizenry against the center" (Derrick 2010: 357). After the ruling of the Constitutional Court of the Russian Federation in 2002, no wider protests took place. This change in the relation between the local and federal level, as well as the *de facto* dominance of the Russian element which is still prevalent in Tatarstan in many fields today, may contribute to the fact that distancing seems to be an option not realizable and therefore is mentioned more rarely.

5.2 One script for one Tatar nation? Attitudes inside and outside of Tatarstan

Another aspect of Tatar nation-building which was often connected to the issue of the introduction of a Latin script for Tatar arose from the fact that, as mentioned earlier, only one third of ethnic Tatars in the Russian Federation live within the borders of the Republic of Tatarstan, while about two thirds reside in other units of the Federation. This caused problems regarding the question for whom the script change was planned and whom it would concern in practice. It soon became clear that the question could be extended to questions such as: who had the power to plan such a script change and, when talking about the "right of the Tatar nation to decide this issue," who defined the boundaries of this Tatar nation and how?

In the early 2000s, Tatars from other parts of the Russian Federation weighed on the debate, but they were often accused of being manipulated and used by federal authorities. Nevertheless, as Derrick (2010: 369) observed "Although it appears Moscow used the Tatar diaspora to inflame controversy, many Tatars living beyond the borders of Tatarstan indeed are anxious about being cut off from their contemporary national culture."

Despite this, Tatars of the Republic of Tatarstan took the leading role or, as Musina (2004: 77) puts it, "represent[ed] the principal focus of the *natsiia* [the Tatar nation]." This was due to the fact that the leadership of Tatarstan, to a certain degree, had the possibility to enact laws or decrees through which it could influence the language situation. According to Musina (2004: 77), "to a large degree, ethnosocial processes among Tatars within the republic determine the level, direction, and rates of development of the entire Tatar people." The Tatar authorities tried to include those Tatars who live outside the borders of Tatarstan by including a "Tatar language beyond the borders" component in its measures, e.g. the Language Program for the Years 2004–2013 (Respublika Tatarstan 2005: 21) explicitly mentioned both Tatar language use in Tatarstan and outside its borders.

In this debate, the issue of the Tatars living outside the borders of the Republic of Tatarstan led to heated discussions and provided a pretext for 10 deputies of the Russian parliament who opposed the script changed to place a draft which led to the adoption of an amendment to Art. 3, § 5 of the Federation's Language Law in 2002 (cf. Section 2) before the State Duma. Sokolovskii (2007: 18) describes the reason which led to the draft as follows:

> In the opinion of the draft law's authors, the arbitrary switching of the language of a titular people from one alphabet to another – by decision of the leadership of one constituent republic – violates the rights of representatives of this ethnic group who live outside "their" republic. "If we all – each of Rossiia's peoples – return to our old script," Deputy Bicheldei [deputy from the Republic of Tuva, RB] argued in justification of the necessity of the draft law, "then we shall destroy the unity of our peoples, the country's single educational space. And that is already a political question, a question of preserving Rossiia's integrity."

One example for the fierce debate is the September 14, 2001 open letter in the *Российская газета* [Russian Gazette] addressed to the Deputies of the Republic of Tatarstan (Khaibullov et al. 2001) and signed by Tatar intellectuals living throughout the Russian Federation, but outside the Republic of Tatarstan. With this letter, the signees militated against the change to a Latin alphabet for the Tatar language. The letter was debated controversially in the next months. It was reprinted by several newspapers released in the Republic of Tatarstan, mostly accompanied by comments containing strong criticism.

The language used in this letter is interesting. In almost every sentence, the authors use personal and possessive pronouns, such as мы [we] and наш [our]. The Russian adjective *родной*, was translated, depending on the context, as "native," "home," or, respectively, "our," or "our own" and was used quite often in connection with phrases like *татарский язык* [Tatar language], *культура* [culture] and *земля* [soil]. In addition, *историческая родина* [historical home-land] was also mentioned twice and lexical phrases denominating some kind of family relationship were used. On one hand, this is meant to address the readers of the letter in an emotional way. For example, in an appeal at the end of the letter, implored "With hope and optimism we appeal to you, dear ladies and gentlemen deputies, compatriots! Let us develop, and not destroy, improve, but not reshape our native Tatar language! Let us do it in such a way that our children understand what their fathers and mothers speak and write about!" (Khaibullov et al. 2001).

On the other hand, these kinds of phrases are used to express the authors' belonging to the Tatar nation in rather abstract contexts, and do not express real family affiliations. Thus, the authors used phrases like *мы, дети татарского народа* ["we, the children of the Tatar nation"] or *наша святая задача, как сынов и дочерей татарского народа* ["our holy duty, as sons and daughters of the Tatar nation"]. In this way, they also tried to evoke a sense of togetherness in the "other Tatars," the ones living within the boundaries of the Republic. The description of what exactly the "holy duty" consisted of could be understood as expressed here "Wherever we live, our holy duty, as sons and daughters of the Tatar nation, is to be united and to be spiritually indivisible in the name of the preservation of the nation, its integrity, in the name of the prosperity of the native culture!" (Khaibullov et al. 2001).

On the other hand, in official documents released by the Republic of Tatar-stan, the issue of Tatars living inside and outside the borders of Tatarstan was handled with care and often not mentioned explicitly. One example is an appeal by the parliament of the Republic of Tatarstan, which was written in November 2002 (Gosudarstvennyi Sovet RT 2002) and contained a petition to suspend the changing of the federal Law on Languages. The argumentation is nearly exclu-sively based on the legislature, i.e., the signees argued that language policy was the responsibility of the republics, that the addition of the new paragraph to the federal law "contradicts the Constitution of the Russian Federation" and that it is also incompatible with international legal acts. The appeal was written in using an objective voice, without any emotional reference to persons. In the entire document, not one reason for the introduction of a Latin alphabet for the Tatar language was mentioned. The authors' arguments were legislative. The issue of the Tatar population living outside the republic was also not mentioned. A reason for that may be the fact that the officials wanted to avoid accusations of separatism and causing ethnic tensions.

However, in our interviews, the issue of Tatars living outside the republic did emerge periodically. The first comment, made by a staff member of the Kazan municipality education department, explained why, apart from other reasons, the introduction of a Latin alphabet would be difficult. The public official stated that "All the more as there are many Tatars in other regions as well, not only in Tatarstan. Even more than there are Tatars in Tatarstan – statistically only 30%. Only 30% of the Tatars [live] in Tatarstan" (personal communication, Tatar, *1964, male; Tatar, *1979, male).

Another comment, made by a person working in the Department of Education of the Republic of Tatarstan, also pointed to the fact that there are many Tatars living outside the republic's territory:

> The reason why a Latin alphabet was of current importance and likely will be is that Tatars do live not only in Tatarstan. And very many Tatars who... and many, more than in our republic, live not only in the regions [i.e., of the Russian Federation], but abroad. And these Tatars don't have any other possibility to learn the language and communicate, than by the way of a Latin alphabet. That is, in this context, the Latin alphabet is used anyway. This approach which was suggested is another, they clearly do not learn the [Cyrillic] script and those tools which are accessible for them electronically, they do not allow, well, the use of the Cyrillic script, and they do not have a special necessity and this is a big problem for them. [...] That is, we give them our textbooks, and they cannot use them [to learn Tatar]. They would need [material] not in an [unfamiliar] language, but in Tatar language, but in a way that it is written in a [familiar] script. That is, so that they understand it and can learn in a familiar script. (personal communication, Tatar, *1952, male)[16]

This interviewee referred to a point which was often downplayed or overlooked by highlighting the fact that more Tatars live abroad (i.e., outside the Russian Federation) than live in Tatarstan. It is estimated that the number of Tatars all over the world is about eight million (Zakiev 2002: 354). According to the 2010 Russian Census, about 5.3 million of them live within the Russian Federation and of those, slightly more than two million live in the Republic of Tatarstan. This indicates that about 2.7 million Tatars live abroad in other FSU

---

16 The interviewee did not express his thoughts coherently and so, certain words were added in square brackets.

countries,[17] Europe, US, or Australia.[18] The question remains: do all these people with Tatar origin living abroad, especially those living in great distance to the Republic of Tatarstan, still regard the Tatar language as an important part of their identity and are willing to improve Tatar or maybe acquire it?

However, during the course of the interview, this interviewee changed his mind and added, thinking about the consequences such a step would have for the Tatars living outside the republic, but within the Russian Federation, by saying "And then, we do prepare textbooks, tutorials for children in Tatar schools in the regions of the Russian Federation. If we introduced a Latin alphabet, there would be absolutely no textbooks for them" (personal communication, Tatar, *1952, male).

A larger concern, namely that the introduction of a Latin script would inflict damage on the unity of the Tatars, was also expressed by President Shaimiev when he addressed the participants of the third World Congress of Tatars. He posed the following question,

> During the last Congress [the second World Congress of Tatars in 1997, RB] we made the decision to convert the Tatar language to a Latin script. The law on the restoration of the Latin alphabet for the Tatar language has not been canceled. Nevertheless, I myself have some doubts concerning the timing of the conversion, and this is connected with the preservation of the unity of our nation. [...] It could happen that Tatarstan shifts to a Latin script, but in the remaining territory of Russia, the Tatars will use a Cyrillic script. Doesn't that weaken our nation? (*"Выступление Президента"* 2002)

In the end, the issue played a great role in the discourse on the introduction of a Latin script for Tatar. The fact that a larger population of Tatars lives outside

---

17 Zakiev (2002: 354) explicitly named Uzbekistan, Kazakhstan, the Ukraine, Kyrgyzstan and Tajikistan. In this context, it is important to keep in mind that amongst the countries of the former Soviet Union, only a few have changed their script to a Latin alphabet, so that Tatars living in these other countries (e.g., Kazakhstan, Ukraine, etc.) are used to the Cyrillic script as the alphabet of the official language of the respective country (and Russian as an important language as well) just like it is the case in the Russian Federation.

18 Unfortunately, no data with the exact number of Tatars in the respective countries outside the former Soviet Union were available. Baskakov (2000: 455) gave a number of Tatars in the countries of the former Soviet Union as 42, 845, but did not have any data about Tatars living in other countries of the world, e.g., in Europe or Australia. According to the numbers given in Table III on a Tatar website (http://web.archive.org/web/20121318563800/http://www.kcn.ru/tat_en/politics/dfa/diaspor/diaspor.htm, accessed 05/11/2014), those numbers could in actuality be much lower. Furthermore, it is doubtable whether or not the knowledge of Tatar among the members of the Tatar diaspora is widespread; but certainly, the assumption is correct that they do not know the Cyrillic script, but the Latin letters. Those are in most cases used for the official language of the country they live in, but in some cases also for the writing of Tatar (Sebba 2006: 106).

of Tatarstan further problematizes the process of building a Tatar nation and is often used as an argument by opponents of the Latin script, especially by those expressing their concerns about the "unity of the Russian Federation" or the like. Nevertheless, supporters of the Latin alphabet keep this in mind as well when talking about their anxiety for the "unity of the Tatar nation" which, in their opinion, should be one inseparable entity.

6 Concluding thoughts

In this chapter, two elements of nation-building were considered. It turned out that the motives of "creating a distance" and "unity of the nation" have shifted over time. While the reality of the Tatar diaspora within and outside of the Russian Federation is still considered important and discussed, discoursal distancing of the Tatar nation from the Russian element seems to be less important than in the past. As previously mentioned, this is probably to a certain degree due to the fact that Tatarstan as part of the Russian Federation felt increasing pressure from the federal government which got stronger over the last few years, but did not cause serious resistance, even after the ruling that forbade the introduction of the Latin script. Derrick (2010: 369) explains the "mild response" with the "disconnect between Tatar state and Tatar nation"; another aspect is the fact that every citizen of Tatarstan is automatically a citizen of the Russian Federation as well and thus has a "Russian" (in the sense of the Russian российский) identity. This could be another reason why the issue of distancing from the Russian element is not that easy as it might have been at the beginning of the 1990s when the degree of autonomy and sovereignty for Tatarstan was considerably higher than it is today.

Concerning the introduction of a Latin script, the change of the relevant federal law in 2002 was a clear signal that the Russian Federation would not allow its subjects a grade of autonomy which was considered as a threat for the unity of the state. One interesting aspect that could not be touched in this chapter due to limitations of space is the fear which opponents of a script change often mentioned, namely the fear of some kind of influence from Turkey. To whatever extent this threat might be real or not, is not easy to evaluate. Unseth (2008: 1) sees "a language community's choice of script as a decision about how to visually represent their language, to represent their identity". In the case of Tatarstan, this choice was restricted from federal authorities. Nevertheless, debating about a script change might already be a good option to create some kind of consciousness for the own group and for the necessity of differentiating from "the other"; something that was and still is an important issue in the nation-building processes in post-Soviet regions where people are in search of their nation's identity. A comparison of similar debates and processes in different communities can provide interesting insights, as well as a closer look at opinions expressed by ethnic Tatars from outside the Republic of Tatarstan could give a hint about the significance the issues language and nation-building have in Tatar communities.

References

Alparov, Gibad, Salakh Atnagulov, & Shigap Ramazanov. 1934. *Правила орфографии татарского литературного языка* [Rules for the orthography of the Tatar literary language]. Kazan: Tatgosizdat.

Anderson, Benedict R. 1998. *Imagined communities: Reflections on the origin and spread of nationalism*, 8th edn. London: Verso.

Azimova, Nigora. 2008. Linguistic developments in post-Soviet Uzbekistan. In Ernest Andrews (ed.), *Linguistic changes in post-communist Eastern Europe and Eurasia*, 195–203. Boulder, CO: East European Monographs.

Baldauf, Ingeborg. 1993. *Schriftreform und Schriftwechsel bei den muslimischen Russland- und Sowjettürken (1850–1937): Ein Symptom ideengeschichtlicher und kulturpolitischer Entwicklungen* [Script reform and script change at the Muslim Turks of Russia and the Soviet Union (1850–1937)]. Budapest: Akadémiai Kiadó.

Bartholomä, Ruth. 2010. Religion und Sprache als Faktoren in der Identitätsbildung der Tataren (Republik Tatarstan, Russische Föderation) [Religion and language as factors in identity-building processes of the Tatars (Republic of Tatarstan, Russian Federation)]. In Sibylle Baumbach (ed.), *Regions of culture – regions of identity: Kulturregionen – Identitätsregionen*, 159–173. Trier: WVT Wissenschaftlicher Verlag Trier.

Baskakov, Nicolai. 2000. Татарский язык [Tatar language]. In G. D. McConnell (ed.), *Письменные языки мира. Языки Российской Федерации: Социолингвистическая энциклопедия* [The written languages of the world. Languages of the Russian Federation: Sociolinguistic encyclopedia], 436–477. Moscow: Academia.

Bowring, Bill. 2010. The Russian constitutional system: Complexity and asymmetry. In Marc Weller & Katherine Nobbs (eds.), *Asymmetric autonomy and the settlement of ethnic conflicts*. Philadelphia: University of Pennsylvania Press, 48–74.

Bruchis, Michael. 1984. The effect of the USSR's language policy on the national languages of its Turkic population. In Yaacov Ro'i (ed.), *The USSR and the Muslim world: Issues in domestic and foreign policy*, 129–148. London: Allen & Unwin.

Cashaback, David. 2008. Assessing asymmetrical federal design in the Russian Federation: A case study of language policy in Tatarstan. *Europe-Asia Studies* 60(2). 249–275.

Clement, Victoria. 2008. Emblems of independence: Script choice in post-Soviet Turkmenistan. *International Journal of the Sociology of Language* 192. 171–185.

Crisp, Simon. 1989. Soviet language planning since 1917–53. In Michael Kirkwood (ed.), *Language planning in the Soviet Union*, 23–45. London: Macmillan Press.

Derrick, Matthew. 2008. Revisiting "sovereign Tatarstan". *Journal of Central Asian and Caucasian Studies* 3(6). 63–86.

Derrick, Matthew. 2010. Contested autonomy: Tatarstan under Putin (2000–2004). *USAK Yearbook of International Politics and Law* 3. 355–382.

Edwards, John. 2009. *Language and identity: An introduction.* Cambridge: Cambridge University Press.

Faller, Helen M. 2011. *Nation, language, Islam: Tatarstan's sovereignty movement.* Budapest: Central European University Press.

Federal'naia Sluzhba Gosudarstvennoi Statistiki [Russian Federation Federal State Statistics Service]. 2010. *Итоги Всероссийской переписи населения 2010 года* [Results of the Russian census of 2010]. http://www.gks.ru/free_doc/new_site/perepis2010/croc/perepis_ itogi1612.htm (accessed 5 November 2014).

Fierman, William & Jala Garibova. 2010. Central Asia and Azerbaijan. In Joshua A. Fishman & Ofelia García (eds.), *Handbook of language and ethnic identity. Disciplinary and regional perspectives*, Vol. 1, 423–451. Oxford: Oxford University Press.

Fishman, Joshua. 2007. Language and ethnicity: The view from within. In Florian Coulmas (ed.), *The handbook of sociolinguistics* [Blackwell Handbook in Linguistics 4], 327–343. Malden: Blackwell.

Frings, Andreas. 2007. *Sowjetische Schriftpolitik zwischen 1917 und 1941: Eine handlungstheoretische Analyse* [Soviet script policy between 1917 and 1941: An action-theoretical analysis]. Stuttgart: Steiner.

Garibova, Jala. 2009. Language policy in post-Soviet Azerbaijan: Political aspects. *International Journal of the Sociology of Language* 198. 7–32.

Garibova, Jala. 2011. A pan-Turkic dream: Language unification of Turks. In Joshua A. Fishman & Ofelia García (eds.), *Handbook of language and ethnic identity: The success-failure continuum in language and ethnic identity efforts*, Vol. 2, 268–281. Oxford: Oxford University Press.

Garipov, Yagfar Z. & Helen M. Faller. 2003. The politics of language reform and bilingualism in Tatarstan. In Farimah Daftary & François Grin (eds.), *Nation-building ethnicity and language politics in transition countries* (LGI Books 2), 163–183. Budapest: Open Society Institute.

Giljasov, Iskander. 1994. *Tatarstan-Rußland: Innerstaatliche oder zwischenstaatliche Beziehungen?* [Tatarstan-Russia: Domestic or international relations?]. In Bernd Heidenreich, Klaus Heller & Eberhard Schinke (eds.), *Rußlands Zukunft: Vorträge eines gemeinsamen Seminars mit der Hessischen Landeszentrale für Politische Bildung* [Russia's future: Lectures of a joint seminar with the Regional Center for Political Education, Hessen], 195–204. Berlin: Duncker & Humblot.

Glück, Helmut. 1984. Sowjetische Sprachenpolitik [Soviet language policy]. In Helmut Jachnow, Klaus Hartenstein & Waltraud Jachnow (eds.), *Handbuch des Russisten: Sprachwissenschaft und angrenzende Disziplinen* [Handbook of the specialist of Russian studies: Linguistics and neighboring disciplines], 519–559. Wiesbaden: Harrassowitz.

Gosudarstvennyi Sovet Respubliki Tatarstan. 2002. Обращение Государственного Совета Республики Татарстан к Президенту Российской Федерации В. В. Путину [Appeal of the State Council of the Republic of Tatarstan to the President of the Russian Federation, V. V. Putin]. Republic of Tatarstan website. http://19972011.tatarstan.ru/?DNSID=01f9fad73 d22a986af089bebf113f351&node_id=1769 (accessed 5 November 2014).

Graney, Katherine E. 2001. Ten years of sovereignty in Tatarstan: End of the beginning or beginning of the end? *Problems of Post-Communism* 48(5). 32–41.

Grenoble, Lenore A. 2003. *Language policy in the Soviet Union.* Dordrecht: Kluwer.

Haarmann, Harald. 1995. Multilingualism and ideology: The historical experiment of Soviet language politics. *European Journal of Intercultural Studies* 5(3). 6–17.

Haarmann, Harald. 2006. Language planning: Graphization and the development of writing systems. In Ulrich Ammon, Norbert Dittmar, Klaus J. Mattheier & Peter Trudgill (eds.), *Sociolinguistics = Soziolinguistik*, 2nd edn., 2402–2420. Berlin: Walter de Gruyter.

Jung, Matthias. 1996. Linguistische Diskursgeschichte [Linguistic discourse history]. In Karin Böke, Matthias Jung & Martin Wengeler (eds.), *Öffentlicher Sprachgebrauch: Praktische, theoretische und historische Perspektiven* [Public language use: Practical, theoretical and historical perspectives], 453–472. Opladen: Westdeutscher Verlag.

Jung, Matthias. 2000. Diskurshistorische Analyse als linguistischer Ansatz [Discourse historical analysis as a linguistic approach]. *Sprache und Literatur in Wissenschaft und Unterricht* 86. 20–38.

Khaibullov, Airat-khazrat et al. 2001. Нам, татарам, не все равно [We, the Tatars, do care]. *Вечерняя Казань*, September 15, 2001. Republic of Tatarstan website. http://1997-2011. tatarstan.ru/?DNSID=17e3694ae6fb5c4fac7df3499d7d0a93&node_id=985 (accessed 5 November 2014).

Khasanova, Gul'nara. 1997. Language and sovereignty: The politics of switching to the Latin alphabet in Tatarstan. *Prism* 3(16). http://www.jamestown.org/single/?no_cache=1&tx_ttnews[tt_news]=19920&tx_ttnews[backPid]=219 (accessed 5 November 2014).

Khisamova, F.M. 2004. *Татарский язык: лингвистические основы возврата к латинице = Татар теле: Латин әлифбасына кайтуның фәнни нигезләре* [The Tatar language: The linguistic and scientific foundations of a return to the Latin alphabet]. Kazan: Shkola.

Kreindler, Isabelle T. 1982. The changing status of Russian in the Soviet Union. *International Journal of the Sociology of Language* 33. 7–40.

Kreindler, Isabelle T. 1995. Soviet Muslims: Gains and losses as a result of Soviet language planning. In Yaacov Ro'i (ed.), *Muslim Eurasia: Conflicting legacies*, 187–203. London: Frank Cass.

Menzel, Theodor. 1927. Der 1. Turkologische Kongreß in Baku [The first Turkological congress in Baku]. *Der Islam* 16. 1–76 and 169–228.

Minnullin, Kim, Timur Akchurin, Gulshat Baleyeva, & Evgeniy Sultanov (eds.). 2006. *Языковая политика в Республике Татарстан: политико-правовое регулирование* [Language policy in the Republic of Tatarstan: Political-legal regulations]. Kazan: Magarif.

Musina, Rozalinda N. 2004. Ethnosocial development and identity of contemporary Tatars. *Anthropology & Archeology of Eurasia* 43(2). 77–93.

Respublika Tatarstan [Republic of Tatarstan]. 1992. Конституция Республики Татарстан [The Constitution of the Republic of Tatarstan]. State Council of the Republic of Tatarstan. http://www.gossov.tatarstan.ru/konstitucia/ (accessed 5 November 2014).

Respublika Tatarstan [Republic of Tatarstan]. 2004. *Закон Республики Татарстан от 25 июня 2004. О государственных языках Республики Татарстан и других языках в Республике Татарстан: Государственная программа Республики Татарстан по сохранению, изучению и развитию государственных языков Республики Татарстан и других языков в Республике Татарстан на 2004–2013 году.* [The Law of the Republic of Tatarstan on the official languages of the Republic of Tatarstan and the other languages in the Republic of Tatarstan: The official program of the Republic of Tatarstan for the preservation, learning and development of the official languages of the Republic of Tatarstan and the other languages in the Republic of Tatarstan for the years 2004–2013]. Kazan: Tatarskoe Knizhnoe Izdatel'stvo.

Respublika Tatarstan [Republic of Tatarstan]. 2013. *Закон Республики Татарстан от 12 января 2013 года №1-ЗРТ. Об использовании татарского языка как государственного языка Республики Татарстан* [Law of the Republic of Tatarstan, January 12, 2013, №1-ZRT. About the use of the Tatar language as the official language of the Republic of Tatarstan]. *Rossiiskaia Gazeta.* http://www.rg.ru/2013/02/19/tatarstan-zakon1-reg-dok.html (accessed 5 November 2014).

Rom-Sourkova, Olga. 2004. *Die sprachliche Situation in der Russischen Föderation: Gesetzgebung und Wirklichkeit* [The language situation in the Russian Federation. Legislation and reality]. Berlin: BWV Berliner Wissenschafts-Verlag.

Sebba, Mark. 2006. Ideology and alphabets in the former USSR. *Language Problems and Language Planning* 30(2). 99–125.

Sebba, Mark. 2007. *Spelling and society.* Cambridge: Cambridge University Press.

Smith, Anthony D. 1991. *National identity.* London: Penguin.

Sokolovskii, S. V. 2007. Alphabets and elites: Script in contemporary Russia as a political symbol. *Anthropology & Archeology of Eurasia* 46(1). 10–35.

Spitzmüller, Jürgen & Ingo H. Warnke. 2011a. *Diskurslinguistik: Eine Einführung in Theorien und Methoden der transtextuellen Sprachanalyse* [Discourse linguistics: An introduction to theories and methods of transtextual language analysis]. Berlin: Walter de Gruyter.

Spitzmüller, Jürgen & Ingo H. Warnke. 2011b. Discourse as a "linguistic object": Methodical and methodological delimitations. *Critical Discourse Studies* 8(2). 75–94.

Suleymanova, Dilyara. 2010. International language right norms in the dispute over Latinization reform in the Republic of Tatarstan. *Caucasian Review of International Affairs* 4(1). 43–56.

Sycheva, Lidia. 2001. *Казанский дневник* [Kazan Diary]. *Молоко/Русское поле.* http://moloko.ruspole.info/node/40 (accessed 05/11/2014).

Tabouret-Keller, Andrée. 2007. Language and identity. In Florian Coulmas (ed.), *The handbook of sociolinguistics,* 315–326. Malden: Blackwell.

TASSR Verxovnьj Sovetь Prezidiumь. 1939. Tatarstan ASSR Verxovnьj Sovetь Prezidiumь Ukazь: Tatar Jazuьn Latin Alfavitьnnan Rus Grafikasь Nigzendəge Alfavitqa Kycery turьnda [Ukaz of the Supreme Soviet of the ASSR Tatarstan: About the shift of the Tatar script from the Latin alphabet to an alphabet on basis of the Russian script]. *Sovet Məktəbe* 5. 4–5.

Tenishev, Edkham, Ninel' Gadzheneva, Lyudmila Pokrovskaya, Gayoz Donidzye, Akhnef Yoldashev, Nikolay Baskakov, Anna Koklyanova, Kenesbay Mussayev, & Gennadiy Melnikov. 1968. Тюркские языки [Turkic languages]. In F.P. Filin (ed.), *Советское языкознание за 50 лет* [Soviet linguistics for 50 years], 250–275. Moscow: Nauka.

Unseth, Peter. 2008. The sociolinguistics of script choice: An introduction. *International Journal of the Sociology of Language* 192. 1–4.

Verkhovnyi Sovet Respubliki Tatarstan. 1990. *Декларация Верховного Совета Республики Татарстан от 30 августа 1990 г. N 334-XII. О государственном суверенитете Татарской Советской Социалистической Республики* [The declaration of the Supreme Soviet of the Republic of Tatarstan from August 30, 1990, No 334-XII. About the state sovereignty of the Tatar Soviet Social Republic]. Republic of Tatarstan. http://1997-2011. tatarstan.ru/?node_id=234 (accessed 5 November 2014).

Wertheim, Suzanne. 2012. Reclamation, revalorization, and re-Tatarization via changing Tatar orthographies. In Alexandra M. Jaffe, Jannis K. Androutsopoulos, Mark Sebba & Sally Johnson (eds.), *Orthography as social action: Scripts, spelling, identity and power,* 65–102. New York: Mouton de Gruyter.

Wright, Susan. 2004. *Language policy and language planning: From nationalism to globalisation*. Basingstoke: Palgrave Macmillan.

Yemelianova, Galina M. 1997. The national identity of the Volga Tatars at the turn of the 19th century: Tatarism, Turkism and Islam. *Central Asian Survey* 16(4). 543–572.

Zakiev, Mirfatykh 2002. Татарский язык [The Tatar language]. In Vladimir Neroznak (ed.), *Государственные и титульные языки России: Энциклопедический словарь-справочник* [The official and titular languages of Russia: Encyclopedic lexicon], 354–370. Moscow: Academia.

Выступление Президента республики Минтимера Шаймиева на III Всемирном конгрессе татар. Полный текст [Speech of the President of the Republic, Mintimer Shaimiev, on the occasion of the 3rd World Congress of Tatars. Full text]. 2002, August 29. ИА Regnum. http://www.regnum.ru/news/polit/50666.html (accessed 05/11/2014).

Перевод письменности Татарстана на латинский алфавит вызван политическими причинами [Tatarstan's script change to a Latin alphabet is due to political reasons]. 2001, September 15. *News.mail.ru.* https://news.mail.ru/politics/arc80091/ (accessed 5 November 2014).

Acknowledgements

The data presented in this chapter were collected within the framework of the project "Majority or minority? Constructions of identity in the debate about the language policy of Russian-Turkic speech communities in the Republic of Kazakhstan and the Republic of Tatarstan (Russian Federation)", has been conducted at the Giessen Center for Eastern European Studies (*Gießener Zentrum Östliches Europa*) at the Justus-Liebig-University Gießen (Germany) since January 2010. Funding for the project was provided by the German Research Foundation (*Deutsche Forschungsgemeinschaft*). I am also grateful to the anonymous reviewers for their helpful comments and suggestions on earlier drafts of this chapter.

Ablimit Baki Elterish

10 Language Use Among Uyghur Students in Xinjiang, PR China

Abstract: This article examines the impact of an abrupt change of the medium of instruction in Uyghur classes at universities throughout the Xinjiang region, which is located in western China at the beginning of the 21st century, from Uyghur, a minority language, to Chinese, the language of the majority. This change in language policy has caused language change to occur in many areas, particularly in the area of language use among young Uyghurs. A mixed method approach was adopted to find out the patterns of language use among the participants about three years after the policy change. A language use questionnaire adapted from Baker (1992) was used to elicit the participants' beliefs regarding the status and functions of Uyghur, Chinese and bilingualism, as well as patterns of language use in domains. A total of 219 questionnaires were used for data analysis. Interviews were also conducted to support the quantitative results. The findings suggest that there is a full impact of the change of language policy upon the patterns of language use among the students. This study contributes to the understanding of language change in lesser known sociolinguistic areas like China's Xinjiang region.

Keywords: language use; language change; bilingualism; Uyghur; Chinese

1 Introduction

At the beginning of the 21st century, China began to shift its economic development focus from its coastal and southern areas westward, with Xinjiang province targeted as an important region to be developed. This shift in economic policy was soon followed by an abrupt change in the language policy for ethnic minority education in Xinjiang. In 2004, the regional government launched a new Chinese language initiative under the umbrella of bilingual education. Under this policy, universities throughout Xinjiang were required to change their medium of instruction (MOI) in ethnic minority classes from their native languages to Chinese. A low level of Chinese language proficiency of ethnic minority people, particularly the ethnic minority students, which has resulted in a slow process of linguistic and cultural integration of Uyghurs into Chinese society, was constructed by the top policy makers as a possible key root cause of both sluggish economic development and ethnic tension of the region. The abrupt changes in various policies, i.e., language policies, which has, in turn, changed traditional patterns of language use among ethnic minority students in the educational sphere is believed to have impacted patterns of language use in other domains. The aim of this study is two-fold, to (a) investigate the general beliefs of the status and function of Uyghur, Chinese and bilingualism, and (b) examine the patterns of language use in four domains among Uyghur university students in Xinjiang.

2 Background information

Approximately 4,000 km. from Beijing, Xinjiang province is situated in the far north-western part of China. In fact, Xinjiang lies within geographic Central Asia (Figure 10.1). Xinjiang's international border stretches over 8,000 km. and

Figure 10.1: Map of Xinjiang
Source: http://www.johomaps.com/as/china/chinamap1.html (accessed 22 September 2010). Permission obtained.

is adjacent to eight different countries, three of which are located in Central Asia. In 2010, the Chinese Census stated that the population of Xinjiang was 21.8 million people made up of a number of ethnic groups. The principal ethnic group in this region are Uyghurs, whose number makes up 43.3% of the population. There are also a dozen more other minor ethnic groups. Uyghurs and other minor ethnic groups are all labelled as the national minorities. The Han Chinese, whose population was less than seven percent in 1949, now make up 41% of the population in the region and although they are a minority in Xinjiang, they are the overwhelmingly ethnic majority of China.

Accordingly, Uyghur and Chinese are the two major languages in Xinjiang. These two languages are typologically different and they are mutually unintelligible. The Uyghur language is classified as a distinct language belonging to the Eastern Turkic branch of the Altaic language family (Hahn 2007: 379). Chinese is in the Sino-Tibetan language family (Li and Thompson 1989: 2) and is the native language of the Han Chinese. These two languages also differ greatly in writing. Written Uyghur is an alphabetic language and the current written script is a combination of the Persian and Arabic alphabets. Written Chinese uses characters instead of an alphabet.

In terms of differences between the ethnic groups, Uyghurs are indigenous to Xinjiang, whereas Han Chinese migrated from inland China into Xinjiang particularly since 1949 for various political and economic reasons (Howell and Fan 2011). Uyghurs are a relatively homogeneous group who understand one another despite some regional dialects of their native language. In addition, the Uyghur language is used as a "lingua franca" among the speakers of ethnic minority languages in Xinjiang (Dwyer 2005: 12). Chinese is comprised of a number of unintelligible "dialects" and Putonghua, the standard Chinese language, which is often referred to as Mandarin Chinese, and is widely used in Xinjiang as a lingua franca by ethnic Chinese speakers of the various Chinese dialects.

The Uyghur and Chinese languages also have different legal statuses. By law, the status of Uyghur in Xinjiang is the same as or even higher than that of Chinese. According to China's Law on Regional Autonomy, Uyghur, as the regional language in Xinjiang, shares co-official status with Chinese. An imperative of the regional government on language use in Xinjiang (XZB 2011) stipulates that a Uyghur text prevails over the Chinese one on any official or public signs in Xinjiang. This is because Xinjiang Uyghur Autonomous Region (XUAR), the official name of the region, is named after the Uyghurs. This is exemplified by many official signs on which the Uyghur script is always above the Chinese characters (Figure 10.2). In reality, however, Uyghur is an ethnic minority language at the regional level, while Chinese is the only national language of the country. In recent years, Chinese has become more dominant in many areas of

Figure 10.2: Official signs in Kashgar, Xinjiang. The text the left sign says "The People's Government of Kashgar City, Xinjiang Uyghur Autonomous Region" and the text right sign says "The Standing Committee of the People's Congress of Kashgar City".

Xinjiang. In education and administration, Chinese has replaced Uyghur as a part of the recent change of the language policy. There is a tendency for the Chinese language to be dominant in business as well (Becquelin 2004: 376).

The education system in Xinjiang follows that of the Chinese education system, which can be roughly divided into two parts: basic education and higher education. Basic education is further subdivided into primary school (six years), junior middle school (three years) and senior middle school (three years). Attending primary schools and junior middle schools (nine years) is compulsory according to the Compulsory Education Law of China. Attending senior middle schools, however, is optional, and is only for students who want to progress to a university. Higher education normally lasts four years for an undergraduate program.

Since the incorporation of Xinjiang as a province (PR) of China in 1949 until the launch of the new Chinese initiative in 2004, the Xinjiang education system had adopted a policy of separate schools for ethnic minority and Han majority students (Baki 2012: 7; Yee 2003: 450). The key issue in these two types of schools was the medium of instruction (MOI). In a Han majority school, Chinese is always used as the medium of instruction. Uyghur is not taught to the Han Chinese students, but English is taught as a preferred foreign language subject from grade three. In an ethnic minority school, the MOI was the native language of the ethnic minority students and Chinese was taught as a second language from grade three until they graduated from middle school. Ethnic minority students attending this type of schools were perceived to have low levels of proficiency in Chinese (Tsung and Cruickshank 2009). However, this current practice of the basic education system is undergoing rapid changes in Xinjiang where these two types of separate schools are being merged, and the MOI is transitioning to only Chinese with the native language of the ethnic minority students taught as a school subject only (Tsung and Cruickshank 2009).

In higher education, there are two streams of classrooms within a university: ethnic minority classrooms and Han Chinese classrooms. All first year ethnic minority students spend one additional year studying intensive Chinese in *yukeban* (预科 [Chinese preparatory classes]) before starting their degree program. After passing all examinations in *yukeban*, ethnic minority students are allowed to proceed to the four-year undergraduate program at universities. These two streams of classrooms continue till the students graduate from university. Before the change of the language policy in 2004, education in ethnic minority classrooms at universities in Xinjiang consisted of full instruction in their native languages and Chinese was taught as a subject for the first two years only. Now, however, all courses in ethnic minority classrooms are taught in the Chinese medium only.

The concept of bilingualism is useful here for understanding considerable differences in language practice between the north and the south, the urban and the rural. According to Appel and Muysken (2006: 2–4), bilingualism can be represented by three criteria: (1) by the number of bilingual speakers; (2) by the distribution of ethnic groups; and (3) by the composition of the society of each of the ethnic groups. Based on these three criteria, bilingualism in Xinjiang can be characterized into three categories: (1) monolingual Uyghurs versus monolingual Chinese; (2) bilingualism in North Xinjiang versus monolingualism in South Xinjiang; and (3) bilingualism in urban Xinjiang versus monolingualism in rural Xinjiang.

The first type of bilingualism is characterized by the co-existence of monolingual Uyghurs and monolingual Han Chinese in Xinjiang. This type of bilingualism fits into the concept of societal bilingualism (Appel and Muysken 2006: 2). According to this concept, each group in a society is monolingual with a few bilingual individuals. In the case of Xinjiang, Uyghur is spoken by the Uyghurs, while Chinese is spoken by the Han Chinese. For most of the Uyghurs, Chinese is a second language acquired at school or in the community (Baki 2012). The majority of the Uyghurs are monolingual with a small percentage of Uyghur-Chinese bilinguals. Xu (2001: 238) reported that in the late 1980s, only 10% of the Uyghurs in Xinjiang were bilinguals. This kind of situation continued for another two decades. Beydulla (2012: 194) reported that nearly 82% of the Uyghurs could not read Chinese when the new language policy was launched. The percentage of Uyghur bilinguals has increased rapidly over the past 10 years as a result of the recent promotion of the Chinese language in schools and universities and a rapid increase of Uyghur students attending Chinese schools both in and outside Xinjiang. Similarly, very few Han Chinese can speak Uyghur because Uyghur is not taught at Chinese schools, and they see no need to learn it (Yee 2003: 446). Interaction between the two groups has remained negligible, or superficial, in spite of three decades of the official campaign on national unity launched by the regional government in 1982.

Additionally, both Uyghurs and Han Chinese tend to live in compact communities with people belonging to the same ethnic group. In many aspects, the case of Xinjiang resembles bilingualism in colonial Hong Kong, where the Chinese and the English-speaking communities led basically disjunctive lives with the existence of a relatively high degree of "social distance" and "enclosure" (Luke and Richards 1982: 55). It can be said that this type of societal bilingualism in Xinjiang is the direct result of the education system in this region.

The second type of bilingualism in Xinjiang is characterised by the existence of bilingualism in North Xinjiang versus the existence of monolingualism in South Xinjiang. North and South Xinjiang have significantly different ethnic distribution. According to the Chinese Census 2010, the majority of the Uyghurs are heavily concentrated in the South, with three-quarters of Xinjiang's Uyghur population living in the Tarim Basin. The majority of the Han Chinese, on the other hand, is concentrated in the North. Most of the Uyghurs living in North Xinjiang are bilingual. In contrast, the majority of the Uyghurs who live in South Xinjiang tend to be monolingual.

A third type of bilingualism is characterised by the existence of bilingualism in urban Xinjiang versus the monolingualism more prevalent in rural Xinjiang. Ma's (2003: 128) comparison of the occupational structure of Uyghurs and the Han Chinese in Xinjiang may shed light on this type of bilingualism in Xinjiang. Ma (2003) found that in urban Xinjiang Uyghurs number less than 20% compared to 63% of Han Chinese. In rural Xinjiang, over 80% of the Uyghurs compared to nearly 37% who are the Han Chinese are farmers. Urban Uyghurs comprise of professionals, leaders of the state department and enterprises, office staff, workers in commerce, services, manufacture and transport, and urban dwellers. Many of these urban Uyghurs are bilinguals to varying degrees. They speak some Chinese learned at schools for various purposes in society. Therefore, bilingualism is the norm in urban Xinjiang. Rural Uyghurs are primarily farmers. Very few rural Uyghurs can speak any Chinese, and many of them manage no more than a few simple phrases of Chinese (Hess 2009: 412). Thus, monolingualism is the norm in rural Xinjiang.

However, there is a sliding scale of the current three types of bilingualism in Xinjiang. With the rapid increase in the number of young Uyghur bilinguals due to the Chinese MOI education, the high speed of urbanization, and the ever-growing number of Han Chinese migrant workers to all parts of Xinjiang due to the improvement of the infrastructure, bilingualism is spreading to rural Xinjiang and South Xinjiang as well. Consequently, Chinese is becoming a dominant language and Uyghur is being marginalized not only in administration and business alike, but also in the education domain.

A bilingual society like that of Xinjiang is a rich setting for the study of language use. In such a bilingual society, "one social group comes into contact with a second social group possessing a different language; each group then develops ideas about the other group's language vis-à-vis its own" (Eastman 1983: 30). Students who are actually receiving bilingual education gradually establish not only attitudes about different languages, but also increase the awareness of choosing a specific language in communicating with others.

3 Theoretical framework

Sociolinguistic studies often focus on language use among bilingual students within specific bilingual society. In a bilingual society in which two languages are present, often a minority language and a majority language, each of the languages has specific status and functions within the minority and the majority communities. Although various factors influence this, the minority language is generally chosen as the language of the family and is used in situations related to family life, while the language of the majority is used in the situations of education and business. This kind of language behaviour of using one language rather than another in a specific context is known as language use (Fasold 1984: 180).

Language use has been studied from different perspectives. The sociolinguistic perspective investigates people's behaviour of language use in specific contexts and sees how the sample population fit into the contexts. Fishman's (1968, 1971) research fits into this perspective. The psychological perspective tries to explore internal reasons and explain why a certain language is used in a certain situation. The work of Giles and Johnson (1981) and Giles and Ryan (1982) belongs to the psychological perspective. The anthropological perspective tries to search for external reasons and explain people's use of one language over another within a cultural context. The work of Watson-Gegeo (1986) also belongs to this perspective.

These situations and contexts are often referred to as "domains" in socio-linguistic literature. Romaine (1996) defines a domain as "an abstraction that refers to a sphere of activity representing a combination of specific times, settings, and role relationships" (576). Sociolinguistic studies often rely on domain analysis of language use to investigate patterns of language use among bilingual speakers. Fishman (1965, 1968) was among the first to develop a model of domain analysis for language use. According to Fishman, one language may be considered as more appropriate than another in particular domains (which are a combination of interlocutors such as participants, locations such as places and times, and topics). The typical five domains for language use originally proposed by Fishman included the family or home domain, the friendship domain, the religious or church domain, the work or employment domain and the education or school domain. Subsequent research, however, expanded Fishman's proposal and created new domains such as business, government, leisure, neighbourhood, and mass media, most of which remain consistent with Fishman's proposal. Normally, it is the minority language that is used in low domains (L) such as family, friendship and neighbourhood, while the dominant language is used in high domains (H) such as education, government, employment and business.

A few studies which relate to language use in Xinjiang have also been conducted by sociolinguists in China. Teng (1998) conducted a survey among 87 Uyghurs in Khotan in South Xinjiang about language use among the Uyghurs. The results of the survey showed that the Uyghur language is widely used in various domains such as school, family and daily life. Teng's study suggests that the ethnic identity of the speaker and his/her interlocutors is far more important than locations and topics in using a language. In Khotan, as well as throughout Xinjiang, an interlocutor's external appearance is often taken as the marker of his/her ethnic identity. According to this marker of ethnic identification, either Uyghur or Chinese is used in all locations and on all topics.

Sheng (2004) conducted similar research into language use among 215 Kazakhs, another Turkic language speaking minority, in a middle school in Urumqi, the capital of Xinjiang. Shen (2004) found that both Kazakh and Chinese are used in public service domains such as shops, bookshops, hospitals, buses, taxis, post offices and banks, while Chinese is used in the leisure and business domains. The use of Kazakh, the native language of the Kazak people, according to Sheng, is gradually being replaced by Chinese at home, especially with siblings. This study suggests that proficiency in the language is a significant factor in language use among the Kazakh students. In another study, Wushou'er

(2006) conducted a survey on language use among 100 Uyghur businessmen in Kashgar and found that language use among the Uyghurs is determined by the ethnicity of their interlocutors, which is similar to the findings of Teng (1998) mentioned earlier.

4 Methodology

The basis of this study is the quantitative method mixed with the qualitative method. As such, questionnaires and interviews have been privileged. The reason behind choosing a mixed method approach was that an over-reliance on a certain single method could induce skewed results and bring about mis-leading generalizations and conclusions (MacKenzie 2008: 66). Questionnaires produced results with quantifiable frequencies so that more information on different variables could be elicited. In addition, interviews were necessary to further develop the findings from the questionnaires. It was expected that taking a mixed method approach in this study could be both helpful in increasing the validity of the research and also widen its scope.

4.1 Questionnaires

The questionnaires used in this study were designed to examine participants' beliefs of the status and functions of Uyghur, Chinese and bilingualism, and lan-guage use in four domains: family, school, leisure, and social. The basis for the questionnaire used for this study was originally developed in 1992 (Baker 1992: 50) to allow researchers to study language attitudes in bilingual situations. This instrument has since been modified and used to study language attitudes in various contexts. Baker's questionnaire was modified and used in the Basque context to measure attitudes towards Basque, Spanish and English in the Basque Autonomous Community (Lasagabaster 2003: 590). Lasagabaster adopted Baker's questionnaire with some modifications e.g., the number of the questions was reduced from the original 20 to 10 and he used the same questions about the three languages to avoid possible bias.

Most recently, the same questionnaire that Lasagabaster had modified on the basis of Baker's and used it in the Basque context has been employed in nine different bilingual regions of Europe (Lasagabaster and Huguet 2007: 11–13) to examine language use. Baker's questionnaire was therefore considered to be a useful instrument because many questions in this questionnaire can be modified to suit this study.

Altogether, the questionnaire on language use in this study had 14 questions, i.e., five on the status and functions of Uyghur, Chinese and bilingualism and nine on language use in the domains of school, family, leisure, and social. Following the previous study of language use in Xinjiang, topics were not considered to be relevant to this study. In scoring the answers to these questions, responses are again on a five-point Likert scale. "Only Chinese" was assigned to five, "Mainly Chinese" was assigned to four, "Both Uyghur and Chinese" to three, "Mainly Uyghur" to two and "Only Uyghur" to one. However, the scores were later recategorized as "Uyghur", "Both Uyghur and Chinese" and "Chinese", because the responses at the extreme ends of the Likert scale were minimal. High mean scores (ranging from four to five) indicated a predisposition to Chinese and low mean scores (ranging from one to two), a predisposition to Uyghur. A midpoint score (three) indicated a predisposition to both Uyghur and Chinese or bilingualism.

4.2 Interviews

Researchers often choose to conduct mixed methods research (Hoare 2001; Lai 2005; Manley 2008; Zwickle 2002). Modelled after previous research which combined questionnaires with interviews, the interview questions used in this project used a semi-structured format were designed to probe at the issues of language use in a greater detail than the questionnaire. These interview questions were divided into five themes: (1) status and functions of Uyghur, Chinese and bilingualism, (2) language use in the school domain, (3) language use in the family domain, (4) language use in the leisure domain, and (5) language use in the social domain.

In order to give an idea of the interviewees' demographic information, a coding system was developed. The first letters represent language background, i.e., "MXJ" stands for monolingual Xinjiang and "BXJ" stands for bilingual Xinjiang. The last number denotes the numerical order. For example, BXJ 01 is a student (01) from bilingual Xinjiang (BX).

4.3 Participants

A total of 250 questionnaires were completed and 219 were accepted as valid for this study. All of the participants came from a university in Xinjiang where students were ethnically divided into Uyghur classes and Chinese classes according to their ethnicities when they started their study at the university.

In the Uyghur classes, although all lectures are delivered by Uyghur lecturers, the MOI is Chinese. Research access was gained with the assistance of former colleagues who were working at the university. The fieldwork took about four weeks during the summer of 2007.

The participants in this study were drawn from a clustered area, i.e., Uyghur university students from a number of classes at the university. Owing to variations in class size and scheduling possibilities, the classes chosen depended on the scheduling availability determined by the lecturers. Nevertheless, careful consideration was given to include students from as wide a variety of departments as possible. The selected classes represented a diversity of specialties and majors, e.g., politics, literature, education, mathematics, physics and English. The students ranged in age from 21 to 24 years old. They were all in their third year at the university, which meant that all students already had two-years of experience of attending lectures instructed in the Chinese language only. Apart from this, they had studied Chinese as a subject at school for about 10 years. Ideally, all of the participants were intended to be Uyghur-Chinese bilinguals with a good command of the Chinese language.

4.4 Procedure

The data for this study was a convenience sample because the questionnaires were administered in classrooms with the help of the former colleagues. Students were informed of the purpose of this study and all of the questionnaires were collected in class. At the end of each questionnaire, participants were asked whether they would be willing to be interviewed at a later date. A total of 48 students agreed to be interviewed. But in the end, a sub-sample of 16 students of different genders and language backgrounds was selected for in-depth interviews. The interviews were conducted in Uyghur and then translated into English by the researcher.

5 Findings

5.1 The beliefs regarding the status and functions of Uyghur, Chinese and bilingualism

Table 10.1 presents the beliefs of the status (Q1 and Q2) and the functions (Q3, Q4 and Q5) of Uyghur, Chinese, or both languages. The results show that Uyghur students generally believe that bilingualism is the norm in Xinjiang.

Table 10.1: Results of Beliefs of the Status and Functions of Chinese, Uyghur and Bilingualism

Questions	N	Uyghur	Uyghur/ Chinese	Chinese	Mean	SD
Q1. Which language(s) do you think best represent Xinjiang at present?	219	82 (37.4%)	117 (53.4%)	20 (9.2%)	2.62	.81
Q2. Which language(s) do you think will best represent Xinjiang in the future?	219	38 (17.4%)	107 (48.9%)	74 (33.8%)	3.18	.81
Q3. Which language(s) is (are) more useful to you?	219	31 (14.1%)	132 (60.3%)	56 (25.6%)	3.13	.73
Q4. In which language can you express yourself better?	219	106 (48.4%)	87 (39.7%)	26 (11.9%)	2.52	.90
Q5. Which language(s) would you like to see your children using to communicate in the future?	219	31 (14.2%)	159 (72.6%)	29 (13.3%)	2.97	.64

The responses to Q1 show that, at present, Uyghur and Chinese (bilingualism) are considered to be the languages that best represent Xinjiang for over half of the participants (53%), while Uyghur is for more than a third (37%) and Chinese for less than a tenth (9%). This variation reflects differences in participants' attitudes toward the status of Uyghur, bilingualism and Chinese. Presently, in the eyes of many Uyghur students, bilingualism is seen as having the highest status in Xinjiang. More choices for Uyghur than for Chinese indicate that Uyghur students give a higher status rating to Uyghur than to Chinese. This again shows the prevalence of Uyghur in the vast region of monolingual Xinjiang.

When it comes to the language(s) that will best represent Xinjiang in the future, as seen in the responses to Q2, a combination of Uyghur and Chinese (bilingualism) was chosen by nearly half of the participants (49%) and Chinese by about a third (34%), but Uyghur was chosen by less than a fifth (17%). Three indications may be inferred from the results. One indication is that the high rating of bilingualism shows Uyghur students' awareness of the spread of bilingualism throughout the region through the intensification of Chinese MOI education. Another indication is that giving a higher status rating to Chinese than that to Uyghur implies that Uyghur students' belief that Chinese will become the dominant language in the region in the future. The last indication is that the low status rating of Uyghur in the future adequately expresses the Uyghur students' feeling of helplessness towards the wider spread of Chinese in the region.

For Q3, nearly two-thirds of the participants say that both Uyghur and Chinese (bilingualism) are the most useful languages (60%). About a quarter agree that Chinese is the most useful (26%), while only a small number (14%) claim that Uyghur is the most useful language. This shows that the majority of the Uyghur students are again oriented towards bilingualism in Xinjiang as far as the usefulness of a language is concerned.

In Q4, nearly half of the participants say that they can express themselves better in Uyghur (48%), whilst only a considerable number (12%) agree that they can express themselves better in Chinese. More than a third (40%), however, say that they can express themselves equally well in both Uyghur and Chinese. This indicates that for nearly half of the students the Uyghur language plays an important role as the language in which they can better express themselves, then comes bilingualism for two-fifths, and Chinese for only a few. As for Q5, the majority of participants claim that they would like to see their children communicate in both Uyghur and Chinese (73%). Only 14.2% claim that they would like to see their children being able to talk in Uyghur and 13.3% chose Chinese. This further shows that Uyghur students have more positive attitudes towards bilingualism in the region.

In line with the quantitative results, the interview findings showed that students believe both Uyghur and Chinese represent Xinjiang at presents, because Xinjiang is an autonomous region of the country. One student noted, "The official name of Xinjiang is Xinjiang Uyghur Autonomous Region. As an autonomous region, both Uyghur and Chinese better represent the language situation of Xinjiang" (BXJ 03, personal communication, 2007).

When it comes to the status of Uyghur and Chinese in Xinjiang, many interviewees expressed the opinion that Uyghur is being replaced by Chinese as a language of higher status. Another student shared,

> From signs displayed in many places in Xinjiang, the status of Uyghur is higher than Chinese. But in reality, the status of Chinese is higher than Uyghur, because Uyghur is just like lip service. To be honest, I don't like it. The status of Uyghur should be higher in Xinjiang, as it is an autonomous region named after the Uyghur people. (MXJ 01, personal communication, 2007)

A few students expressed their worries about the future of their language, as they feel that the Uyghur language is now under some threat. BXJ 07 stated "When I have kids, their first language is going to be Uyghur because I want them to know that we are Uyghur. I would, of course, like them to learn Chinese as well" (personal communication, 2007). MXJ 01 observed that "The Uyghur language will continue to be used by Uyghurs in the next century. But I can see that the language will be used in a greatly reduced form as a home or community language, but not as the language of education and business" (personal communication, 2007). BXJ 14 more personally shared "I care a lot about my language. I don't want to see my language endangered or soon to become extinct" (personal communication, 2007).

On the whole, Uyghur students appear to be fully aware of the current language situation and its future development in Xinjiang. Bilingualism is, and will continue to be, the norm in Xinjiang and will have the highest status, but Chinese will also become more dominant in the region. In spite of this, many young Uyghurs assign high value to their native language, although their responses indicate shift in attitudes.

5.2 Language use in the school domain

Concerning language use outside the classroom, the results in Table 10.2 show that nearly two-thirds of the students report that they use Uyghur on the campus (62%), while nine percent say that they use Chinese.

Table 10.2: Results of Language Use in Schools

Questions	N	Uyghur	Uyghur/ Chinese	Chinese	Mean	SD
Q6. Which language(s) do you use with people on the campus outside the classroom?	219	135 (61.6%)	64 (29.2%)	20 (9.1%)	2.30	.90
Q7. What is the language of the newspapers and magazines you read?	219	73 (33.3%)	115 (52.5%)	31 (14.2%)	2.72	.83
Q8. What is the language of books you read besides your textbooks?	219	77 (35.1%)	109 (49.8)	33 (15.1%)	2.73	.84

It is striking to note that only a scant third of the participants report that they use both Uyghur and Chinese on the campus (29%). This suggests that despite the government's efforts to impose Chinese as a MOI in the Uyghur classroom, the majority of the Uyghur students still live in Uyghur monolingual contexts outside the classroom and their exposure to the Chinese language is mainly limited to the classroom context.

When it comes to the use of the language in reading newspapers and magazines asked in Q7, a third of the students say that they read Uyghur newspapers and magazines (33%) while just over half say that they use two languages (53%), and only a relatively small number use Chinese alone for this activity

(14%). This shows literacy practices are more bilingual. As for the language use in reading books apart from textbooks, just over a third of the students report that they read books only in Uyghur (35%), while half report that they read both Uyghur and Chinese books (50%) and again only 15% read Chinese books only. This indicates that using two languages is common in obtaining knowledge.

On the whole, the language use in the school domain is mainly in Uyghur if the school activity is not related to academic studies; however, both Uyghur and Chinese are used in school and literacy practices related to academic studies. This is a clear difference of using different languages between speaking and reading. The standard deviations for these questions do not produce heterogeneous answers, thus indicating a homogeneous agreement.

It can be noted from the comments below that, although most of the interviewees were fluent in Uyghur and Chinese, their involuntary use of the Chinese language with their interlocutors was limited only to the classroom. Outside the classroom, voluntary use of the Uyghur language was prevalent, because they associate mainly with Uyghur students and teachers. For example, BXJ 05 shares, "I don't know other Chinese students and teachers. Most of my friends on the campus are Uyghurs. So I hang out only with my Uyghur friends. It would be stupid if we use Chinese to talk to each other on campus when all other Uyghur students are using Uyghur only" (personal communication, 2007). Another student, BXJ 15, states "I speak Chinese with my coursemates and teachers in the classroom, but I speak only Uyghur to them outside the classroom on campus. We all feel uncomfortable if we speak Chinese outside the classroom" (personal communication, 2007).

Other students commented that their common use of Uyghur on campus was largely due to the fact that they were not provided with opportunities to interact with the Chinese students, as their dormitories and classrooms are also ethnically separated. For example, "I'm a rep at the Student Union. I meet with my Chinese counterparts on a weekly basis when I can talk with them in Chinese. The rest of the time, I just use Uyghur only" (MXJ 07, personal communication, 2007). Another student MXJ 04 commented "I want to share my dormitory with Chinese students. But the university just does not allow us to do this. We have been separated in the dormitory and in the classroom. I don't like this. I want to make more friends with Chinese students, but I have no opportunity to get to know them" (personal communication, 2007).

Many interviewees agreed that they read books, newspapers and magazines both in Uyghur and Chinese outside the classroom, because there is an abundance of them in the library. Some students reported that they read mainly in Uyghur because it is more difficult to understand Chinese. For example, MXK

06 shares "Yes, I read more Chinese books but I read mainly Uyghur newspapers and magazines, because they are easier to understand" (personal communication, 2007). Similarly, BXJ 05 notes that "Sometimes I try to find books in two languages so that I can refer to the book in the Uyghur language when I do not understand the Chinese book" (personal communication, 2007).

5.3 Language use in the family domain

Table 10.3 presents the results of language use in the family domain. As far as language use in the family domain is concerned, the generational differences are obvious (Table 10.2). Most of the participants report that they communicate almost exclusively in Uyghur at home with their parents (91%) with only nine percent reporting that they use both Uyghur and Chinese when talking with parents. Chinese language use with parents is minimal. This predominant use of Uyghur in the home with parents suggests that parents maintain a strong emphasis on their native language in the family situation, but also reflects a probability that these parents themselves are more likely to have received education in Uyghur MOI schools.

Table 10.3: Results of Language Use in the Family Domain

Questions	N	Uyghur	Uyghur/ Chinese	Chinese	Mean	SD
Q9. Which language(s) do you use at home with your parents?	219	200 (91.4%)	19 (8.7%)	0 (0%)	1.46	.65
Q10. Which language(s) do you use at home with your brothers and sisters?	219	154 (70.3%)	63 (28.8%)	2 (0.9%)	1.87	.87

Compared to the above findings regarding language use with parents, results relating to language use at home with brothers and sisters seem to diverge slightly. Over two-thirds of the students say that they use Uyghur with their siblings at home (70%), while use of Chinese alone is minimal. A notable point is the considerable rise in the use of the two languages in communicating with brothers and sisters. More than a quarter said that they use both Uyghur and Chinese with their siblings (29%). One reason for this might be that this reflects the changing language use patterns by school-aged young people. More students are becoming bilingual through bilingual MOI education at schools and have two languages at their disposal when necessary, especially among siblings. The findings suggest that a gradual shift is taking place in the family situations from using one language to the use of two languages with brothers and sisters, a language shift across time and generations.

Consistent with the quantitative results, the majority of the interviewees claimed that they speak Uyghur at home with their family members because they are used to it. Some students reported that they try to speak some Chinese at home especially with their brothers or sisters, but this is strongly disapproved of by their parents. The main reason why they speak Chinese with their siblings is if they have some secrets to share, but only if their parents are Uyghur monolinguals who do not speak Chinese. This is an example of representations of "instrumental" use of Chinese. For example, "I use the Uyghur language to talk with my parents and siblings at home. My parents would never allow me to speak Chinese at home. Sometimes I say just a few words of Chinese when I talk with my siblings" (BXJ 10, personal communication, 2007). Similarly, BXJ 06 also states "At home, I have to speak Uyghur, or my parents will tell me to say it again in Uyghur" (personal communication, 2007). And MXJ 03 shares "Yes, I use Chinese with my siblings only when I have something secret to share with them, and when I do not want my parents to know what I am talking about, because they don't speak Chinese" (personal communication, 2007).

In general, students were positive about speaking Uyghur at home with their family members although one can see that there is an infiltration of Chinese at home, particularly among the younger generation when they want to share some secrets. This explains, to some extent, why some Chinese is spoken at home, as shown in the results of the quantitative data.

5.4 Language use in the leisure domain

The data in Table 10.4 suggests that Uyghur students seem to prefer using two languages, Uyghur and Chinese, to a remarkable extent, in these two activities.

Table 10.4: Results of Language Use in the Leisure Domain

Questions	N	Uyghur	Uyghur/ Chinese	Chinese	Mean	SD
Q11.What is the language of the TV programmes you watch?	219	38 (17.3%)	129 (58.9%)	52 (23.8%)	3.06	.84
Q12.What is the language of songs you listen to and sing?	219	59 (26.9%)	129 (58.9%)	31 (14.2%)	2.80	.81

Nearly two-thirds of the students say they use both Uyghur and Chinese in watching television (59%), and the same proportion say they listen to and sing songs in Uyghur and Chinese (59%). This strongly implies that many of the Uyghur students are bilingual and bicultural, to some extent. Uyghur is used to a lesser extent in watching television. Slightly less than a fifth say that they watch only Uyghur programmes (17%), compared to nearly a quarter who say they watch only Chinese programmes (24%). This reflects the availability of more Chinese TV programmes. As listening to and singing songs often involves linguistic proficiency and cultural orientation, we might then expect that more Uyghur would be used as the language of music, as most Uyghurs are fans of Uyghur pop singers. But over a quarter say they listen to and sing only Uyghur songs (27%) as compared to 14% of the students who use only Chinese for this activity (14%).

In Xinjiang, Uyghur students' choice of a language for listening to the kind of music and television programmes that they enjoy is more likely to be determined by the language proficiency, content, quality and quantity of the programmes. As seen below, for most of the interviewees, watching news programmes in Chinese is more difficult than watching films in Chinese which is, in fact, linked to language proficiency.

> I often watch news in Uyghur, because it is easier to understand. But when I watch films on TV, I try to watch Chinese films, even if I don't understand all of them, because there are more films to choose from on the Chinese channels. (BXJ 08)

> I never watch news programmes in Chinese. The newsreaders speak too fast to for me to follow. (MXJ 11)

> There are more channels in Chinese. I watch Chinese programmes if there are some good films and live football matches. (MXJ 04)

> Sometimes I feel that translated programmes from Chinese into Uyghur are more exciting, especially movies. The quality of the dubbing is very good. I find it more exciting to watch television programmes, especially films in Uyghur. (BXJ 08)

> I listen to and sing mainly Uyghur songs. And I can sing them at any time I want to, without any hesitation. I can also sing some Chinese songs, but I don't like to sing them in public places because people don't like it. (BXJ 05)

> I like Uyghur songs. I also like foreign songs such as Indian, Pakistani and Turkish songs, because I feel they are closer to me. I don't like Chinese songs very much, because I don't understand the lyrics and I also feel culturally distant. (BXJ 07)

5.5 Language use in the social domain

The results in Table 10.5 show that about two-thirds of the students use Uyghur (68%) with their friends when they go home. The use of Chinese on its own is again minimal with friends (1%). A notable point, similar to that in the previous domain, is the increased use of two languages among friends. Nearly a third say that they use both Uyghur and Chinese (31%). The results show that there is a strong loyalty to the native language among most of the Uyghur students when they communicate with friends. On the other hand, the results indicate that using two languages seems to be taking place among over 30% of the Uyghur students in the friendship domain.

Table 10.5: Results of Language Use in the Social Domain

Questions	N	Uyghur	Uyghur/ Chinese	Chinese	Mean	SD
Q13.Which language(s) do you use with your friends when you go home?	219	148 (67.6%)	68 (31.1%)	3 (1.4%)	2.05	.83
Q14.Which language do you use when you go shopping?	219	35 (16%)	150 (68.5%)	34 (15.5%)	3.00	.72

The economic development forces both monolingual and bilingual Uyghurs to come into contact with more and more Chinese shop owners who speak Chinese only. The data reflects this sociolinguistic situation in Xinjiang. Table 10.5 shows that the majority of the participants use two languages when shopping (69%) whilst an equal percentage of the participants report that they use either only Uyghur (16%) or only Chinese (16%). The use of two languages in the business reflects the dominance of using two languages in the business sphere. This illustrates that bilingualism is the major trend in business, although a small number of the students only use one of the languages when buying things.

Many students explained during the interviews that they have to choose a language, i.e., if talking with friends in the neighbourhood during the holidays or if they go shopping. The main reason for the predominant use of Uyghur with friends is expressed to be mainly because Uyghur students do not have Han Chinese friends to use Chinese with them. This corresponds to the findings in section of 5.2. For example, MXJ 08 shared "I don't have Chinese friends, and it is impossible to use Chinese among Uyghur friends" (personal communication, 2007). MXJ 03 goes further, stating "I don't hang out with Chinese people. All my friends that I go to parties with are pure Uyghur. We all speak Uyghur to each other, and we laugh at those who speak Chinese" (personal communication, 2007).

Uyghur students expressed that their choice of language depends on the situation, particularly on the ethnicity of the person with whom they are talking.

I often go shopping in bazaars where all of the sellers are Uyghurs. I do shop sometimes in the city centre, where I buy stuff at Chinese shops. I speak Chinese or Uyghur there, depending on with whom I talk. (BXJ 07, personal communication, 2007)

Many places have Uyghur and Chinese staff. I speak Uyghur if a Uyghur staff member is serving me, but I have to speak Chinese if I'm going to talk with a Chinese staff member, because the Chinese people do not speak our language. (BXJ 09, personal communication, 2007)

As far as my daily life is concerned, I don't use Chinese very often. All of my friends are Uyghur, and we feel awkward talking to each other in Chinese. I use Chinese only when I buy goods from Chinese sellers. Even in a lot of shops owned by Chinese there are Uyghur shop assistants with whom I only use Uyghur. (MXJ 12, personal communication, 2007)

One of the main reasons why Uyghur students do not have Han Chinese friends is stated as Uyghur and Han Chinese students are institutionally separated on the campus. As many as 11 students wrote in the third part of the questionnaire, in which students are asked to feel free to write down any further comments, that they do not understand why the university do not allow Uyghur students to be mixed with Han Chinese students in the university dorms. According to theses students, sharing a dorm with Han Chinese students could strengthen the understanding of the students from Uyghur and Han Chinese background. This may also increase their chances of using Chinese on the campus.

6 Concluding thoughts

This study has looked into language use among Uyghur university students in Xinjiang. It has shown that although Uyghur students give their highest ranking to bilingualism in Xinjiang, they give higher status to the Uyghur language over Chinese. The perceived social status of a language is closely related to language vitality. Baker (2006: 62) maintains that when a majority language is seen as giving higher social status, a shift towards the majority language may occur. But this study does not reveal such a result. The higher rating of the status of Uyghur is perhaps another indication that Uyghur students are unwilling to shift towards Chinese and unwilling to be assimilated into a Han-dominated society. This higher rating of Uyghur as opposed to Chinese is also perhaps closely related to the sociolinguistic, historical, and political contexts of Xinjiang. Minority people like the Uyghurs in Xinjiang may have "violent" language attitudes which may contradict the actual status of their language in a Han dominated society. This is in agreement with Zhou (1999), who found that Tibetans upgraded their own language, Tibetan, a low status language, in the social-status dimension.

The results show that the patterns of language use in the school, leisure and social domains are mainly Uyghur but in the family domain, there is an overwhelming use of Uyghur. These results correspond with the results for Tibetans given by Wan and Wang (1997), who found that Tibetans use the Tibetan language at home with family members and also outside with people belonging to the same ethnic group. The results are partially similar to Xi and Cai's (2004) study of the language attitudes of Uyghur students in Urumqi. Xi and Cai found that an overwhelming majority of Uyghur students (86%) speak Uyghur in the family. The use of mainly Uyghur in the school, leisure and social domains suggests that speaking Chinese in these domains has not gained public acceptance. Uyghurs use Chinese only when they have to speak with people belonging to the Han Chinese group. Chambers (1995) argues that any differences in language use which are not considered to be due to linguistic reasons can be viewed as identity-oriented language use as far as the speaker is concerned. This use of language may or may not be conscious. The emphasis on the predominant use of Uyghur in the home, particularly with parents, is an indication of the strong maintenance of the native language, and this contributes to the representation of Uyghur identity. This corresponds to the previous discussion on positive attitudes towards Uyghur among the Uyghur students.

One implication of this study concerns the response of Uyghur students to the state language policy in Xinjiang. Rudleson and Jancowiak (2004: 300) categorized three modes of Uyghur response to state policy. First is acculturation, which is defined as adaptation to the Chinese policy both actively and passively. Uyghurs follow this path instrumentally when they learn the Chinese language. The second is nonviolent resistance, which refers to those Uyghurs who are mistrustful of the Chinese policy but oppose it in non-violent ways. And third is violent resistance, fierce anti-government action conducted by a small number of Uyghurs.

In this study, the Uyghur participants' responses reflect the second mode, i.e., non-violent resistance. This type of response may result in conflict at certain stages. Dwyer (2005) argues that, for both urban and rural Uyghurs, ethnic identity is linked to religious and linguistic identity. Young Uyghurs will only become radicalized if they sense that their language and religion are under threat (the third option). In Xinjiang, the removal of the Uyghur language from higher education may certainly be viewed as a threat, a step towards assimilation and an attempt to enforce monolingualism. In this context, further promoting the Chinese language, under the umbrella of bilingual education, may produce a counter-reaction among the Uyghurs. Some may regard compulsory instruction through the medium of Chinese in place of their own native language as a direct attack on their language and culture. This may push some people to despair, or even lead to radicalisation, which will inevitably lead to the third type of Uyghur response to state policy if the right policy prescription is not adopted. This is harmful to the ultimate goal of ethnic unity in Xinjiang.

The researcher fully understands that the results to be reported in this study may not be generalised to the population of all Uyghur students in Xinjiang owing to the convenience sampling method and the size of the participant pool. However, the results can be considered representative of the population of the university, which was one of 18 universities in Xinjiang and raises a number of issues for future research.

References

Appel, Rene & Pieter Muysken. 2006. *Language contact and bilingualism*. Amsterdam: Amsterdam University Press.

Baki, Ablimit. 2012. Language contact between Uyghur and Chinese in Xinjiang, PRC: Uyghur elements in Xinjiang Putonghua. *International Journal of Sociology of Language* 215. 41–62.

Baker, Colin. 1992. *Attitudes and language*. Clevedon: Multilingual Matters.

Baker, Colin. 2006. *Foundations of bilingual education and bilingualism*. Clevedon: Multilingual Matters.

Becquelin, Nicolas. 2004. Staged development in Xinjiang. *The China Quarterly* 178. 358–378.

Beydulla, Mettursun. 2012. Rural economy, environmental degradation and economic disparity: A case study of Deryabuyi, Xinjiang. *Central Asian Survey* 31(2). 193–207.

Chambers, Jack K. 1995. *Sociolinguistic theory: Linguistic variation and its social consequence*. Oxford: Blackwell.

Dwyer, Arienne M. 2005. The Xinjiang conflict: Uyghur identity, language policy, and political discourse. *Policy Studies* 15. East-West Center Washington.

Eastman, Carol M. 1983. *Language planning: An introduction*. San Francisco: Chandler & Sharp.

Fasold, Ralph. 1984. *The sociolinguistics of society*. Oxford: Blackwell.

Fishman, Joshua A. 1965. Who speaks what language to whom and when? *La Linguistique* 1(2). 67–88.

Fishman, Joshua A. 1968. Sociolinguistic perspective on the study of bilingualism. *Linguistics* 39. 21–49.

Fishman, Joshua A. 1971. *Sociolinguistics: a brief introduction*. Rowley, MA: Newbury House Publishers.

Watson-Gegeo, Karen Ann. 1986. The study of language use in Oceania. *Annual Review of Anthropology* 15. 149–162.

Giles, Howard & Patricia Johnson. 1981. The role of language in ethnic group relations. In John C. Turner & Howard Giles (eds.), *Intergroup behaviour*, 199–243. Oxford: Blackwell.

Giles, Howard & Ellen B. Ryan. 1982. Prolegomena for developing a social psychological theory of language attitudes. In Ellen B. Ryan & Howard Giles (eds.), *Attitudes towards language variation: Social and applied contexts*, 208–223. London: Edward Arnold.

Hahn, Reinhard F. 2007. Uyghur. In Lars Johanson & Eva A. Csato (eds.), *Turkic languages*, 379–396. London: Routledge.

Hess, Steve. 2009. Dividing and conquering the shop floor: Uyghur labor export and labor segmentation in China's industrial east. *Central Asia Survey* 28(4). 403–416.

Hoare, Rachel. 2001. An integrative approach to language attitudes and identity in Britanny. *Journal of Sociolinguistics* 5(1). 73–84.

Howell, Anthony & Cindy C. Fan. 2011. Migration and inequality in Xinjiang: A survey of Han and Uyghur migrants in Urumqi. *Eurasian Geography and Economics* 52(1). 119–139.

Lai, Mee-ling. 2005. Language attitudes of the first postcolonial generation in Hong Kong secondary schools. *Language in Society* 34. 363–388.

Lasagabaster, David. 2003. Attitudes towards English in the Basque Autonomous Community. *World Englishes* 22(4). 585–597.

Lasagabaster, David & Angel Huguet (eds.). 2007. *Multilingualism in European bilingual contexts: Language use and attitudes*. Clevedon: Multilingual Matters.

Li, Charles N. & Sandra A. Thompson. 1989. *Mandarin Chinese: A functional reference grammar*. Berkeley: University of California Press.

Luke, Kang-kwong & Jack C. Richards. 1982. English in Hong Kong: Functions and status. *English World-Wide* 3(1). 47–64.

Ma, Rong. 2003. Economic development, labour transference, and minority education in the West China. *Development and Society* 32(2). 125–145.

Mackenzie, Robert. M. 2008. *A quantitative study of the attitudes of Japanese learners towards varieties of English speech: Aspects of the sociolinguistics of English in Japan*. University of Edinburgh, Scotland: PhD thesis. http://www.era.lib.ed.ac.uk/bitstream/1842/1519/5/McKenzie_thesis07.pdf (accessed 27 March 2008).

Manley, Marilyn S. 2008. Quechua language attitude and maintenance in Cuzco, Peru. *Language Policy* 7. 323–344.

Romaine, Suzanne. 1996. Bilingualism. In William C. Ritchie & Tej K. Bhatia (eds.), *Handbook of second-language acquisition*, 571–604. San Diego: Academic Press.

Sheng, Guiqin. 2004. Wulumuqi shi Hasake zu xuesheng shiyong Hanyu xianzhuang fenxi [An analysis of the current practice of using Chinese among Khazakh students in Urumqi] *Yuyan Yu Fanyi* [Journal of Language and Translation] 2004(02). 36–40.

Teng, Xing. 1998. Zhongguo Xinjiang Hetian Weiwu'er zu Wei Han shuangyu jiaoyu kaocha baogao [A research report on Uyghur-Chinese bilingual education for Uyghurs in Khotan, Xinjiang, China] *Minzu Jiaoyu Yanjiu* [Journal of Minority Education Research] 4. 20–38.

Ruddleson, Justin & William Jankowiak. 2004. Acculturation and resistance: Xinjiang identities in flux. In S. Frederick Starr (ed.), *Xinjiang: China's Muslim borderland*, 299–319. London: M.E. Sharpe.

Tsung, Linda T. H. & Ken Cruickshank. 2009. Mother tongue and bilingual minority education in China. *International Journal of Bilingual Education and Bilingualism* 12(5). 549–563.

Wan, Minggang & Jian Wang. 1997. Zangzu shuangyu ren shuangyu taidu de diaocha yanjiu [An investigation of bilingual attitudes of Tibetan bilinguals]. *Xinlixue Bao* [Journal of Psychology] 29(3). 294–300.

Wushou'er, Gulizha'er. 2006. Kashi cong shang renyuan yuyan shiyong xianzhaung diaocha fenxi [An investigation and analysis of the current practice of language use among the traders in Kashgar] *Xinjiang Zhiye Daxue Xuebao* [Journal of Xinjiang Vocational University] 14(3). 37–39.

Xi, Lin & Hao Cai. 2004. Weiwu'er, Menggu zu da xuesheng shuangyu taidu de bijiao yanjiu [A comparative study of bilingual attitudes of Uyghur and Mongolian university students]. *Xinjiang Daxue Xuebao (Shehui Kexue)* [Xinjiang University Journal (Social Science)] 32(1). 139–142.

Xu, Shiyuan. 2001. *Bingwei yuyan yanjiu* [A study on endangered languages]. Beijing: Press of the Central University for Minorities.

XZB. 2011. *Xinjiang Weiwu'er Zizhiqu Renmin Zhengfu Bangongting guanyu jinyibu guifan shiyong Min Han liangzhong yuyan wenzi de tongzhi* [Notice of the People's Government of the XUAR on further standardisation of the use of the minority and Chinese languages booth in speech and writing]. No 57 Document of the General Office of Xinjiang.

Yee, S. Herbert. 2003. Ethnic relations in Xinjiang: a survey of Uygur-Han relations in Urumqi. *Journal of Contemporary China* 12(36). 431–452.

Zhou, Minglang. 1999. The official national language and language attitudes of three ethnic minority groups in China. *Language Problems and Language Planning* 23(2). 157–174.

Zwickle, Simone. 2002. *Language attitudes, ethnic identity and dialect use across Northern Ireland border: Armagh and Monaghan*. Belfast: Queen's University Belfast Press.

II Globalization and Language Change in Central Asia

Leroy Terrelonge, Jr.

11 Language Policies and Labor Migration: The Case of Tajikistan

Abstract: Labor migration to Russia has become a major economic lifeline for households in Tajikistan. Furthermore, the ability to speak Russian helps migrants more easily adapt to living and working in the receiving country. Since the fall of the Soviet Union, however, the role of the Russian language in Tajikistani society has steadily diminished as a result of changing government language policies and demographics. This chapter focuses on the narrative accounts of Tajikistani migrant workers who have worked in Russia in order to examine how Russian language competency affects migrants' ability to secure housing, navigate relationships with law enforcement, integrate socially, and find work while abroad in Russia.

Keywords: labor migration; Tajikistan; Russia

1 Introduction

When Tajikistan became an Autonomous Soviet Socialist Republic (ASSR) under the Uzbek Soviet Socialist Republic (SSR) in 1924 and then later became a SSR in its own right, Soviet language planners chose the Tajik language as the language of the newly formed administrative unit, regardless of its multilingual constituency. Under its policy of *korenizatsiya* [nativization], the Soviet regime believed that the most effective way to gain the trust and loyalty of local populations was through recruiting and building up a native cadre of administrators that was loyal to Moscow; one approach used to achieve this was to promote the language of the titular ethnic group. In the Tajik case, the Soviet government exerted considerable effort to induce non-Tajik speaking (mainly ethnic Russian) communist party officials working in the Tajik SSR to learn the Tajik language. Thus, for a short period of time, Tajik was a prestige language in the Tajik SSR. Soon thereafter however, Moscow officials determined that native recruits were "unreliable" because they were subject to local pressures and adapted central directives in the context of local requirements. Moscow subsequently relied on ethnic Russians to occupy positions of leadership. Thus, from the mid- to late 1930s, the Soviet administration began to slowly abandon its policies of *korenizatsiya*, including language policies. Teresa Rakowska-Harmstone (1970) described this change in policy, noting that "in the 1920s the presence of the Russian cadres in the borderlands was regarded as temporary, but in the 1930s the continuous political leadership of the central cadres – consisting mainly of ethnic Russians – came to be regarded as a permanent feature." What followed was a major influx of ethnic Russians that brought a smaller, pre-existing Russian population to 10% of the total Tajik SSR population by 1939 (Rakowska-Harmstone 1970). The change in policies and the arrival of large numbers of Russians heralded a change in status for the Tajik language. From that time on until the dissolution of the Soviet Union, Russian would play a central role in the public sphere of the Tajik SSR.

Starting in 1938, it became compulsory to study the Russian language in all schools throughout the Soviet Union. Knowledge of Russian became a prerequisite for career advancement and for full participation in Soviet society, and its status was further cemented by the mass conscription of soldiers from around the Soviet Union in the run up to World War II.[1] The Russian language continued to enjoy undisputed preeminence until Soviet leader Mikhail Gorbachev's policy of *glasnost'* in the late 1980s. The accompanying relaxations on censorship permitted nationalists, including those of Tajik descent, to protest the inferior status afforded to their languages (Landau and Kellner-Heinkele 2012).

The primacy accorded to Russian continued to erode as a result of the collapse of the Soviet Union and the ensuing outbreak of civil war in Tajikistan. By 1989, the Tajik SSR government passed a language law designating Tajik as the state language and requiring its teaching in all schools, and with the breakup of the Soviet Union in 1991, newly independent Tajikistan's Constitution, adopted in 1994, also identified Tajik as the state language. Similar to the other Central Asian republics, however, this document made an explicit provision for Russian as the language of interethnic communication. Russian's status further deteriorated in the aftermath of the civil war that raged in Tajikistan from 1992 to 1997. By the end of the war, 40,000 to 80,000 people had been killed, 600,000 were internally displaced, and 80,000 fled Tajikistan to bordering Afghanistan (Human Rights Questions 1996). Besides the scars the war left on Tajikistan and its inhabitants, it led to a mass emigration of Russian speakers and reinforced the country's persistent poverty, both of which contributed to the diminished role of the Russian language in Tajikistan.

---

1 Russian was the common language for these soldiers and they were strongly discouraged from using regional languages. A Kazakh man who served in the Red Army recounted that if he spoke Kazakh with a friend, his superiors would tell him his native language was a language for "the school yard" and mete out physical punishment (personal communication, 2012).

According to the Soviet census conducted in the Tajik SSR in 1989, ethnic Russians numbered 388,481 out of a total population of 5.1 million, i.e. 7.6% of Tajikistani residents were ethnic Russians ("Ethnic composition, language skills, and citizenship" 2010). As a result of the war and the increasingly uncertain situation for Central Asia's ethnic Russians after the fall of the Soviet Union, the census conducted in 2000 showed Tajikistan's ethnic Russian population decreased to just 17.5% of its Soviet-era amount ("Ethnic composition, language skills, and citizenship" 2010). The outflow of ethnic Russians continued into the following decade, and the 2010 census in Tajikistan reported that the ethnic Russian population was just fewer than nine percent of the number of Russians counted in the 1989 census ("Ethnic composition, language skills, and citizenship" 2010). These ethnic Russian emigrants presumably left Tajikistan for Russia. Of course, it was not only Russians that left Tajikistan for Russia; anyone with the resources to leave for Russia did so, and these tended to be well-educated individuals with high levels of Russian language ability.

As ethnic Russians and other elite Russian speakers fled Tajikistan's cities, particularly Dushanbe and Khujand, they were replaced by displaced persons from the southwest of Tajikistan and also from Kulob, the birthplace of Tajikistan's President Emomali Rahmon, and many of these displaced persons have opted not to return to their former homes. Newcomers to the capital city, Dushanbe, tended to speak Russian worse than previous city dwellers. One reason for this is that inhabitants of rural areas were farther removed from the Russian-speaking elite that concentrated in urban areas. A second reason is that rural areas in particular lacked a solid education infrastructure and did not receive enough education funding from the government to spend adequately on language instruction.

2 Tajikistan's language policy and its education infrastructure

Today, Tajikistan's education system continues to be one of the casualties of the country's pervasive poverty. During the transition to independence in 1991, the government spent 8.9% of GDP on education. After the onset of the civil war, this number dropped to 2.4% of GDP in 1995 and continued to fall until it reached 2.07% in 1999 (Landau and Kellner-Heinkele 2012). One consequence of this was low teacher salaries, i.e., the average teacher salary is currently around $50 USD per month. The Tajikistani government has offered incentives of free health care, subsidized property ownership, and exemption from compulsory military service in order to entice young Tajikistanis to become teachers. Despite these enticements, the low salary continues to be an impediment for recruiting new teachers (Navruzshoh and Najibullah 2012).

Another tactic the government has implemented in order to remedy the country's teacher shortage was to provide free education to students of pedagogical institutes in exchange for a commitment to teaching for at least three years. However, Tajikistan's education minister reported in 2009 that, of the 4,700 recent graduates who volunteered for this program, only 3,158 reported for teaching duty at the appointed time (Trilling 2009). The Tajikistani government has had to rely on high school-age teachers in some remote areas, paying them $20 USD a month to teach primary school classes. Other critics have complained about the curriculum of Tajikistani schools, claiming it is too ideological and does not include enough emphasis on math, science, and critical thinking skills (Trilling 2009). For help with curricular issues, Tajikistan turns to Russia. For example, the Russian Federation sent 200 Russian language instructors to Tajikistan's northern Sughd province in August 2012 ("Moscow sends 200 Russian language teachers" 2012).

The Tajikistani education infrastructure generally continues to face numerous challenges; however, these issues become magnified when looking at specific areas, e.g., Russian language education. However, it should be noted that challenges related to Russian language education are not unique to 21st century, independent Tajikistan. Even during the Soviet period, Russian instruction in Tajikistani schools was fraught with challenges. There was a shortage of qualified Russian teachers in general and available educators were reluctant to leave urban areas for the difficult living conditions in rural areas. There was also much concern about teacher pedagogy and the adequacy of teaching materials (Rakowska-Harmstone 1970). Moving into the post-Soviet period, there has been little, if any, improvement. And since the official language of Tajikistan is Tajik, along with it being the primary Medium of Instruction (MOI), there should be less of a demand for Russian MOI education since most Tajikistani students complete their studies in Tajik with Russian offered as a foreign language supplement for two to three hours per week (Landau and Kellner-Heinkele 2012). On the supply side, there are only a few Russian MOI schools, limiting the number of students that can pursue a Russian MOI education. For example, the Russian Ministry of Foreign Affairs issued a report claiming that there are four students for every one place in a Russian medium school (Landau and Kellner-Heinkele 2012).

However, despite the lack of supply and Tajik's official prestige (i.e., Tajik being the official state language), many parents still consider the quality of education in a Russian MOI school more rigorous than in a Tajik MOI school. According to one study, 96% of respondents expressed a desire to study Russian. This was the highest percentage from among the Central Asian republics which were included in the survey (Landau and Kellner-Heinkele 2012). Similarly, in a Gallup poll conducted in 2007, respondents from 10 post-Soviet nations were asked how important they thought it was for children in their country to learn Russian. Again, Tajikistan topped the list with 98% responding learning Russian was either very or somewhat important (Gradirovski and Esipova 2008).

The value that Tajikistani citizens accord to learning Russian is strongly linked to the fact that large numbers of Tajikistanis seek work in Russia, with domestic poverty being a major push factor. Although the country has never been prosperous, the civil war that raged between 1992 and 1997 stunted domestic economic growth by causing many highly trained and qualified specialists trained during the Soviet period to flee, consequently draining the country of valuable skill and talent.[2] Today, Tajikistan is the poorest Central Asian country with a per capita GDP in 2012 of $2,300 USD. Fifty-three percent of the population lives on the equivalent of US$40 per month while 17% earn less or have no declared source of income (Landau and Kellner-Heinkele 2012). Since the country is 93% mountainous, only seven percent of the land is arable, severely limiting job opportunities in the agricultural sector. Consequently, many Tajikistani citizens have made the difficult decision to leave their families and travel outside the country in search of work in order to send back remittances, the Russian Federation being the main receiving country for such migrant workers.

In general, after the United States, the Russian Federation has the world's second highest number of immigrants. The Russian Federal Migration Service reports that there are close to 11 million immigrants in Russia, and though figures vary, an estimated 1.1 million of these immigrants (10%) are Tajikistani citizens (Ergasheva 2013). Russia also has the distinction of being the country with the largest number of undocumented migrant workers; according to the OECD, illegal migrants make up between 6.5 and 7.5% of Russia's workforce (as cited in Kalinnikov 2012). Furthermore, migrant labor provides up to eight percent of Russia's GDP. In an interview, Konstantin Romodanovsky, the head

---

2 A good example is a man in Dushanbe who worked as an electric engineer for a factory. When I asked how he got a job as an electrical engineer when his degree was in agriculture, he told me, "There was a war on and there was no one else to do the job" (personal communication, July 2013).

of the Federal Migration Service, explained the importance of migrant labor in Russia, saying "We don't need this prattle over whether Russia needs or doesn't need immigrants. We need them like we need air." He went on to say, "If only Russians would remember that our courtyards and streets did not become as clean as they have ever been by magic", referring to the fact that many migrant laborers take on low-paying service sector jobs ("Russia in desperate need of immigrants" 2010). It is clear, then, that migrant workers are a vital part of the Russian economy for various reasons, including its declining population (Eke 2006).

Despite remittances from labor migration to Russia being perceived as significant, due to current education realities, Tajik migrant laborers in particular are less prepared than previous generations to move to Russia and find work. According to one study performed by the Center for Migration Studies, more than 20% of immigrants to Russia from Central Asia do not speak Russian and 50% are unable to fill out a simple form in Russian (Smolyakova 2011). Yet, despite their lack of preparation, they must nevertheless provide for their families, so they still move to Russia anyway and in increasing numbers. Their low level of Russian competence and unfamiliarity with legal provisions that affect them, however, create dangerous situations for migrant workers as the experiences in the rest of this chapter illustrate.

3 Methodology

This chapter focuses on the impact of the Tajikistani government's language policy post-independence on the Tajik migrant experience by focusing on narrative accounts of migrant workers' lived experiences, i.e., issues related to adjusting to life in Russia and their experience in the workplace. These interviews were conducted during the summer of 2013 in Dushanbe, Tajikistan, with five migrant workers. The individuals were selected because they represent a diversity of educational and socio-economic levels, as well as differing levels of Russian language fluency. Interviews were conducted in either Persian/Tajik or Russian, based on the preference of the interviewee and included a list of around 30 questions. These questions focused on interviewees' educational background and Russian language proficiency, as well as their experience finding housing/ jobs and their interactions with Russians, particularly with law enforcement representatives. The interviewees' profiles are listed in Table 11.1.

Table 11.1: Participant Profiles

Pseudonym	Gender	Age (years)	Marital status	Language competencies	Level of education	Notes
Aseddin	Male	24	Single	Tajik; Russian	Completed three years of higher education in a technical college.	From the Rasht region of Tajikistan. Travels seasonally to work in construction and, occasionally, as a taxi driver. He has traveled to Russia four times (first in March 2009) and left for his fifth trip shortly after our interview. He has worked mainly in and around Moscow in construction and as a taxi driver.
Momin	Male	22	Single	Tajik; Russian; Uzbek	No higher education experience.	From the Rasht region of Tajikistan. Travels seasonally to Moscow to work as a taxi driver. He has worked mainly in and around Moscow as a taxi driver.
Zohir	Male	31	Married with two children	Tajik; Russian; Uzbek; English; Turkish	Has a Bachelor's degree in Economics/ Marketing.	From the city of Kulob, Tajikistan. He has worked in Moscow and the Perm region (just over 700 miles northeast of Moscow) in the construction industry.
Umed	Male	21	Single	Tajik; Russian; English	Third year university student in agro-business and marketing.	He has worked in Moscow, Chelyabinsk (932 miles east of Moscow), and the Sverdlovsk region (880 miles northeast of Moscow). He has worked mainly in construction, in a nightclub, and in the market.
Farhad	Male	30	Married with two children	Tajik; Russian; Turkish; English	Has completed a professional degree and completed his schooling in Russia.	He is a banker in Dushanbe. He has attempted to work in Russia, but had issues with citizenship and work authorization. He has also traveled widely in the US.

4 Findings

4.1 Language issues (pre-migration)

Even before leaving for Russia, the effect of language policy on Tajikistanis' access to information and services regarding the migration process is mixed. Since the overwhelming majority of potential migrants get their information through kinship and other informal networks, in one sense, the effect of the official state language policy (Tajik MOI and lack of Russian language education resources) have little impact on the exchange of information. The main problem in this case however, is that there is little guarantee that the information provided to the migrants is reliable and accurate, which could adversely affect their planning process. More widespread use of privately owned employment agencies may help increase the reliability of information for migrants; however, the use of these agencies as a resource is limited owing to various constraints. For example, the fact that migrants must sign contracts written in Russian raises questions as to how much is explained to or translated for migrants about the conditions of their employment.

People looking to services provided at government centers do not suffer from language barriers; however, these sites are often difficult to reach and lack adequate staffing to address the range of matters under their purview. Non-governmental organizations (NGOs) attempt to provide information and services in Tajik and help fill in the gaps that the government is unable to provide. Additionally, the range of resources that is available on the Internet remains inaccessible by large segments of the general population because they are written in Russian and because of limited access to the internet due to power shortages. Prior to departure then, migrants are often primarily if not purely dependent on hearsay from people within their social networks, which leads to the reproduction of certain types of knowledge which may (or may not) be true.

4.2 Language challenges (upon arrival in Russia)

4.2.1 Housing

One of the first things that new arrivals need to take care of is finding housing. There are three main ways that Tajikistani migrant workers find housing in Russia. They can: (1) stay with family members who are already living in Russia; (2) live in employer-provided housing, or (3) rent a living space on their own.

The first option involves one's *avlod* [kinship] network which helps organize communities and families in Tajikistan and extends across borders to Tajikistani communities abroad. Because so many Tajikistani citizens have migrated to Russia, many migrants have family members who live permanently in Russia and consequently, make space for visiting family members while they are on work assignments. The second option is to live in employer-provided housing. In many cases, however, the housing provided is generally considered unsuitable for human occupancy. Migrants have been documented living dormitory-style, inside condemned buildings with crumbling walls and no gas, running or hot water, or even glass in the windows ("Tajikistan releases Russian and Estonian pilots" 2011). And while employer-provided housing is initially attractive to migrant workers because it defrays their cost of living, it may end up taking a toll on their health.[3] The close quarters and lack of sanitation often breed sickness, e.g., infectious and respiratory illnesses like tuberculosis. The third option for migrants is to rent a living space on their own. The challenge with this is that Russian landlords often refuse to rent to Tajikistanis (personal communication, 18 July 2013). And when apartments are available, they are expensive. According to one rental site, the average price for a one-bedroom apartment outside the Moscow city center was 32,080 rubles ($894 USD at the time this was written) ("Cost of living calculator" n.d.). When compared to a migrant's average salary of $455 to $605 USD per month, the costs can be prohibitive unless they are shared between a number of workers ("Race to the bottom" 2013). However, if one could find groups of people to share a residence, this could help the group offset this cost.

In general, finding housing in Moscow can be a difficult experience for migrant workers, especially when they cannot rely on the assistance of family members, but a lack of Russian language skills only further disadvantages migrant workers who decide to find housing on their own. It is possible that they find information about available units through migrant networks, but barring this, all information about apartment availability is in Russian and landlords will be Russian speakers. This makes communication difficult and often exposes them to exploitation by unscrupulous landlords.

---

3 Having the right preparation (education and Russian language skills) can decrease the risk of falling victim to these living conditions. Zohir explained to me that of the two times he lived in Russia, once he lived alone in a regular apartment that he picked out himself, but that in that case, the apartment was paid for by his company. The other time he lived with an older woman in a room she rented out in her building. Again, it is worth noting that he had more education and a higher level of skills than many other migrants (personal communication, 18 July 2013).

4.2.2 Law Enforcement

The relationship between Tajikistani migrants and the police is largely an adversarial one with harassment and extortion from the police side and, consequently, feelings of suspicion and distrust from the Tajikistani migrant workers. Migrants regularly experience police raids at the workplace and at home. They are often stopped and detained on the street based on appearance alone. If they are unable to produce the necessary documents to satisfy the police, or are not able to defend themselves and their presence in Russia adequately, they can be arrested and taken to police stations where they are sometimes subjected to violence and mistreatment. Tajikistani migrant workers have even reported to researchers that some police officers have learned how to solicit bribes in the Tajik language so there is no misinterpretation of what they are after, regardless of the migrant's level of Russian knowledge ("Tajikistan: Exporting the workforce" 2011).

In a 2003 survey, 97% of the construction workers who were interviewed described the relations with law enforcement agents the worst problem they faced while abroad (Olimova and Bosc 2003). Particularly since many migrant workers who work in construction have lower levels of education and are not familiar with their rights and obligations under Russian law, they are more inclined to fear law enforcement authorities because they (1) do not understand the basis for detentions and (2) believe that encountering a police officer puts them at high risk for exposure to police abuses. Moreover, this population is also more likely to have ambiguous migration status, making these concerns justifiable. Thus, migrants go to great lengths to avoid coming into contact with police officers. For example, since workers are most vulnerable while moving around the city by foot, they avoid leaving their worksite. If they must leave their worksite, one popular option for avoiding police officers is to complete as much of the journey as possible by taxi (Olimova and Bosc 2003). Another popular option for migrant workers is to clean or provide other types of free manual labor for police stations as a form of preemptive or preventative bribery so that officers do not detain the migrant workers in that area. However, if migrants do not volunteer these services themselves, in some places, they are detained by police officers and forced to perform the manual labor anyway ("Are you happy to cheat us?" 2009).

From the other side, police perception of Tajikistani migrant workers is also quite low. They are seen as moving targets for migration violations and are widely considered to be "the fundamental reason for the high crime level" ("Tajikistan: Exporting the workforce" 2011). This assertion, however, is contradicted by figures released by Russia's Interior Ministry in 2012, showing that all foreigners, including migrant workers, account for only two percent of crimes committed (Sadykov 2013).[4] Motivations for poor treatment of migrant workers by police are tinged with racism, but the main reason is likely economic. Russia's police force has been described as very corrupt for many years, which is not surprising because they are vested with a great deal of power for little pay. Before wide scale anti-corruption reforms to the police force were introduced in 2011 in order to trim the overall size and increase pay, a police lieutenant received a monthly salary of $360 (Krainova 2011).[5] It is hard to picture how police officers could live on such a salary, especially in the capital, Moscow, which is regularly ranked as one of the most expensive cities in the world in which to live.[6] For police officers looking to supplement their paltry income, migrant workers become an attractive target because they frequently violate Russian migration legislation and because of their vulnerability, they lack the ability and/or incentive to report police abuses. The inability to communicate well in Russian adds to migrants' vulnerability; some migrants are unable to report on police abuses because they lack the necessary language skills to do so. In a 2003 survey, 16% specified that [the lack of] Russian-language skills were a key factor in their relations with the police. They claimed that it was easier to get rid of the police if you knew Russian well (Olimova and Bosc 2003: 72).

My interviewees further confirmed the reality of these various issues. All five participants stated that they never had any problems with police and attributed this to the fact that their documents were always in order and they spoke Russian well enough to answer the officers' questions if they were stopped. One man, Momin, said that the police had enough experience dealing with migrant workers that they could instinctively deduce from a migrant's behavior whether or not his documents were in order, but that otherwise, in his experience, migrants were generally left alone. However, between having the correct documents and speaking Russian, Momin and his friend, Asleddin, noted that it was more important to be able to speak Russian. According to Momin,

---

4 There has been much politicization of crime statistics related to migrant workers, with some interpreting different data sources suggesting that up to 50% of crimes are committed by migrants. These assertions rely on data that make it difficult to impossible to tease out the role of migrants specifically, and rely on witness testimony, which can be unreliable because of the prevailing attitude towards migrants (Tselikov 2013).

5 The amount has since tripled to between $1,170 and $1,600 USD per month (Krainova 2011).

6 In 2011, it came in 14th place in a semiannual survey conducted by ECA International (a global HR firm) (Wong 2011).

> Even if your documents are not in order, if you know Russian well they won't bother you... but if you don't know Russian well they will treat you badly. That's the Russian character, after all – they are nationalistic. If you don't remain silent when they ask you questions, and you can even challenge them as to why they are questioning you [sic]... If you remain silent they will cheat you and fine you and otherwise mistreat you. (personal communication, 14 July 2013)

His friend, Asleddin, added "Yeah, if you don't know the language they will [expletive] with you as much as they can" (personal communication, 14 July 2013). Another migrant worker, Zohir, explained his interactions with the police.

> For me personally their behavior was good. But other friends and acquaintances who were there with me in that city, they lived there longer (five to six years), but they always said that police are bad and treated them badly. They stopped me on many occasions in the metro, out on the street, in stores, in trading centers (malls), at my workplaces and asked [for my documents]. I always showed my documents. They were in order, my passport was in order, visa and registration were there, so they sent me on my way. There was no problem. (personal communication, 18 July 2013)

When pushed for further analysis on why some of his friends had fallen victim to police abuses, Zohir said, "When they don't have their documents or cannot speak Russian, they demand money from them and empty out their wallets" (personal communication, 18 July 2013).

What I observed from the interviews I conducted with migrant workers was that once migrants are stopped for questioning by police officers, a large determining factor in whether or not that individual would be fleeced for bribes or otherwise abused by officers was his level of Russian fluency. If a Russian officer determined that a foreigner has limited ability to communicate in Russian, this lowered the inhibition to refrain from exploiting the detainee. This is because it is assumed that one's language knowledge is indicative of an individual's embeddedness in a society. Those whose knowledge of the local language is low are probably either itinerant with little knowledge vis-à-vis recourse for police abuse, or are low-prestige members of society who are less likely to have access to the resources to pursue recourse (or may be denied recourse by virtue of their low status). If that is the case, then lower or no Russian language proficiency among migrants can be correlated to the likelihood of police abuse, which will only become worse as Russian language education in Tajikistan continues to decline.

4.2.3 Social integration

Apart from the broader politics, relationships between Russians and Tajikistani migrant workers are difficult to form because of the inability of many migrant workers to integrate into life in Russia. Because of the fear of being stopped by police, many migrant workers choose not to leave their work and living sites, and so remain shut off from contact with Russian people and Russian society. Olimova and Bosc (2003: 121) observed that migrant workers "create a semi-isolated micro-society which largely precludes the possibility of adaptation to the receiving society." In his interview, Zohir corroborated this observation, sharing that

> From personal experience I know that they do not come into much contact with Russian people. They speak mostly among themselves and do not go out anywhere. One person will go out and buy the things they need and they just work in these places. For this reason they have many problems with learning language in these places. But apart from these people there are many who go out and speak with Russian people. They become friends with and speak with Russian speakers and they learn Russian well. But most do not do that. They don't often go out and do not learn. (personal communication, 18 July 2013)

Because they do not mix, this perpetuates feelings of mistrust between foreign-born migrants and local Russian residents. While two of my interviewees, Momin and Asleddin, generally harbored favorable impressions of Russian people, they judged their perceived lack of moral values, observing that Russian children did not listen to their parents "as all Muslims do until the end of their lives", and claiming that children start to drink, smoke, and carouse at eight years old. They also found it quite egregious that many women in Russia smoked, asserting that 95% of women in Moscow smoked while the statistic was reversed in Tajikistan (according to them only five percent smoked in Tajikistan) (personal communication, 14 July 2013).

While Russian authorities have made some attempts to facilitate better social integration experiences for migrants, these programs have, for the most part, been unsuccessful. In May 2013, Moscow authorities ended a program entitled "Museum for Migrants" because it was ineffective and was not supported by either the Federal Migration Service or the migrants themselves. This program, launched in 2012, was intended to educate migrant workers about Russian cultural values by offering free access to museum exhibits on Russian history and culture. In another program, designed by a Russian-based NGO, a handbook was published to teach migrant workers about their legal rights, local Russian customs, and other information useful for recent immigrants. But while there were no problems with its content, the illustrations used in the publication drew the ire and criticism of human rights advocates and journalists. This was because the publication depicted migrant workers as anthropomorphized tools (a spatula, a paintbrush, a paint roller, and a broom) and local Russian residents as human beings ("Tools of tolerance" 2012).

Figure 11.1: Depiction of Tajikistani migrant workers as tools
Source: France24 ("Insulting" Russian guide depicts migrant workers as tools 2012)

In their interviews, Momin and Asleddin, confirmed that there was a pervasive negative attitude towards Tajikistani migrant workers. However, they drew interesting distinctions in the types of people who were responsible for harming migrant workers. Momin commented saying "90% of the 'new' Russians are racist. The older people who grew up under the Soviet Union understand us and treat us well. But they are now old and the 'new' Russians hate us" (personal communication 14 July 2013). To which Asleddin added "And there were Russians living in the provinces who find themselves in monetary distress and move to Moscow because there are higher wages. When they become rich they show their hatred towards us and call us names. But the Muscovites themselves are not bad people" (personal communication, 14 July 2013).

Momin's comments support the generally perception among migrants that older people who lived under the Soviet Union are more tolerant of diversity and that the younger generations have been more susceptible to the creeping influence of nationalism. Asleddin, in his comments, though, distinguished between longtime urban residents of Moscow, who he implies treat migrants generally well, and rural internal migrants to Moscow, who may have more conservative views and distrust foreigners more than urbanites. What's more, Muscovites got a pass from both Momin and Asleddin in terms of violence and discrimination towards Tajikistanis. When asked if they had ever fought/clashed with Russian citizens, Asleddin said he had not, and Momin, while replying affirmatively, was quick to add that he never had any problems with ethnic Russians, but instead mentioned a host of ethnic minorities – some Russian citizens and others nationals of former Soviet republics. Dagestanis, Azeris, and Uzbeks are the ethnic groups Momin claimed to have clashed with. He was particularly negative about Uzbeks, whom he claimed had only recently started migrating to Russia and were taking Tajik workers' places for much less pay, making it harder for Tajiks to earn a living. In his words, "If it were not for the Uzbeks, Tajiks would live like kings" (personal communication 14 July 2013). Asleddin confirmed what Momin reported.

Zohir further supported Asleddin and Momin's thoughts. When I asked him if he had any bad experiences with Russian citizens, he replied, "There are good people and bad people because this is Moscow we are talking about. It's the same all around the world, in every country and region... there were good people and bad people and I mostly met the good ones" (personal communication, 18 July 2013). When asked about the experience of his friends, he recalled an occasion where one of his friends was attacked by a group of men in the metro. They demanded his money and belongings. According to Zohir, his friend emphasized "I saw that they were not Russian. Russians do not do these things" (personal communication, 18 July 2013) When I pressed him on the identity of the assailants he said,

> They were people who had come from other countries. They speak Russian... he [the friend] said "they took my phone"... they took what he had on him, then they let him go. Then others I heard they told me that on the streets they are held up... But not by Russians usually. They stop them, take their money, telephone, documents... but thank God that never happened to me. (personal communication, 18 July 2013)

Another migrant worker, Umed, believed that Russians were motivated by an irrational fear of Tajikistanis, but that as long as migrants knew Russian well that no one would try to harm them. If not, they could be subject to mistreatment at the airport, by police, and by Russian citizens. Umed also said that he had no problems with ethnic Russians, and like the other migrant workers interviewed, blamed Russian citizens from the Caucasus (Chechens and Dagestanis) for conflicts with Tajikistani migrant workers in Russia (personal communication, 25 July 2013).

In general, language skills play an important role in Tajikistani migrants being able to adapt to working and living in Russia. Olimova and Bosc (2003: 116) noted that "Education, and in particular language skills, facilitate interaction with governmental authorities and law enforcement bodies in the receiving country as well as contact with the society at large." In finding housing, a lack of Russian language proficiency complicates the task of migrant workers who must find an apartment on their own instead of with family or through their employers. With the police, the level of Russian language skills appears to be a strong predictor of how likely a migrant is to be extorted, detained, or abused by law enforcement officials. And finally, while the role of language in the relationship between Tajikistani migrant workers and local Russian citizens is not the primary defining characteristic of racism and xenophobic stereotypes, it does contribute to the continued isolation of migrant workers and their failure to be integrated into the communities in which they work. Because there is little interaction between migrants and Russians, there is little understanding of how the others live. This reinforces stereotypes between the groups and keeps tension high. Thus, decreased Russian skills contributes to the increased marginalization of Tajikistani workers and erecting barriers to the interchange between migrants and local citizens that could potentially ease the distrust and tension between different populations.

4.3 Language and labor

In addition to housing challenges and an increased likelihood of police harassment, the lack of Russian language skills has serious repercussions for the job options available to migrants. Almost as a rule, those who do not speak Russian well occupy poorly remunerated, low-skilled, low-prestige jobs. The jobs that migrants hold in Russia tend to be segregated by national group. Kyrgyzstani migrants are mostly employed in street-sweeping jobs in wealthy areas, Uzbekistani migrants most often work in trading and in marketplaces, and Tajikistani migrants are mostly concentrated in the construction sector (Gorst 2011). In a 2006 survey that was conducted, respondents (Tajikistani migrant workers) confirmed this fact: 62% said they work in construction and building. Other popular jobs for Tajikistani migrant workers were service sector jobs in gardening, housework, or restaurants (25% of respondents) and positions in industry and transportation (eight percent of respondents). A further four percent worked in agriculture (A survey of political engagement and enfranchisement, 2006).

The high percentage of Tajikistani workers in the construction business makes the migration flows coming out of Tajikistan subject to the idiosyncrasies of this industry. The biggest example is the seasonality of the migrants' movements. During the harsh Russian winters, work available on construction projects decreases and there is less work available for the migrant workers. The seasonality of the industry means that Tajikistani workers in large numbers divide their time between their homes in Tajikistan and their jobs in Russia, leaving for Russia in mid-spring and returning to Tajikistan in mid-fall. Of course, a return trip to Tajikistan requires money and migrant workers may prefer to stay in Russia during the off-construction season and find employment in another sector. Asleddin described how he would earn money during winters in Moscow,

> I worked as a taxi drives for four or five months during winter. I would work at night on Fridays and Saturday. The other days it was unclear if there would be customers. But when they spend time in café, come out drunk, and don't want to get behind the wheel, then they order taxis. But during the last three or four years, they have decided to get rid of *patenty* for taxi drivers, and if they find out that you are working as a taxi driver they can take away your license. (personal communication, 14 July 2013)[7]

Language skills are a major determinant of the types of jobs that Tajikistani migrant workers find in Russia. Unfortunately, these skills are on the decline. In the first mass emigrations from Tajikistan, ethnic Russians and highly skilled/ educated Tajikistanis fled to Russia, then younger, less highly skilled Tajikistanis who were still educated under the Soviet education system started to migrate, followed by today's reality of very young migrants with poor educational backgrounds and lack of Russian language skills. Combined with a broader trend of lower-skilled migration, continued de-emphasis of Russian in the national language policy effectively limits the employment options for migrant workers and restricts them to low-pay, low-skilled labor.

---

7 *Patenty* mentioned by Asleddin is a way for foreign workers in Russia to obtain permission to work for private individuals (as gardeners, drivers, cooks, etc.). They were introduced in 2010 and allow foreigners to purchase their continued work permission for 1,000 rubles per month ("Protecting Tajik migrants' rights" 2013). Migrant workers have tended to look favorably on the introduction of *patenty* because it gives them a way to work legally in Russia and the Russian Federal Migration Service also likes this system because more workers have declared themselves to the authorities and in so doing make themselves available for tax collection ("Tajikistan releases Russian and Estonian pilots" 2011). Starting in 2013, however, *patenty* are only valid for three months unless the holder has an employment agreement.

4.3.1 The role of intermediaries

There are Tajikistanis who want to go to Russia but find it difficult, most often due to a combination of language difficulties, unfamiliarity with how to get to there, or find work once they are there. Some enterprising individuals have recognized that there is a need for services to help people with difficulties navigating the migration process and provide support at different price points. One popular option that is used to channel these services to migrant workers is the "brigade system".

The brigade system is a way for Russian companies employing migrant workers to outsource the hiring of workers and offload their legal risks onto a third party. In this system, a brigade leader is contracted to perform a specified task. The brigade leader assembles a team by recruiting from among his compatriots. In theory, this setup should work well in the Tajikistani context because of the tight familial connections, but in practice, these relationships often turn exploitative. Once individuals join the brigade, they become reliant on the brigade leader for a range of needs from migration documentation to sending money home to family. Consequently, these leaders have a great deal of influence over the lives of the migrant workers they recruit and often mistreat their employees. Apart from brigades, there are individual employment recruiters, private or state employment agencies, diaspora networks, and agencies assisting in obtaining residency registration and work permits. Ninety percent of these intermediaries are informal and subject to very little oversight. As a result the system is quite prone to abuse. Legal recourse tends to be elusive; if migrants seek help from authorities, their efforts can be frustrated because intermediaries also typically have the protection of at least one important official (Olimova and Bosc 2003).

Despite the numerous instances of exploitation at the hands of intermediaries, it is quite possible for migrants to avoid the abuses cited here by having the right preparation prior to leaving the country. Zohir shared about his two experiences in Russia. The first time he was there to build a heating plant in Perm and the second to build a shopping mall in Moscow. He is currently in Russia working on a project in St. Petersburg. Before leaving for Russia, he completed a correspondence Bachelor's course in marketing and studied/spoke Tajik, Russian, Uzbek, Turkish, and English at very high levels. Though the work he performs in Russia is still in the construction arena, because of his language skills and higher level of education, he is not dependent on intermediaries to help arrange his employment and travel abroad. Instead, he uses a popular Russian website for job postings (e.g., www.hh.ru) and negotiates the salary and other arrangements on his own. Because of the security of his position, he has been able to invite his wife and children to come and live with him during some of projects when he works in Russia (personal communication, 18 July 2013). His friend, Farhad, has also managed to escape some of the more negative aspects of migration to Russia, with the large caveat that he was never a "migrant worker" in Russia. He attended a Turkish high school in Dushanbe where he learned Turkish, English, and Russian (in addition to his native Tajik), spent three months in North Carolina through the U.S. State Department's Work and Travel program, and then studied in Moscow. He now lives in Dushanbe with a prestigious job at one of the country's biggest banks (personal communication, 28 July 2013).

The accounts of these individuals show how intertwined the themes of education and language are and how difficult it is to separate them in identifying the root of the problems associated with migrant workers. Migrants with higher education levels tend to speak better Russian. These individuals also have access to a much wider range of foreign language education opportunities, whereas those with lower levels of education are more likely to be monolingual. Since migrants to Russia who speak Russian well have an increased chance at finding jobs on their own or through other non-exploitative routes, they are less susceptible to exploitation by intermediaries. By contrast, migrants with lower levels of education have a lower level of skills and training, so in addition to relying on intermediaries because of language shortcomings, they are more likely to put up with abusive practices because they have few other options. The phenomenon of exploitation by informal intermediaries, then, is enabled by a lack of educational resources, made more acute by the fact that educational institutions are hard-pressed to provide adequate instruction in Tajik, much less Russian.

In sum, without a strong foundation of Russian language ability before they leave for Russia, migrant workers are unable to integrate enough with the receiving society to acquire new knowledge and skills that they can bring back to their communities in Tajikistan.

5 Conclusion

Language has a significant impact on the experience of Tajikistani migrants adapting to life in Russia, and this chapter has explored the effects on the lives of migrant workers that arise in connection with their Russian language proficiency. First, although before they travel migrants often rely on informal networks for information regarding the migration process, their level of Russian ability plays a determining role in the quality (reliability and accuracy) of the information they can access regarding the migration process. Second, after traveling to Russia, Russian language skills do not have a significant effect on the experience of securing housing for those migrants who live with family or in employer-provided housing, though language skills are important for the subset of migrants who seek out and rent apartments on their own from local landlords. Third, the relationship between Tajikistani migrants and law enforcement is often uneasy due to patterns of mistreatment of migrant workers. The interviewees for this study unanimously identified a lack of Russian language skills as the principle factor attracting police abuse, surprisingly even over race and ethnicity. Furthermore, participants affirmed repeatedly that migrants with higher Russian language skills had fewer negative interactions with law enforcement and rated Russian knowledge as being more important, even, than having proper legal documentation. Fourth, Russian language skills are an important indicator of migrants' ability to integrate into Russian society. Without adequate Russian language proficiency, migrants are less likely to mingle with the local population, which builds mutual mistrust and spawns antagonism between migrants and local residents in Russia. Fifth, Russian language ability determines what jobs migrants are able to hold in Russia. In general, migrants with lower Russian language ability work low-skilled, poorly-remunerated jobs, while those with higher language ability work in higher-skilled and better paid positions. Lastly, since a lack of Russian language skills does not hinder migrants from traveling to Russia to look for work, those who do make the journey are at increased risk for abuse by various intermediaries. Poor language competency creates dependence on these intermediaries, which they often exploit to the detriment of migrants.

An obvious solution to these problems would be the creation of economic opportunities that allow Tajikistanis to stay in Tajikistan. This would lower exposure to the kinds of exploitative situations migrants currently face abroad and reduce disadvantages based on language proficiency. This solution would almost certainly result in fewer instances of exploitation, but knowledge of Russian (or another major world language) must be a vital part of Tajikistan's economic development. Continued low levels of proficiency in major world language will shroud the country in linguistic isolation and make it more difficult for Tajikistanis to access information outside the country. After all, no other countries have Tajik as an official language, and fellow Persian-speaking Iran and Afghanistan use the Perso-Arabic script. It is not likely to be feasible for a small country of eight million people to prosper as monolingual speakers of a non-prestige language, therefore development strategies for Tajikistan must include funds to promote proficiency in a major world language; Russian seems the most likely candidate given Tajikistan's history and geopolitical considerations, though English or Chinese could work just as well. In this context, devoting money to foreign language proficiency should not be seen as a secondary cultural goal, but as a prime catalyst for the country's economic development and future prosperity.

References

A survey of political engagement and enfranchisement of Labor Migrants from Tajikistan. 2006. Washington, DC: International Foundation for Electoral Systems.

"Are you happy to cheat us?" Exploitation of migrant construction workers in Russia. 2009, February. New York: Human Rights Watch.

Cost of living calculator. n.d. *Numbeo.com.* http://www.numbeo.com/cost-of-living/ (accessed May 2, 2015)

Eke, Steven. 2006, June 7. Russia faces demographic disaster. *BBC.* http://news.bbc.co.uk/2/hi/europe/5056672.stm (accessed 2 May 2015).

Ergasheva, Zarina. 2013, April 20. Tajik migrants ill-prepared for work in Russia. *Institute for War and Peace Reporting.* https://iwpr.net/global-voices/tajik-migrants-ill-prepared-work-russia (accessed 2 May 2015).

Ethnic composition, language skills, and citizenship of the Republic of Tajikistan. 2010. Dushanbe: State Statistical Committee of the Republic of Tajikistan.

Gorst, Isabel. 2011, December 16. Russia's migrants living on the edge. http://www.ft.com/intl/cms/s/2/0d1569a0-2607-11e1-856e-00144feabdc0.html (accessed 2 May 2015).

Gradirovski, Sergei., & Neli Esipova. 2008. Russia's language could be ticket in for migrants. *Gallup.* http://www.gallup.com/poll/112270/russias-language-could-ticket-migrants.aspx (accessed 2 May 2015).

Human Rights Questions: Human rights situations and reports of special rapporteurs and representatives. 1996. New York: United Nations. http://www.un.org/documents/ga/docs/51/plenary/a51-483add1.htm

Jonson, Leona. 2006. *Tajikistan in the new Central Asia: Geopolitics, great power rivalry and radical Islam.* London: I.B.Tauris.

Kalinnikov, Kirill. 2012, June 28. Russia leads world on illegal migration – OECD. *RIA Novosti.*

Krainova, Natalya. 2011, July 20. Police pay is tripled in anti-graft fight. http://www.themoscowtimes.com/news/article/police-pay-is-tripled-in-anti-graft-fight/440794.html (accessed 2 May 2015).

Landau, Jacob & Barbara Kellner-Heinkele. 2012. *Language politics in contemporary Central Asia: National and ethnic identity and the Soviet legacy.* London: I.B. Tauris.

Moscow sends 200 Russian language teachers to north Tajikistan. 2012, July 31. *Radio Free Europe/Radio Liberty.* http://www.rferl.org/content/moscow-sends-200-russian-language-teachers-to-north-tajikistan/24662293.html (accessed 2 May 2015).

Olimova, Saodat & Igor Bosc. 2003. *Labour migration from Tajikistan.* Dushanbe: Mission of the International Organization for Migration (IOM).

Navruzshoh, Zarangez & Farangis Najibullah. 2012, November 21. With perks and privileges, Tajikistan seeks to draw male teachers back to schools. *Radio Free Europe/Radio Liberty.*

http://www.rferl.org/content/tajikistan-male-teachers-needed/24777844.html (accessed 2 May 2015).

Protecting Tajik migrants' rights: positive aspects of new migration policy require implementation. 2013. Paris: International Federation for Human Rights.

Race to the bottom: Exploitation of migrant workers ahead of Russia's 2014 Winter Olympic Games in Sochi. 2013. New York: Human Rights Watch.

Rakowska-Harmstone, Teresa. 1970. *Russia and nationalism in Central Asia: The case of Tadzhikistan*. Baltimore: Johns Hopkins University Press.

Russia in desperate need of immigrants – official. 2010, September 30. *Global Nation Inquirer*. http://globalnation.inquirer.net/news/breakingnews/view/20100930-295177/Russia-in-desperate-need-of-immigrantsofficial (accessed 2 May 2015).

Russia slaps ban on alcohol advertising in media. 2012, July 23. *BBC*. http://www.bbc.com/news/world-europe-18960770 (accessed 2 May 2015).

Sadykov, Murat. 2013, June 18. Central Asia: Labor Migrants Caught in Russian Politicians' Crosshairs. http://www.eurasianet.org/node/67135 (accessed 2 May 2015).

Smolyakova, Tatyana. 2011, September 21. ФМС: Более 20 процентов мигрантов не знают русского языка [FMS: More than 20 percent of migrants do not know the Russian language]. *Российская газета* [Russian Gazette]. http://www.rg.ru/2011/09/21/migraciya.html (accessed 2 May 2015).

Tajikistan: Exporting the workforce – at what price? 2011, September. Paris: International Federation for Human Rights.

Tajikistan releases Russian and Estonian pilots. 2011, November 22. *BBC*. http://www.bbc.com/news/world-europe-15835483 (accessed 2 May 2015).

Tools of tolerance? St. Pete leaflet depicts cartoon migrant workers. 2012, October 19. *Russia Today*. http://rt.com/art-and-culture/petersburg-migrant-guide-city-811/ (accessed 2 May 2015).

Trilling, David. 2009, May 12. Tajikistan: Dushanbe confronts dysfunction in education sector. Eurasianet.org. http://www.eurasianet.org/departments/insightb/articles/eav051309b.shtml (accessed 2 May 2015).

Tselikov, Andrey. 2013, August 30. The politics of Moscow's migrant crime statistics. https://globalvoicesonline.org/2013/08/30/the-politics-of-moscows-migrant-crime-statistics/ (accessed 2 May 2015).

Wong, Venessa. 2013, August 23. World's most expensive cities 2011. http://www.bloomberg.com/bw/slideshows/20110608/world-s-most-expensive-cities-2011 (accessed 2 May 2015).

Dilbarhon (Dilia) Hasanova

12 English Education in Uzbekistan

Abstract: Because of its unique role globally and in an effort to catch up with the Western world, English has become the most widely learned foreign language in Central Asia. Nowadays, Central Asian people realize that the knowledge of English is an essential skill for those who are eager to achieve personal growth, better careers, and advanced education. Moreover, the fact that English is the most widely learned foreign language could be perceived as Central Asia's response to globalization and modernity. The penetration of English into educational domains in post Soviet countries, along with controversies around the reasons for its spread and functions in social domains have become popular issues explored in a number of empirical studies (Ciscel 2002; Dimova 2003; Dushku 1998; Fonzari 1999; Petzold 1994, Petzold and Berns 2000) since the downfall of the Iron Curtain. Yet, even though it has been more than two decades since English has gained a new status in the former Soviet republics, many functions and the growth of this global language in Central Asia, particularly in Uzbekistan, still remains unexplored. This study, the first of its kind, uses qualitative methods to investigate the spread and impact of English language in educational domains in the Republic of Uzbekistan following the political changes of 1991.

Keywords: English education; World Englishes; Uzbekistan

1 Introduction

The spread of foreign languages and local people's motivation to learn them are not new phenomena in Uzbekistan. In fact, as a result of various political, social, and economic changes, there have been a number of significant language events in Uzbekistan in the 20th century, e.g., the Romanization of pre-existing Arabic-based alphabet in 1923 (Uzman 2009), the spread of the Russian loan words in the Uzbek lexicon, the adoption of the Cyrillic script in 1940, the replacement of the Cyrillic alphabet with a modified Latin script in 1993, the disempowerment of the Russian language after the collapse of the Soviet Union, and the wide spread of the English language in the educational system in the late 1990s (Hasanova 2007a, 2007b, 2007c).

This chapter investigates the use of English in the educational domains in the Republic of Uzbekistan, which was and is a multilingual nation in Central Asia, both before and after the collapse of the Soviet Union. This study was specifically provoked by the linguistic ambiguity that was created in Uzbekistan in the wake of the collapse of the Soviet Union. This significant geo-political event opened a new phase for local and foreign languages in Uzbekistan and while the Uzbek language has regained its status as the national language, Russian has lost its status as the language of power. Consequently, English has become the most widely learned foreign language in the country (Hasanova 2007a, 2007b, 2007c).

This chapter has several additional objectives. First, because the findings of the larger study were mainly based on primary data that was collected from classroom observations and interviews with English teachers and students, implications and conclusions drawn from this study can serve as a resource for English teachers, teacher trainers, and curriculum developers to make improvements in the English education domain in Uzbekistan. Second, by revealing sufficient information regarding the spread of English in language change and shift in this context. Finally, by investigating the role of English in educational system in Uzbekistan, the study responds to Margie Berns' (2005) call for the need to have more research and scholarship on profiling the range and depth of uses and users of English in Expanding Circle Countries, i.e., countries where English is not the dominant language of the broader population.

1.1 Uzbekistan: An overview

Uzbekistan has a population of 28, 661, 637 ("Uzbekistan", 2014). Eighty percent of its citizens identify themselves as being ethnically Uzbek, while the remaining 20% consist of Russians (5.5%), Tajiks (5%), Kazakh (3%), Karakalpak (2.5%), Tatar (1.5%), and an unidentified (2.5%). Uzbek, the official language of the country, is spoken by 74.3% of population, followed by Russian (14.2%), Tajik (4.4%) and other (7.1%) ("Uzbekistan" 2014). The Uzbek language is a member of the Turkic language family; however, present day standard Uzbek includes a significant number of Arabic, Persian, and Russian loan words. Most Uzbeks are bilingual in their first language and Russian; others can be considered multilingual since they can communicate in three or more mutually incomprehensible languages, e.g., Russian, Tajik, Tatar, Karakalpak, and Persian.

Uzbekistan became the Uzbek Republic in 1924 and then, the Uzbekistan Soviet Socialist Republic (SSR) in 1925. Under the Soviet regime, industry in Uzbekistan was concentrated on growing cotton with the help of irrigation,

Figure 12.1: Map of Uzbekistan

mechanization, and chemical fertilizers and pesticides, causing serious environmental damage. "In June 1990, Uzbekistan was the first central Asian republic
to declare that its own laws had sovereignty over those of the central Soviet
government" ("Uzbekistan" 2012).

2 Methods

This study used various qualitative methods in order to provide a brief history
of teaching and learning English as a foreign language during the Soviet time
and to describe and analyze the functional allocations of English in educational
contexts in post-Soviet Uzbekistan in depth. In order to get unbiased data on the
role and functions of English in post-Soviet Uzbekistan, it was imperative that I
examined my positionality as a researcher who, at the time of data collection,

was affiliated with an American university. As an educator, I am a product of the Soviet and post-Soviet education. However, my perspectives as a researcher and my beliefs and knowledge about research and research methodologies are the result of the American education. Hence my position as a researcher is on the periphery of an insider, who was born, raised, and educated in Uzbekistan, and also of an outsider, who lived and studied in the USA during the course of study. The fact that I lived in the USA and visited Uzbekistan once a year (2002–2007) led me to a concern over the objectivity of my respondents' answers to my research questions and their attitudes towards me. Moreover, I was also concerned that as a result of the sour relationship between Uzbekistan and the USA following the Andijan massacre in 2005 and the government's tight control of the "free speech", my potential respondents would feel uncomfortable to talk about the use and spread of English in the country. Hence it was vital for me to provide my informants with the information about me, my family, my place in the community, my research, and my life in the USA. This disclosure became part of my research and enabled me to establish rapport and to gain the research participants' trust.

2.1 Research sites

The fieldwork for this study was conducted in Bukhara city. Specifically, the following institutions and public and private schools were chosen as research sites, i.e., Bukhara State University (BSU), two urban and one rural public school, the Regional Language Learning Center (RLLC), one private language learning center, and a shopping plaza.

The selection of these sites was based on the following criteria. First, the aforementioned research sites were suitable for obtaining information and for recruiting potential research participants necessary for the study (McMillan & Schumacher 1997). Second, I was familiar with the social system of the city and the cultural and language backgrounds of the local people. Third, since I had worked as an English faculty member at Bukhara State University, an English teacher at one of the local schools, and an instructor at a public language center prior to pursuing my graduate studies in the USA, it was not difficult for me to establish rapport with my research participants. Hence, the permission to collect data was granted to me in all sites. Finally, I decided to conduct the research in Bukhara because the city (unlike Tashkent, the capital city, where English learners have access to ample resources) could better reflect the reality of the use of English in the urban educational domains throughout the country, thereby allowing for the generalization and application of the findings to other cities in Uzbekistan.

2.2 Methods

The data collection methods for this study are based on naturalistic inquiry, where research takes place in real world settings and the researcher does not attempt to manipulate the phenomenon of interest (Patton 2002). In order to explore my research topic in a real-world situation, I spent three consecutive summers in Bukhara (2004–2006) collecting data. All in all, the data for this study was collected from both primary and secondary sources. Primary sources included guided interviews (in person and telephone), close-ended questionnaires, and observation notes. Secondary sources included books, print materials (advertisements, announcements, newspaper articles, etc), and other empirical studies exploring the sociolinguistic profile of English in Eastern Europe after the collapse of the USSR.

2.3 Participants

In order to find information-rich subjects, this study used mixed sampling strategies. More specifically, participants were recruited using purposeful and stratified random sampling methods (McMillan and Schumacher 1997). Participants for this study were chosen purposefully to ensure diversity vis-à-vis the uses and users of English in the educational sectors. Before selecting my subjects, I considered several selection criteria such as participants' educational background, English as a Foreign Language (EFL) learning experiences, international travel experiences, and social interests.

2.3.1 Participant profiles

A total number of 233 subjects participated in the study, i.e., 95 undergraduate students, 91 secondary school students, 15 members of the Bukhara English Youth center, 23 English teachers, four Peace Corps volunteers, a representative from an international educational agency, and four parents. Tables 12.1 and 12.2 present the information regarding respondents' age and sex.

A total number of 201 participants (62 male and 139 female) returned completed the instrument. Out of all respondents, 75.9% identified themselves as Uzbek, 11.3% as Tajik, 9.4% as Russian, and other (3.4%). The majority of respondents (78.3%) had never traveled outside of the country and 21.2% respondents who had traveled abroad had visited Russia, Tajikistan, Kazakhstan, and the USA. All respondents indicated that they had background knowledge in English, e.g., they had taken EFL courses in secondary school.

Table 12.1: Age Distribution of Participants

Participants' age	Number of participants
<18	113
19–24	103
25–34	11
35–44	3
>44	3

Table 12.2: Participants' Gender

Participants' gender	Number of participants
Male	79
Female	153
N/A	1

3 English during the Soviet period

Formal teaching of English as a Foreign Language (EFL) in Uzbekistan started when the Soviet government released a decree in 1932 promulgating "the necessity of providing every secondary school graduate with the knowledge of a foreign language" (Ornstein 1958: 382). It is noteworthy that even though the Soviet government realized the importance of learning foreign languages for social and political reasons, little attention was given to foreign language learning, particularly to the English language. In fact, in the early 1930s and on, by and large, English was "considered the language of Western imperialism... Moreover there was a very powerful censorship of student exposure to contemporary British and American literature, art and lifestyles" (Jacques 1995; cited in Dushku 1998: 372). Consequently, instead of seeing the knowledge of English as a tool to help students gain understanding in culture, tradition, and literature of the countries where it was spoken natively, English teachers focused on producing qualified translators of technical and scientific materials and selected British and American literary works (Garrard 1962).

Because of Soviet government censorship, the emphasis in foreign language courses was on improving grammatical competence of EFL learners. The majority of class time was devoted to analytical readings, grammatical analysis of sentences, translation exercises, and mastering grammar rules. Students were required to construct sentences in the target language with the help of well-studied grammar rules. Primary attention in English education was given to developing students' theoretical understanding of complex grammatical structures rather than helping them to apply their knowledge in real life situations. Moreover, the approach to teaching EFL was "formal and rigid, with no appeal to the children's interest and with no consideration for the children's ability to acquire language patterns by imitation" (Kreusler 1963: 434).

3.1 English in secondary schools

For most Soviet learners, English and other foreign language classes (e.g., German, French, and Spanish) started in the fifth grade. In fifth and sixth grades, English classes were offered four hours a week, while students in grades seven through 10 had three hours a week. In general, students had to take a total of 660 hours of foreign-language classes by the end of grade 10 with the academic year stretching for about 33 weeks. It is noteworthy that the allocation of foreign-language teaching hours differed in Russian and Uzbek MOI schools. It was essential for Uzbek students to master the Russian language before they started learning foreign languages because Russian was considered not only the language of friendship and interethnic communication within the Soviet Union but also it was the second mother tongue of non-Russian Soviet people (Abell 1959). Hence, "in the parts of the Soviet Union where education [was] conducted in the native language and where Russian ha[d] to be learned as a second language, the hours given to the study of a foreign language [were] somewhat fewer" (Abell 1959: 72).

More specifically, in non-Russian MOI schools, "students generally average [d] one hour less weekly of foreign language instruction, which reduced the number of contact hours by approximately one third" (Ornstein 1958: 383). In addition, since most of the teaching materials and textbooks were designed and written by prominent Russian scholars, it was also permitted to introduce a foreign language in non-Russian schools in sixth grade, by which point students were expected to have gained at least a medium level of proficiency in the Russian language (Ornstein 1958).

As far as students' accomplishment in foreign language learning is concerned, by the end of the end of 10th grade, EFL learners were expected to have "an active vocabulary of 2,400 to 2,600 words, as well as the ability to read in an hour 5,000 words of a text taken out of the material used in class, with the help of dictionary, 1,700 words of an unfamiliar text containing no more than 15% new words" (Abell 1959: 73). Soviet secondary school students' proficiency in a foreign language was assessed on their final-state examination grade. State examinations usually consisted of the following sections: read aloud, translation of a piece of literature or scientific article with the help of dictionary, an oral examination about a text, and a text recitation on a specific topic.

3.2 English in higher educational institutions

In higher education during the Soviet times, at least one course in a foreign language like English, German, French, or Spanish was a required component of the university curricula. This class was two hours per week and was required for all students in the first four of the five-year university program.

The aim of these classes was to help students develop as rapidly and as completely as possible the ability to read technical books and articles in their specialty. The languages most frequently studied were English and German (Abell 1959: 75).

The teaching curricula of most university level EFL teachers reflected the importance of grammar and phonetics. In classes "students perfect[ed] their pronunciation in individual drill sessions, in which the student [was assigned] to criticize his own speech and point out his mistakes" (Nash 1971: 9). Emphasis on grammar and phonetics, and rigid teacher-centered methods resulted in students having high proficiencies in reading, writing, and translating, while their proficiency in listening and speaking were lower.

As for the variety of English used and learned in the Soviet schools and higher educational institutions, only one variety of English was used, i.e., British English or Received Pronunciation (RP). Nash (1971), who studied the place of English in the USSR, offers several reasons why the Soviet EFL educators insisted on teaching RP. She posits,

> First, it was believed by educators to be the most universally intelligible and socially desirable pronunciation of English. Second, textbooks and pronunciation manuals were traditionally based on the works of British phoneticians, who made detailed linguistic descriptions of that variety of English. Third, because almost all English language teachers in the Soviet Union [were] non-native speakers who have been trained in RP by other non-native speakers, it would have been highly impractical, in the absence of a large number of native speakers, to introduce other English accents. (Nash 1971: 10)

Despite the inflexible didactic methods used in the classrom (Abell 1959), the lack of audio-visual aids and suitable teaching materials (Ornstein 1958), and the cultural deprivation arising from the Soviet government's prohibition against travel to Western countries and insulation of citizens from any contact with users of English (Dushku 1998; Nash 1971), the English language maintained its place as one of the most popular foreign languages in Soviet-era schools. Moreover, the place of English in educational institutions was secured for the years ahead due to the Soviet commitment to stay curent with the world's scientific publications and literary works and desire to learn more about the cultures and societies they were prohibited from having access to (Evgeniy Astanov, personal communication, July 2004).[1]

4 English in post–Soviet Uzbekistan

This section aims to explore the role of English within the domains of foreign language education in Uzbekistan after 1991. After gaining independence, as the country opened up to West, and as EFL teacher trainers started offering different seminars and workshops to expose Uzbek EFL teachers to the latest methods and theories in the field of ESL/EFL, it became apparent to the Uzbek educators that the teaching methods inherited from the Soviet times were no longer adequate to meet global educational standards. In order to meet and satisfy the ever-growing needs of language learners, more up-to-date teaching methods and materials reflecting the latest developments in language learning and teaching were needed.

4.1 Educational reforms implemented after independence

One of the first educational reforms implemented in the education system in the wake of independence was the establishment of the Uzbek language as sole official language of the country. As a result, the number of Uzbek language classes and subjects to be taught in Uzbek increased dramatically, sometimes at the expense of other subjects and especially the Russian language classes. In addition, all local and regional administrative offices were required to encourage their employees to take Uzbek classes if they were not proficient in it. The Ministry of Education (MoE) invested special efforts in organizing and developing the teaching of the Uzbek language. A special committee worked on implementing the teaching of Uzbek for adults, employing a new book for schools published by the *O'qituvchi* Press in Tashkent (Landau and Keller-Heinkele 2001: 81).

---

1 Pseudonyms were used in this study in order to protect the privacy of research participants.

Along with the changes mentioned above, the Law on Education resulted in the decentralization of the education system and placed the responsibility for implementing fundamental changes in teaching curricula to local schools and educational institutions. This meant that local teachers had more freedom to design their lesson plans and select textbooks and other teaching materials that would be appropriate for their students. Other curriculum changes included addition of new subjects such as economics, presidential works, and environmental studies. The revision of the social studies curricula and teaching materials was especially important because they had to reflect the up-to-date information regarding the political and economic changes that took place after the downfall of the Soviet Union.

With Uzbekistan's increasing collaboration with the developed countries and local peoples' growing awareness of the importance of learning foreign languages, this resulted in significant changes in the foreign languages curricula. Today, foreign language teachers are encouraged to implement new methods in teaching English that focus more on learner-centered classrooms.

4.2 English as a Foreign Language in the post-Soviet Uzbek education system

This subsection takes a closer look at English language education in post-Soviet Uzbekistan by examining the status of EFL in preschools, secondary schools, and higher education. Along with presenting some statistics about English education and describing the structure of English language classrooms and expected learner outcomes, this section also examines pressing problems of teaching and learning English in post-Soviet Uzbekistan. It is worth noting that all the information presented in this subsection is based on the findings of the present study because the Uzbek government does not provide any statistics on the place of English in schools and other educational institutions.

On December 10, 2012, Islam Karimov, the president of Uzbekistan, signed a decree "On measures to further foreign language learning system" ("President resolves to improve" 2012). This decree, along with the Law on Education, aimed at providing world-class education to the Uzbek youth. As the decree outlined "starting from 2013/2014 school year foreign languages, mainly English, gradually throughout the country will be taught from the first year of schooling in the form of lesson-games and speaking games, continuing to learning the alphabet, reading and spelling in the second year (grade)" ("President resolves to improve" 2012).

4.2.1 English in preschools

Uzbek children can take their first EFL class as early as in preschool, which includes children from ages four to six. According to a MoE report, approximately seven percent of children study foreign languages in preschools. It should be noted that English education is not a mandatory part of preschool curriculum; hence the government provides little or no funding for it. Consequently, preschools that offer English at this stage require an additional enrollment fee. This fee is charged in order to pay English teachers to purchase necessary teaching materials and technical equipment. These preschool English teachers design their own curricula, lesson plans, and teaching materials (Shahnoz Aminova, personal communication, September 2005).

After finishing preschool, some schools require six and seven year old children to take an Elementary School Entrance Examination, which is held in the form of an interview. During these pre-admission interviews, students are tested on their knowledge of alphabet, basic math and their ability of story telling and poem recitation. Elementary schools do not test their students on their knowledge of a foreign language. However, if a child can say a few words in English or other foreign languages can help make a good impression on interviewers.

4.2.2 English in secondary schools

As a result of the decentralization of educational system, the central government no longer specifies what foreign language should be taught in secondary schools. According to Firuza Haitova, a regional methodologist, local educational offices are authorized to conduct a survey on what foreign languages are most frequently requested by local schools, students, and their parents. That said, in a 2004 survey conducted by the Local Educational Office reported that out of 38 secondary schools in Bukhara, 32 (84.2%) offered EFL courses, three (7.9%) schools offered German, two (5.2%) offered French, and one (2.6%) offered Hebrew (Educational developments in Uzbekistan 2004). All schools also offered Russian as a second foreign language (Feruza Haitova, personal communication, July 2004).

In order to meet the needs and demands of their EFL learners, many schools have reduced the overall number of class hours for Russian courses in order to introduce English (Landau and Keller-Heinkele 2001). In the early 2000s, secondary schools offered three hours of foreign language classes a week, while specialized foreign language schools offered six to eight hours of teaching a foreign language. According to Mrs. Sattarova, the Director of Employment Department, in all schools and other educational establishments Russian language teaching hours were decreased by as much as 50%, while English language classes increased by 35–40% percent since the late 1990s (Mrs. Sattarova, personal communication, June 17, 2004).

In terms of curriculum, the National Teaching Standards and Curricula (2004), which is a manual published by the Uzbekistan MoE for secondary school teachers, succinctly describes what EFL learners at secondary public schools are expected to achieve before completing their education. Generally, most local EFL teachers follow the requirements of this manual, designing their lesson plans accordingly. The manual divides the English language learning process into two stages.

In the first stage, students are expected to acquire the basic skills in foreign languages. In other words, during the first couple of years, students focus on reading and writing in English. At this stage, English teachers are expected to focus on developing learners' listening comprehension, communication skills, pronunciation, and intonation. This first stage is to help students acquire basic grammatical and lexical materials and to be able to create new sentences and speech patterns based on textbook models. Among the skills learners are expected to acquire during stage one include: distinguishing letters from sounds; comprehending recorded speech and being able to recreate text using "correct" pronunciation; forming grammatically correct sentences with specific words and word combinations; and creating new texts with the help of lexical and grammatical materials acquired during the period of learning.

In the second stage, which is during grades seven through nine, students continue working on listening comprehension, speaking, reading, and writing. At this level, a lot of attention is paid to developing students' independent and creative thinking. By the end of the second stage, learners should be able to demonstrate: understanding and recognizing lexical patterns not in written texts and independent sentences; identifying the meaning of unknown lexical patterns from the context or being able to translate them with the help of dictionaries; speaking on a given topic with the help of active vocabulary; forming grammatically correct and complex sentences including a knowledge of subordinate clauses; and being able to compare, contrast, analyze, and synthesize (National Teaching Standards and Curricula, The 2004).

In order to receive a certificate of completion of secondary education, highschool students take national examinations in a range of subjects. According to state standards, in order to pass the English language examination, students are expected to achieve some level of proficiency in the following. In terms of reading, students should be able to comprehend texts in a foreign language and be able to identify the main points of those texts, understanding literature and sociopolitical articles published in newspapers and journals in a foreign language, and be able to read 300 words in 10 minutes (National Teaching Standards and Curricula, The 2004). Additionally, students should also be able to:

- Recognize 80–90% of texts that contain five percent of unfamiliar words;
- Identify the main idea of 1.5 to two pages of text with 70% unfamiliar vocabulary;
- Express their ideas fluently (in short descriptions, through storytelling, or making comments);
- Communicate successfully; and
- Develop the skills needed for effective dialogues.

Based on the availability of English teachers, classrooms, and other resources, English classes are divided into two groups with 10–15 students in each group. English teachers are expected to coordinate with each other while designing their lesson plans. While younger teachers try to follow the manual requirements and are eager to sustain students' interest in classes by incorporating different activities to explain grammar rules and discuss required topics, experienced teachers still prefer their traditional methods. As one teacher with 25 years of teaching experience explained,

> When I attended seminars organized by American organizations, they taught us different educational games we could use to explain grammar and other topic. When I started using them, students made a lot of noise; they did not listen to each other. I remember having a bad headache after that class. Next time I had to explain the same thing in my traditional way. All students were quiet and attentive; once they understood how many mistakes they make in their oral speech, they started paying even more attention. Right now, my students use correct tense forms when they speak in English. (Madina Serova, personal communication, June 2005)

In the classrooms I observed, students showed a keen interest in all class activities and teachers were enthusiastic about explaining new materials. Most school children seemed to be eager to learn English. My observations also revealed that the students tried to take advantage of any opportunity outside the school to practice their oral English (for example, chat with invited speakers and tourists). The analysis of the survey demonstrated that most secondary school students learned English because it provided them with better career opportunities. Table 12.1 summarizes 201 respondents' answers to the question "Why do you learn English?"[2]

---

2 In total, 233 surveys were distributed and 201 completed surveys were returned (85% return rate).

The findings in Table 12.1 show that 55% of respondents take English classes in order to have better career opportunities in the future. Interestingly, even though English is a required subject at school, only three percent of respondents noted that they learn English because it was a mandatory subject. My one-on-one interviews also revealed that younger Uzbeks are enthusiastic to learn English because the knowledge of English, similarly to the Hungarian context (Petzold 1994), is associated with a more prosperous life.

4.2.3 English in higher education institutions

Today, all college and university students are still required to take two to four hours of foreign-language classes a week. Based on their background in learning foreign languages at secondary schools, students can choose English, German, French, or Spanish as their FL in college. However, since the early 1990s, a number of departments in higher educational institutions (HEIs) have been including English as a required subject in their teaching curricula. For example, at Tashkent State University, in the departments of economics, management, international relations, and sciences, intensive courses in English are compulsory. At Bukhara State University, students in the department of economics are expected to know English, not only to do well at their foreign languages classes but also to pass some core subjects. Needless to say, English is the most popular major in the faculties of foreign languages. More recent development on foreign language education in Uzbekistan, i.e. the education decree signed by President Karimov in 2012 "envisaged that university modules, especially in technical and international areas, will be offered in English and other foreign languages at higher education institutions" ("President resolves to improve" 2012).

A survey conducted in spring 2005 revealed that in the Faculty of Foreign Languages at Bukhara State University, out of 771 students, 528 (68.5%) majored in English, 120 (15.5%) in German, 75 (9.7%) in French, and 48 (6.2%) majored in Russian (Hasanova 2007a, 2007b, 2007c). At the Uzbek State University of World Languages in Tashkent, out of the 3,801 students enrolled in the Faculties of English Philology, German Philology, Romance Philology, and Russian Philology, and Education (for upgrading teachers' skills) about 60% of students majored in English (Landau and Keller-Heinkele 2001: 177).

4.2.4 Teaching English as a foreign language: methods and approaches

In order for Uzbeks to be competitive in most international-level professional/ work spheres, they have to acquire not only linguistic proficiency but also demonstrated communicative competence in English. As a result, the basic goal of the new curriculum was to equip students with the adequate knowledge that meets the demands of the global education. Hence, foreign language teachers were encouraged both by local and international teacher trainers to put more emphasis on improving language learners' communicative competence. It was during this time that communicative language teaching (CLT) was spread as a new approach in language teaching in Uzbekistan. Over the last two decades, CLT has been promoted and supported in teaching conferences both by local and international English educators and curriculum developers as a "new trend in teaching English" in the country (Matskevich 2002). CLT was introduced to Uzbek teachers as a way of teaching where communicative competence is developed with the help of communicative activities such as group work, pair work, and role plays in a learner-friendly (i.e., in which learners are not afraid of making mistakes and feel comfortable in expressing themselves) socio-academic environment.

It has been almost two decades since Uzbek English teachers were exposed to communicative language teaching. Nevertheless, the data I collected through interviews showed that CLT in Uzbekistan is perceived more as a topic of discussion for teaching conferences rather than an approach to be implemented in classroom teaching. While most teachers reported that they were aware of the fundamentals of CLT and incorporated communicative activities in their classrooms, in practice, however, they were still mostly using traditional methods in teacher-centered classrooms. Moreover, findings also revealed that the majority of the EFL teachers had little theoretical knowledge of what CLT was about and consequently, mostly perceived CLT as an oral-based method to language teaching with little or no grammar.

In order to understand the disparity between teachers' responses to interview questions and their classroom practices, I asked English teachers to explain what they understood by CLT. The results of the survey demonstrated that the majority of respondents (89.6%) noted that they thought that the main principle of CLT was to help students improve their speaking and communication skills. As one teacher explained, "In my opinion communicative language teaching method is teaching students to speak and communicate with people. We should increase their oral speech" (Aziz Norov, personal communication, September 15, 2005).

Observation notes collected in summer 2005 also documented that in "communicative" classrooms, teachers embedded conversational or conversation-focused activities as often as they could because they believed that these activities were more effective than the form-focused ones in helping students develop their speaking skills. As a result of strong emphasis on speaking, EFL teachers also tried to teach grammar inductively, using different games, in order to give students more opportunities to speak in English and improve their oral speech.

4.2.5 English outside the classroom

English outside the school or other domains in which to use English is mostly available to those who live in urban areas. Uzbek children look for opportunities to use English outside the school in order to satisfy their curiosity about different cultures and to develop their speaking and listening skills both with native and non-native speakers of English. Because of the growth in the tourist industry ("Travel and tourism in Uzbekistan" 2011) in Uzbekistan, contact with foreigners has become more common and much easier than it was during the Soviet time. The most popular places where locals can meet with foreigners and practice their English are parts of cities with historical architecture.

Thousands of tourists come to post-Soviet Uzbekistan all year round. The most tourist-attracting places are old cities such as Bukhara, Samarqand, and Khiva. While doing my fieldwork, I observed that Uzbek children were eager to have a chance to see and to have conversations with foreigners. Hence they took advantage of any opportunity to use their English and make contacts with foreigners. The most contact between local children and foreigners occur when tourists need directions or want to buy souvenirs at local bazaars. My observations of local children's contact with tourists showed that local children feel really excited to be able to use English to greet tourists, to find out how they are doing, and to ask them where they come from. The only language local children use with tourists is English; they keep talking in English, even when tourists say they come from non-English speaking countries (observation notes, June 2005).

4.2.5.1 English clubs

Another opportunity for people to learn English informally are through local English clubs. A number of English clubs were established with the initiative of the US Peace Corps and local educational offices in late 1990s. These clubs were one of a few places where local people of different ages and educational backgrounds could practice their English language skills, gain a deeper understanding and appreciation of English speaking cultures, participate in debates, play different games, and borrow English language literature and movies. The members of these clubs had to follow the English-only language policy, even in the absence of native speakers (Kahramon Yusupov, personal communication, July 2005). Unfortunately, in July 2005, all Peace Corps programs were suspended "because the Peace Corps was unable to ensure proper documentation from the Uzbekistan government" ("Peace Corps Suspends Program" 2005). As a result, local English club members were deprived of the opportunity to have casual conversations with the native speakers in friendly and welcoming environment.

It is worth noting that the suspension of the Peace Corps hasn't stopped the popularity of the English language in the country. The US Embassy in Tashkent continues a weekly English Club called the Chay Chat Club. "The group gathers each Friday afternoon for a discussion led by a native English speaker. Topics vary, but tend to focus on American culture, policies and society or on issues of global importance" ("Practice Your English" 2014). Unfortunately, this opportunity is available only to the English learners who live in Tashkent.

4.3 Problems and challenges facing English education

There have been some positive changes in the foreign language education since a 2012 decree regarding teacher training and curriculum development was passed. However, phone interviews conducted in January of 2014 with the local EFL teachers along with a news article analyzing the "current system of organizing language learning" revealed that current learning standards, curricula revisions, teacher training and workshops, and learning and teaching resources do not satisfy the requirements/standards mentioned in the president's decree ("President resolves to improve" 2012). According to my interviewees and the limited literature that is available on education, the education sector in Uzbekistan still faces a number of serious problems mainly due to the lack of financial support.

First, local schools are very slow in implementing new approaches in teaching foreign languages due to insufficient pre- and in-service teacher training. Local teacher-training institutions lack personnel who have expertise in new methodologies for teaching EFL, hence they are unable to provide local EFL teachers with the necessary training. Second, even though EFL teachers may receive training offered by local and international teacher trainers on current teaching methods and approaches, they lack the skills and resources to implement the latest methods in their classrooms; hence grammar translation methods are still widely used.

Third, the shortage, lack of availability, and prohibitive cost of textbooks pose a serious obstacle in incorporating new approaches in classroom teaching. Most teachers (especially in rural schools) still rely on the textbooks that are inherited from the Soviet times, and on the blackboard as the main (if not only) teaching resources. Tape recorders and overhead projectors are used rarely. Owing to the shortage of financial support, local schools and other educational institutions (with exception of a few) are unable to provide their teachers with audio-visual equipment, photocopiers, computers, and overhead projectors.

Even if tape-recorders and headphones are available in some schools, they are not used regularly for instructional purposes. EFL teachers use the available technical equipment only or mostly for "demonstrative" purposes, i.e., when they are scheduled to have demonstrative classes. The major reason for why EFL teachers prefer not to use the technical materials regularly is because they are concerned that technical equipment might be damaged or wear off due to frequent use. As Umida, an EFL teacher, commented,

> There is a huge shortage of technical equipment. Our school administrators have struggled for three years before we got a tape recorder and headphones for our lab. I don't want my students to break anything in the lab, that's why we use them very rarely. I don't want to spend my teacher's salary to repair broken equipment. The government never reimburses any expenses the teacher spends on repairing school equipment. That is the reason why I prefer to use textbooks, index cards, and visual aids instead of whatever technical equipment we have at school. (personal communication, June 2005)

Umida went on talking about how little attention the government pays to financing secondary school education. She also noted that at different meetings and conferences school administrators usually talk about what should be done to increase the quality of education instead of laying out a clear plan for how to achieve desirable results.

Fourth, even though the 2012 decree on education "envisages 30% salary increase for foreign language teachers in rural areas, 15% increase for those in other areas" ("President resolves to improve" 2012) local teachers are still looking for better financial opportunities outside of educational domains, i.e., as a result of low salaries and fringe benefits, most public school English teachers are leaving their teaching positions in order to work at better-paid non-governmental organizations. Moreover, "the teaching profession lost its social respect as teachers began to be more concerned about personal survival than educating children" (Huttova & Silova 2002: 17). As a result, some public schools (especially in rural areas), started recruiting applicants for teaching position who have no formal college education and hold only EFL certificates. As Erica, a Peace Corps Volunteer noted, "Most of the teachers I worked with never majored in English language and were therefore not familiar with teaching methods" (Erica Smith, personal communication, October 2005). The shortage of skillful teachers, obviously, leads to a concern over the quality of English education and the qualification of school graduates.

Finally, availability of English outside of educational domain is almost non-existent (except in Tashkent) and hence EFL learners and teachers do not have any opportunity to practice their language in real-life environment. The Agency for Press and Information of the Republic of Uzbekistan was tasked to prepare and broadcast language-learning programs and significantly increase access to international educational resources. However, none of my informants confirmed watching or listening to any foreign language programs on national cable TV or radio (personal communication, January 2014).

5 Conclusion

On the basis of the role of English in the Uzbek educational domains over the last century described in this chapter, I have attempted to show that the demand for English in post-Soviet Uzbekistan has increased to the extent that beginners' English classes are offered as early as in preschool. At the university level, English is not only the most popular foreign language but is also the preferred language in technical and international fields. Since 1990 a number of projects, including the 2012 legislation of foreign language education, have been undertaken by the MoE and other organizations to implement curriculum changes and to improve the quality of English education in Uzbekistan. However, in practice, curriculum changes have only been partly implemented largely because of insufficient financial support and teacher training. To improve English education and to make it more responsive to learner needs will require appropriate textbooks and teaching materials, improved teacher training, and adequate teacher salaries. Without such urgent improvements, teachers will be discouraged from devoting sufficient time and energy to their professional development, and, above all else, to their students' educational success.

References

Abell, Marcelle. 1959. Foreign language teaching in the USSR. *The Modern Language Journal* 43 (2). 72–78.

Berns, Margie. 2005. Expanding on the expanding circle: where do WE go from here? *World Englishes* 24(1). 85–93.

Ciscel, Matthew. 2002. Linguistic opportunism and English in Moldova. *World Englishes* 21(3). 403–419.

Dimova, Slobodanka. 2003. Teaching and learning English in Macedonia. *English Today* 76(19). 16–22.

Dushku, Silvana. 1998. English in Albania: Contact and convergence. *World Englishes* 17(3). 369–379.

Educational developments in Uzbekistan. 2004. http://www.bibl.u-szeged.hu/oseas/uzbek.html (accessed on 5 December 2005).

Fonzari, Lorenzo. 1999. English in the Estonian multicultural society. *World Englishes* 18(1). 39–48.

Garrard, J. G. 1962. The teaching of foreign languages in the Soviet Union. *The Modern Language Journal* 46(2). 71–74.

Hasanova, Dilia. 2007a. Teaching and leaning English in Uzbekistan. *English Today* 23(1). 3–9.

Hasanova, Dilia. 2007b. Broadening the boundaries of the Expanding Circle: English in Uzbekistan. *World Englishes* 26(3). 276–290

Hasanova, Dilia. 2007c. Functional allocations of English in post-Soviet Uzbekistan: Pedagogical implications for English language teachers. West Lafayette, IN: Purdue University dissertation.

Huttova, Jana & Iveta Silova. 2002. *Education development in Kyrgyzstan, Tajikistan and Uzbekistan: Challenges and ways forward*. Budapest: Open Society Institute.

Kreusler, Abraham. 1963. Foreign languages for young children in the USSR. *The Elementary School Journal* 63(8). 432–440.

Landau, Jacob & Barbara Keller-Heinkele. 2001. *Politics of language in the ex-Soviet Muslim states*. Ann Arbor, MI: The University of Michigan Press.

Matskevich, L. 2002. *New trends in teaching English in Uzbekistan*. No longer available online. (accessed on December 10, 2005)

McMillan, James & Sally Schumacher. 1997. *Research in education*. Harlow: Addison-Wesley.

Nash, Rose. 1971. The place of the English language in the USSR. *Review Interamericana* 1(1). 1–13.

Ornstein, Jacob. 1958. Foreign language training in the Soviet Union – a qualitative view. *The Modern Language Journal* 42(8). 382–392.

Patton, Michael. 2002. *Qualitative evaluation and research methods*, 3rd edn. Newbury Park, CA: Sage.

Peace Corps suspends program in Uzbekistan. 2005. http://www.peacecorps.gov/media/forpress/press/1043/ (accessed 23 January 2014).

Petzold, Ruth. 1994. *The sociolinguistics of English in Hungary: Implications for English Language teaching*. Purdue, IN: Purdue University dissertation.

Petzold, Ruth & Margie Berns. 2000. Catching up with Europe: speakers and functions of English in Hungary. *World Englishes* 19(1). 113–124.

Practice your English at the Chay Chat Club. n.d. US Embassy website. http://uzbekistan.usembassy.gov/chaychat.html (accessed on 23 January 2014).

President resolves to improve foreign language learning. 2012. *Uzbekistan National News Agency*. http://uza.uz/en/society/president-resolves-to-develop-foreign-language-learning-system-11.12.2012-3147 (accessed 22 January 2014).

National Teaching Standards and Curricular, The. 2004. Uzbekistan Ministry of Education. Tashkent, Uzbekistan: Ministry of Education.

Uzbekistan. 2014. *The CIA World Factbook*. https://www.cia.gov/cia/publications/factbook/geos/uz.html (accessed on 23 January 2014).

President resolves to improve foreign language learning system. 2012, December 11. *Uzbekistan National News Agency.* http://uza.uz/en/society/president-resolves-to-develop-foreign-language-learning-system-11.12.2012-3147?ELEMENT_CODE=president-resolves-to-develop-foreign-language-learning-system-11.12.2012-3147&SECTION_CODE=society&print=Y (accessed in January 2014).

Uzman, Mehmet. 2009. Romanization in Uzbekistan past and present. *Journal of the Royal Asiatic Society* 3. 112.

Travel and tourism in Uzbekistan. 2011. *Euromonitor.* http://www.euromonitor.com/travel-and-tourism-in-uzbekistan/report (accessed on 1 April 2014).

Uzbekistan. 2012. *Infoplease.* http://www.infoplease.com/ipa/A0108128.html (accessed January 24 2014).

Elise S. Ahn and Juldyz Smagulova
Afterword

As mentioned in the preface, the idea for this book emerged out of conversations that we had while organizing a thematic stream on language issues in Central Asia at the 19th Sociolinguistics Symposium in Berlin, Germany. While we were discussing and developing the stream description and then later, reviewing submissions, we were struck by how much language-related research in and around Central Asia has remained focused on macro-level policy documents and maintaining strict, essentialist dualisms between Soviet and post-Soviet socio-political and various ideological underpinnings. This type of research, while important, framed language-related issues to neat boxes or relationships when the reality is often much messier.

As our contributors have demonstrated, the relationship in and between different ethno-linguistic communities and the state in Central Asia is a complex one. In this way, many of the chapters in this book can be considered to be examples of the "vertical case study", which "strives to situate local action and interpretation within a broader cultural, historical, and political investigation" (Vavrus and Bartlett 2006: 96). According to Vavrus and Bartlett (2006), the vertical case study is situated in a site and then studied in its broader socio-political-cultural context. This is an example of the type of interdisciplinary language research that Sue Wright (2004: 2–3) calls for, i.e., inquiry "within the political and social sciences, acquir[ing] information from economics and law, and set[ting] the events and processes that affect language choice and change within a historical framework." This type of work highlights the interaction between different levels of governance as well as the providing a local perspective on change "on the ground."

However, further complicating language, and more broadly, social science research in the region is the geo-political instability. For example, since we started this book project, Russia has reasserted itself as the major political player in Eurasia vis-à-vis the conflicts in Crimea and Ukraine which has been accompanied by a resurgence in "new Cold War" discourse in American media. And because of international sanctions and plunging oil prices, the value of the Russian ruble plummeted, which has had substantial reverberations throughout Central Asia but particularly in Tajikistan and Uzbekistan because of the large number of migrant workers from those countries that work in Russia and send back remittances. This dynamic structurally affects access to resources particularly within lower income communities, which can lead to further socio-economic stratification.

Geo-political instability not only affects the different socio-economic contexts which shape and structure people's lives and livelihoods, it has also led to greater restriction and control on the type of research which can be done within the region, which subsequently limits what informs public debates regarding public policies and the way they are being produced and implemented.

But what the ripple effects of these political events have highlighted is the continued connectedness within and between the local, regional, and global, which has implications for future areas of research in the region. For example, as Sarah Kendzior (2014) argued in a piece on Uzbek activism and Twitter, where two Uzbek activists conducted a hunger strike in order to get an audience with President Islam Karimov, their voices were unheard amidst the deluge of tweets because the Uzbek language choice was limited both in terms of receptivity as well as communicability. Brooke Bolander (2015) discussed the complex relationship that Ismaili Muslims in Khorog, Tajikistan have with learning English. While English is proffered by the Aga Khan IV as the language of wider communication (students in Aga Khan-established schools use Shugni, Tajik, Russian, and English), people often see English education as taking time away from learning Tajik, which holds more opportunities in terms of higher education, and by extension, future career opportunities.

As the region (and the world) continues to become increasingly interconnected, under-researched areas like language and transnational spaces both physically and virtually (e.g., communication via social media outlets) and the complexity of their ideological underpinnings both illustrate and provide insight into the dynamics of multilingualism, identity construction, and the way language becomes a means through which to see different (and changing) ideological agendas. We hope that this volume contributes to this broader area of research and anticipate more empirically-based work that provides insight into this socio-politically complex and ethno-linguistically rich context.

References

Bolander, Brook. 2015. Language ideologies in multilingual Khorog, Tajikistan. *Anthropology News*. http://www.anthropology-news.org/index.php/2015/04/15/english-or-russian/ (accessed 10 May 2015).

Kendzior, Sarah. 2014, October 1. Can minor languages make a revolution? Uzbekistan and the codes of activism on the internet. *The Common Reader*. https://commonreader.wustl.edu/c/languages-revolution-internet/ (accessed 10 May 2015).

Vavrus, Frances & Lesley Bartlett. 2006. Comparatively knowing: Making a case for the vertical case study. *Current Issues in Comparative Education* 8(2). 95–103.

Wright, Susan. 2004. *Language policy and language planning*. London: Palgrave Macmillan.

Appendix

Table A1: Interview Response Table

Participant	Details	Interview Summary
1	Female, head of a local company (geological prospecting of oil & gas reserves), works between Almaty, Aktau and Astana. First interview on 25 October 2010 and onwards. In total, 4 interviews conducted	Has been in business for about 20 years. Has worked for government and national companies. Now runs her own (family) business related to oil and gas. Due to the nature of her work, does regular trips to the western region of KZ. Has got extensive network connections in the oil & gas industry. Speaks English and knows very well about the challenges of technical translation. When needed, does technical translation herself, from English to Russian and from Russian to English (the latter is more challenging since the main source of technical vocab. is English). Reports that there were serious issues related to misunderstanding and miscommunication due to translation incompetence and lack of terminology; illustrates by giving several examples when the government withdrew the license from a company which failed to submit correctly filled in technical documentation; there are more and more cases like that because there are at least 3 government-level bodies (2 ministries and 1 agency), besides local authorities, that monitor the industry. Failure to comply with regulations can be caused by inability to deal with technical documentation, and with technical language in particular. Has offered her assistance in the current research by referring to key people and companies in the industry.
2	Male, middle management, works for a foreign oil & gas equipment company. Interview on 26 November 2010.	Technical documentation is an integral part of company's activities. However, the company does not keep its own translation department; all the translation work is outsourced to an Astana-based translation bureau. The quality assurance of the documents translated is carried out by the employee who placed the order for translation. The bureau was contacted later for a possible interview or survey but decided to decline the offer.
3	Male, project manager, small local service company. 3 interviews conducted; first in 2 December 2010 and onwards (including Skype connections when he was out off a business trip).	The interviewee now works for a construction service company but previously was employed in a big international oil company. Had been extensively involved in technical translation for about 10 years. Knows a lot about the challenges of technical translation, and shared his experience of overcoming them. Agreed to participate in this research project's activities (survey, interview, discussions and submission of own terminology developed throughout personal practice). Recommended several contacts from relevant fields and former colleagues.

Participant	Details	Interview Summary
4	Female, head of translation department of a big oil joint venture. First interview conducted 24 Feb.2011, after that has been in intensive regular communication through phone and e-mail.	Herself a professional translator; has received 2 university diplomas. Generously shared her translation experience, including the challenges of the work and their solutions (e.g. how to create new terms, etc). Constantly works on upgrading the skills of staff under her by offering trainings and workshops (has asked me to run a workshop to share the research findings). Has kindly agreed to let me use her network contacts of translators for the purpose of this study.
5 & 6	2 males, both are department heads in big oil and gas companies, both interviews on 15 June 2011.	The main purpose of these 2 separate interviews was to gain access to the companies by explaining the goals and objectives of the research. After the agreement was reached, each person recommended people who deal with technical translation in various departments branches.
7	Male, professional translator of an international oil company (prospecting, extracting and drilling activities), first interview on 27 May 2011 (plus subsequent intensive electronic communication).	Does oral and written translations, experience of over 10 years, besides technical does a lot of legal translation. Prefers to use electronic translation resources such as LINGVO or Multitran (which a translators' forum attached to it). Emphasizes the importance of technical and language backgrounds when doing translation, has been undertaking a lot professional development activities.
8	Male, professional translator in small local company (oil extraction), first interview on 26 May 2011 (plus subsequent electronic communication).	Philologist by education but trained himself to be a professional translator. Has been translation business for around 5 years. Shares examples of term creations and challenges associated (e.g. lack of info and narrow specialization, etc). The key is constant professional development. Uses a wide range of electronic tools to assist translation. Developed some templates for technical documentations for his company. Recommended his female colleague from the same department for participation in the study.
9	Male, former professional translator, now project manager in service branch establishment of a big oil company. First interview conducted on 16 June 2011 (plus subsequent intensive electronic communication).	Has given a lot of examples of challenges that exist in technical translation (e.g. ambiguity, lack of information, etc). Has big experience in drafting important contracts at international level.

Participant	Details	Interview Summary
10, 11 & 12	2 females, professional translators of an international oil company (a joint interview session in May 2011).	Dealt mainly with written translation of technical documentation in the company's headquarters. Listed some common challenges of translation; the way to overcome those challenges, according to both interviewees, is constant professional development. Their company offers opportunities for development by organizing regular training sessions at the company's premises or funds training participation in Almaty or Astana.
13, 14, 15, 16 & 17	A big interview session with the group of professional translators (4 females and 1 male) on 4 April 2011.	The translators usually work shifts at oilfield and in the company's main office. Some have philological background (including teaching English), and their overall translation experience is from 5 to 10 years; 2 translators have formal experience brought from other companies in. The main challenges associated not only with English (as a source language for most terminology) but with Russian as well (due to various levels of Russian language among staff) and Kazakh too (where a lot of terminology needs to be developed from scratch). Another challenge is abundance of technical acronyms, which keep appearing with the development of machinery, equipment and tools related to the industry. This requires being constantly alert and updated. The sources to assist in translation include web based dictionaries and glossaries, and also translators' forums. For those who work at an oil field it is easier to deal with some challenging terminology because there are technicians (both local and expat) who they can refer to for help. Experienced translators keep a special notebook of terms where they enter new technical vocabulary or terms. The company supports professional development of their staff by sending them for trainings including overseas. They openly share their experiences among themselves.
18	Female, the head of a section in a big foreign oil company, former technical translator. Interviewed on 26 May 2011 (plus subsequent intensive electronic communication).	A philologist by education, soon after graduation from university went into translation business. Started as a junior translator at an oilfield working in shifts, then in construction sites, thereby gaining practical experience. Her pattern of developing the meaning for a new technical word was the following. For instance, in case an unknown terminology was a spare part of a machine, she would refer to the machine's blueprint, then seek an explanation from a worker who operates that machine, which often happened right on the oilfields. After getting a detailed picture of how the spare part functions and consulting with dictionaries and technical manuals, then she would develop an equivalent which would then go into a Word or Excel format sheet for future reference.

Participant	Details	Interview Summary
19	Female, assistant to a department head, former technical translator. Interviewed on 26 May 2011.	Due to the work schedule, the interview was short (less than 10 min.). The interviewee briefly shared her previous experience of working on an oilfield and how faced the challenges of technical translation. The pattern of dealing with terminology was similar to the previous (#18) interviewee's.
20 & 21	2 males, professional translators in the engineering department of an international oil company (April 2011).	Both translators were interviewed in one office; they talked about their translation experiences. The way they both dealt with translation challenges was to turn to oilfield workers or sometimes to native speakers of English to explain a term or at least clarify the way a particular object (piece of equipment, tool or else) functions to get its meaning. They both keep their own logs where they enter new terms.
22 & 23	2 representatives (male and female) of an agency, which offers professional development and trainings for technical translators. 3 April 2011.	They talked about the services their company offers to oil and gas translators from all over Kazakhstan.

Index

www.ingramcontent.com/pod-product-compliance
Lightning Source LLC
Chambersburg PA
CBHW071352280326
41927CB00041B/2881

9 781501 516269